Borderland Smuggling

NEW PERSPECTIVES ON MARITIME HISTORY
AND NAUTICAL ARCHAEOLOGY

UNIVERSITY PRESS OF FLORIDA

Florida A&M University, Tallahassee
Florida Atlantic University, Boca Raton
Florida Gulf Coast University, Ft. Myers
Florida International University, Miami
Florida State University, Tallahassee
New College of Florida, Sarasota
University of Central Florida, Orlando
University of Florida, Gainesville
University of North Florida, Jacksonville
University of South Florida, Tampa
University of West Florida, Pensacola

Borderland Smuggling

Patriots, Loyalists, and Illicit Trade in the Northeast, 1783–1820

Joshua M. Smith

FOREWORD BY JAMES C. BRADFORD AND GENE ALLEN SMITH, SERIES EDITORS

University Press of Florida

GAINESVILLE   TALLAHASSEE   TAMPA   BOCA RATON   PENSACOLA
ORLANDO   MIAMI   JACKSONVILLE   FT. MYERS   SARASOTA

Copyright 2006 by Joshua M. Smith
All rights reserved
Published in the United States of America

First cloth printing, 2006
First paperback printing, 2019

24 23 22 21 20 19   6 5 4 3 2 1

A record of cataloging-in-publication data is available from the Library of Congress
ISBN 978-0-8130-2986-3 (cloth)
ISBN 978-0-8130-6443-7 (pbk.)

The University Press of Florida is the scholarly publishing agency for the State University System of Florida, comprising Florida A&M University, Florida Atlantic University, Florida Gulf Coast University, Florida International University, Florida State University, New College of Florida, University of Central Florida, University of Florida, University of North Florida, University of South Florida, and University of West Florida.

University Press of Florida
2046 NE Waldo Road
Suite 2100
Gainesville, FL 32609
http://upress.ufl.edu

FOR JEA

Ships are but boards, sailors but men;
there be land-rats, and water-rats, land-thieves and water thieves.

William Shakespeare, *The Merchant of Venice*

CONTENTS

Foreword ix
Preface xiii

1. "The Habit of Smuggling" 1
2. "A Sort of Neutrality" 17
3. "A Commerce of Mere Stone" 33
4. "The Rascals of Passamaquoddy" 49
5. "The Pursuit of Ignominious Gain" 66
6. "Ulmer Was a Rascal" 81
7. "Actual and Unqualified Rebellion" 95
Conclusion: The Memory of Smuggling 109

APPENDIX A.
State of Settlement on Moose, Dudley, and Frederick Islands, c. 1800 121

APPENDIX B.
Enemy Aliens, Eastport, c. 1812–1813 123

Notes 125
Bibliography 145
Index 157

FOREWORD

Water is unquestionably the most important natural feature on earth. By volume, the world's oceans compose 99 percent of the planet's living space; in fact, the surface of the Pacific Ocean alone is larger than that of the total surface of all land bodies. Water is as vital to life as air. Indeed, to test whether other planets or the moon can sustain life, NASA looks for signs of water. The story of human development is inextricably linked to the oceans, lakes, and rivers that dominate the earth's surface. The University Press of Florida series "New Perspectives on Maritime History and Nautical Archaeology" is devoted to exploring the significance of the earth's water while providing lively and important books that cover the spectrum of maritime history and nautical archaeology broadly defined. The series includes works that focus on the role of canals, rivers, lakes, seas, and oceans in history; on the economic, military, and political use of those waters; and on the people, communities, and industries that support maritime endeavors. Limited by neither geography nor time, volumes in the series contribute to the overall understanding of maritime history and can be read with profit by both general readers and specialists.

Joshua Smith's unique study—based on an impressive collection of local, state, and federal records from the United States, Canada, and the United Kingdom—uses smuggling in the Passamaquoddy borderlands of Maine to explore the social construct of border communities and to analyze the creation of the border between the United States and Canada. Smuggling, by its inherent nature, involves the illicit crossing of political boundaries, and given the primitive nature of land transport in the region of Maine, New Brunswick, and Nova Scotia, and the abundance of waterways and predominance of waterborne transport in the area, it is only natural that most smugglers employed watercraft. Both the U.S. and British Canadian governments exerted considerable effort to counter the smuggling. Possessing more of a local or regional than a national identity, the inhabitants of the area resisted these state-created boundaries and the governments' efforts to impose a state-created conformity.

Casting his study in a borderlands premarket perspective, Smith reveals how smuggling became an important construct in the social composition of the local populace. The remoteness of the area and the limited state power also contributed to the desire and willingness of locals to subvert governmental authority. Local connections to family and friends carried far more importance than fealty to some distant, nebulous governmental entity. And in this contest between illicit trade and governmental authority, smuggling almost always won. The American embargo of 1807–9 failed, in part, because of the smuggling at Passamaquoddy, along the Georgia–Spanish Florida border, and at New Orleans. The American government also failed in its attempts to prevent smuggling during the War of 1812. Passamaquoddy smugglers defied British law in 1817 and 1820 when New Brunswick officials attempted to halt the plaster trade.

On another level Smith's study explores the frontier experience of settlers in the region, how the international boundary influenced their lives, and how smuggling connected loyal New Brunswick and republican Maine. Governmental officials attempted to limit, control, or eliminate cross-border commerce. But for the people of the region, this trade was a way to provide for their families while accommodating the economic needs of their neighbors. Smith contends that these people generally spoke of themselves not as smugglers but as "free traders." Afterward, they downplayed their involvement in smuggling altogether, insisting that the illicit activity was conducted by outsiders.

Smith's historical research resembles the work of a detective because smugglers carried out their activities in the shadows of society. Those who found their way into the historical record were perhaps unskilled or simply unlucky. More sophisticated smugglers used the legal system to legitimize their contraband goods and, in doing so, found a way into the historical record. Some smugglers chose to inform against competitors, knowing that a jury of their peers would not prosecute them but that the legal proceedings would curtail their business. Undoubtedly, hundreds of ships, barges, and canoes crossed the invisible boundary dividing the United States and Canada, safely introducing contraband goods into forbidden markets. The prevalence of these illicit activities illustrates how smuggling was inextricably linked to border formation. As such, Joshua Smith's book provides us with not only a rousing story about an illicit activity, but also insights into the creation of borders, governmental control, and seaborne trade.

James C. Bradford
Gene Allen Smith
*Series Editor*s

PREFACE

Smuggling has always been a problem, yet the nature of smuggling is little understood. By definition it is an elusive, secretive, and subtle practice. This book explores smuggling as a social force within border communities, using the Passamaquoddy region on the border between the United States and Canada as a model. Like other forms of crime, smuggling can be used to analyze social economies, attitudes toward violence, and the rise of governmental authority in the decades following the American War of Independence, both in the American republic and in the neighboring British colonies to the north. Moreover, smuggling almost always involved the illicit crossing of political boundaries and as such can reveal popular attitudes toward the creation of national borders.

This work argues that smuggling was inextricably linked with the process of border formation, compelling the state to exert considerable efforts to control its borders. Government efforts to control boundaries often created an equal and opposite effect among border residents, who resisted state-created boundaries through a variety of actions, including smuggling. This constant struggle between the state and smugglers played out in areas like Passamaquoddy, where the boundary line between the United States and British North America was not yet permanently fixed, the local populace on both sides of the boundary often sympathized with smugglers, and state powers were diminished by the region's remoteness. Often the smugglers won these contests; the American embargo of 1807–9 failed because of rampant smuggling at places like Passamaquoddy; the American government also failed to stem smuggling there during the War of 1812. Passamaquoddy's smugglers defied British colonial officials, most notably in 1817 and 1820 when New Brunswick attempted to halt the illicit plaster trade.

These struggles united the region's inhabitants, despite their ideological differences. Throughout the Western world, smugglers and governments engaged in a constant battle. In many cases, this struggle was linked to strengthening commercial impulses and the growing needs of the state to control its borders to tax and regulate trade. Smuggling thus offers an insight into how border formation affects local populations.

This is an effort to bring to light that which was vigorously concealed even two hundred years ago and is even more obscure now. Why dig up this illicit past? It is hoped that given the current debate over North American free trade, readers will find some relevance in a study of borders, government control, and trade. Furthermore, this is an effort to reconcile the increasingly divergent histories of the United States and Canada and to find common ground.

I owe many debts of gratitude to numerous archivists and library staff in both Canada and the United States. On the American side of the border, I thank Stanley Tozeski, George Young, and James Young at the National Archive and Records Administration Regional Records Center, Waltham, Massachusetts; Betsy Paradis of Special Collections, University of Maine; Nicholas Noyes, Bill Barry, Stephanie Philbrick of the Maine Historical Society; Paul O'Pecko at Mystic Seaport; and the staff of the Massachusetts Historical Society. In Canada, I benefited from the assistance given to me by the staff of the Provincial Archives of New Brunswick; Mary Flagg, head of Special Collections at the Harriet Irving Library of the University of New Brunswick; and Timothy Dubé, of the National Archives of Canada.

Little of this research could have been done without generous funding from a number of establishments on both sides of the border. The U.S.–Canada Fulbright Foundation awarded me the luxury of spending an entire academic year in Ottawa. Dr. Chad Gaffield, director of the University of Ottawa's Institute for Canadian Studies, generously provided me with office space. The Canadian Embassy funded research at the New Brunswick Museum and the Provincial Archives of New Brunswick. The Massachusetts Historical Society administered two grants, one of which permitted me to conduct my work at institutions such as the Maine Historical Society, the Baker Library at Harvard Business School, Mystic Seaport Museum, and of course their own grand quarters; my heartfelt thanks go especially to Conrad Wright, who administers the Society's grant programs. The University of Maine's Canadian American Center offered steady support, especially Dr.

Stephen Hornsby. And while all times are hard times at the University of Maine's Department of History, somehow it managed to provide me with funding through the Dunn Account.

My dissertation advisor, Dr. Scott See, provided me with an inexhaustible supply of sound advice. The rest of my committee, Drs. Liam Riordan, Richard Judd, and Jim Gallagher, and of course the insightful Dr. Jacques Ferland, were of inestimable service: my debts to them are numerous.

Many others have contributed as well. While not on my committee, Dr. Julian Gwyn, emeritus of the University of Ottawa, has been a steadfast supporter, as were Canadian scholars Dr. Faye Kert and Dr. David Bell. Dr. Alan Taylor sparked my interest in the Maine frontier and offered some kind advice along the way. Frances Raye, Valdine Atwood, and Wayne Wilcox, all of Washington County, Maine, are local historians who possess a remarkable knowledge of their communities. What would Maine do without people like these? My thanks to all of them.

Finally, I would like to thank my colleagues from graduate school, Hans Carlson, Brian Payne, and Micah Pawling.

I dedicate this work to my wife, Jea. She will always be my love and inspiration; she smuggled my heart away on first sight.

I

"THE HABIT OF SMUGGLING"

Smuggling can be understood in at least two ways. To law enforcers, it was a crime that deprived the state of needed income, threatened the standing order, and undermined deference to political and social leaders. But to others, smuggling was a form of self-help, a way that neighbor helped neighbor in the grim business of survival. When the opposing sides met, even by accident, violence often threatened. For example, after smugglers stumbled across Methodist missionary Joshua Marsden, who was a passenger on a vessel carrying contraband in Digby, Nova Scotia, the minister recorded that

> Digby is given up to smuggling, and at night, when the smugglers came on board, to carry their contraband goods ashore, we were greatly disturbed with their profane and worldly conversation; they continued to grow worse, and at last we reproved them, but this brought upon us a flood of reproach and invective: one of them, to show his importance, quoted a scrap of latin, but upon my calmly telling him we did not deal in scraps, his fury became ungovernable; and I believe, had it not been for fear of the consequence, they would have murdered us both.[1]

Marsden was no prig; he came from modest origins and had sailed before the mast as a common sailor.[2] But smugglers vexed him. Methodism's founder, John Wesley, deemed smuggling as bad as highway robbery, yet Marsden's own deacon who worked under him in the Saint John, New Brunswick, Methodist church, proved to be a smuggler, too. Marsden snubbed his deacon, a pious Loyalist named Stephen Humbert, on the grounds that Humbert engaged in the smuggling trade. The Saint John Methodist community nearly split over the friction between the missionary and the deacon.[3]

The divergence of opinions regarding smuggling was not unique to Saint

John. While lexicographer Samuel Johnson and other members of the privileged class denounced smuggling, other contemporary accounts leaned in the opposite direction. In addressing the new United States Congress in 1789 on the problem of smuggling, Fisher Ames stated, "The habit of smuggling pervades our country. We were taught it when it was considered rather as meritorious than criminal."[4] Ames referred back to the time before the American Revolution, when British imperial attempts to curb smuggling had helped to spark the spirit of revolt. Ames addressed the fact that the Revolution was partly initiated by angry crowds engaged in direct protest against antismuggling policies.

But smuggling was more than an ideological statement or a struggle between the haves and the have-nots. It was an activity participated in eagerly by all levels of society. The political elite of both Nova Scotia and New Brunswick engaged in smuggling; accusations of smuggling even resulted in a duel in Halifax in 1819 between the son of the provincial attorney general and a local merchant.[5] Similarly, Maine's political and economic leaders actively participated in smuggling. William King, the state's first governor, was a well-known smuggler.[6] Those charged with enforcing antismuggling laws found it a daunting task not only because of violent resistance but also because of apathy or resistance from above and often because of their own ambitions or greed.

Sympathy for smugglers surfaces in surprising places. Adam Smith, the famed political economist and a customs officer himself, wrote extensively about smugglers in his *Wealth of Nations*, the book that forms the basis of western liberal economic thought. He insisted that smugglers were essentially honest citizens but that unjust laws "made that a crime which nature never intended to be so."[7] Colonial New York merchants certainly found commercial restrictions "unnatural acts" that stymied mercantile initiative.[8] Little wonder then that smugglers on both sides of the Atlantic referred to themselves as "free traders."

Smuggling had one persistent quality: it always involved crossing a border. An understanding of illicit trade on a global scale places smuggling in the Bay of Fundy well within the normal commercial impulse of the Atlantic world. Bernard Bailyn has found that illicit commerce bound the Atlantic world together, despite mercantilist efforts to keep groups apart.[9] This included groups as diverse as Native American women who carried furs into colonial New York from New France, Acadians who traded furs with Massachusetts Bay, Philadelphians who smuggled French molasses, British merchants who introduced textiles illicitly into New Granada, Cornish smugglers who brought French wine to England, Yankee merchants landing tobacco at night on the Irish coast, and even the introduction of contraband slaves into the United States via Florida.[10] Smugglers brought goods out of countries illicitly, too: Dutch colonists smuggled cotton out of Demerara onto waiting British ships, Americans smuggled provisions out of the United States during Jefferson's embargo, and Loyalists and others from New Brunswick and Nova Scotia brought gypsum to eastern Maine.[11] The scale was enormous everywhere, and the Bay of Fundy was no exception. British Treasury officials investigating New Brunswick's illicit trade estimated that half of all goods brought into the colony were American contraband. This figure included up to seven-eighths of all wine, gin, and brandy; the same proportion of soap and candles; most indigo, tobacco, starch, mustard, and nankeen; and virtually all of the provinces' sailcloth, cordage, and anchors. The same commission found that even in Loyalist Saint John, there were shops filled entirely with American contraband goods, "and, if asked for, that such goods are instantly produced and openly avowed to be such."[12]

Smuggling existed throughout the Atlantic world, at many levels and in different societies. For the struggling poor, the problem was to wrest a living, while for political leaders, the problem was how to better control national wealth to strengthen the state. At first glance one might place smuggling within the tradition of proletarian struggle against the standing order as outlined by E. P. Thompson and more recently by Peter Linebaugh and Marcus Rediker.[13] But while smugglers engaged in all the tumults, riots, and traditional forms of community protest that excite neo-Marxist scholars and others, these "free traders" also seem to have collaborated with the rising middle class and actively—even enthusiastically—engaged in commercial enterprise. These struggles were not necessarily class struggles, but they were clearly a struggle between the state and the populace.

Britain, the foremost commercial nation of the eighteenth- and early nineteenth centuries, and the first to enter the industrial revolution, suffered an astonishing degree of smuggling that threatened both the government's revenues and its authority. British smugglers frequently operated in large, well-armed gangs that openly defied customs officers and even military units. Smugglers broke into customhouses, murdered informants, intimidated the legal system, bribed officials, and rescued compatriots from London's Newgate prison. Even the indomitable British admiral Horatio Nelson found himself unable to stop smuggling in Antigua in the late 1780s, one of the few defeats in his naval career.[14] A member of Parliament described smuggling as a national evil that tore apart the very fabric of British society.[15]

Illicit trade and smuggling-inspired violence required that the Crown mount a sustained and expensive effort to suppress it, often when the government was fighting wars overseas that required the very revenue that smuggling denied. In 1767, the British Crown employed 2,687 men to stop smuggling; by 1783 it employed 4,235. Yet Parliament reckoned that smugglers introduced twenty million pounds of tea and thirteen million gallons of brandy into Britain between 1780 and 1783, and reported that smuggling gangs of up to seven hundred roamed the English countryside.[16] By 1784, nine cavalry regiments and fifty-six revenue cutters in England and Scotland acted to suppress smuggling, at a cost of well over a quarter million pounds.[17] They failed. Parliament responded with several investigations headed by arch-mercantilist Lord Sheffield and ever harsher laws. In 1817, Parliament established a special Royal Navy Coast Blockade Service employing over three thousand personnel to contain smuggling in Kent and Sussex. The cost in lives escalated as well; throughout the 1820s gun battles erupted on England's southern coast. Both smugglers and preventative officers died. The authorities hanged several prominent smugglers and transported hundreds more to distant colonies.

The British government did not successfully curb smuggling until the 1840s when an enormous army of coast guards, combined with lower tariffs, made smuggling difficult and unprofitable. In some ways the destruction of the smuggling trade was a triumph for those espousing Adam Smith's liberal economics, such as David Ricardo and Sir Robert Peel, prime minister in the early 1840s. Peel found that by lowering tariffs and throwing open British ports to the world's shipping, many of the financial incentives to smuggle goods disappeared. Yet at the same time the state had to create a massive enforcement machinery to ensure that trade was carried out legally, so that it could be taxed and regulated. Illicit trade became increasingly furtive, involving concealment and bribery in the ports rather than large gangs on the beaches. In addition the type of smuggled commodities changed: smuggling increasingly became a matter of moving small, high-priced items rather than shiploads of bulky wool or barrels of claret. By 1857 British smuggling was a mere shadow of what it had been due to both increased state control and the effects of free trade.[18]

What drove British smuggling? British historian Cal Winslow perceived smuggling in the same light as poaching and wrecking, a "right" common people possessed according to custom and tradition.¹⁹ Ending smuggling, therefore, required a change in societal views as well. The industrial revolution harkened in a new age that demanded rationalization, professionalization, and respect for the law, and thus played an important part in ending the social economy of smuggling. The smuggler did not fit well into the scheme of modern commerce, which tended to confine international trade to fewer ports with larger and more modern facilities. The transition from mercantilism to economic liberalism put many smugglers out of work and made them conform to new economic realities. Those who remained in the trade practiced it through bribery, subtlety, and concealing cargoes within vessels. This practice, true to the age, was dubbed "scientific smuggling."²⁰

Customhouse corruption further undermined the enforcement of commercial regulation. Britain's tradition of colonial salutary neglect was not unique. The Spanish colonial empire was riddled with corruption and special deals that opened it to foreign traders. British colonial officials, too, evaded the intent of the Navigation Acts through a number of ruses. Over time, these evasions and indulgences became customary. Throughout the Americas, it seems likely that the diligent customs officer was the exception to the rule.²¹

Serious colonial problems with royal customs began in 1762, when Parliament passed an act calling for renewed vigilance on the part of customs officers stationed in North America. Since American colonies had long ignored Crown trade regulations, colonists saw the sudden vigilance of royal customhouse officers as a dangerous precedent. In contrast, the British government saw smuggling as a practice that threatened national security. Before the Revolution, the British government countered smuggling by appointing a host of new customs officers, using the Royal Navy to enforce the Navigation Acts, and even tampering with the colonial vice-admiralty courts that had been very lenient with colonial smugglers. This latter action, especially the removal of vice-admiralty jurisdiction to Halifax, Nova Scotia, alarmed many colonial smugglers, who rightly perceived that renewed imperial vigilance would cut into their profits. Many colonists in commercial coastal areas saw these actions as dangerous innovations that threatened their liberty, even those who later became Loyalists.

The northern commercial colonies were outspoken in their opposition to new customhouse regulations, especially Massachusetts Bay. The means used by Massachusetts varied from legal action to violence. Attorneys such as John Adams and James Otis successfully frustrated Crown officials in court. The irritation of Crown officials with Otis became so intense that a customhouse officer beat him over the head with a cane, permanently debilitating him. When legal methods ultimately failed against the determined royal government, the colonials adopted extralegal methods. Mobs throughout New England met the use of lightly armed revenue cutters with force. Naval vessels met with yet more resistance, including the destruction of HMS *Gaspee* in Rhode Island. Mobs in Massachusetts were equally adamant in obstructing royal customs officials. The most famous incident involved John Hancock's sloop *Liberty* in 1768, which directly resulted in the garrisoning of Boston with regiments of regulars. Bostonians harassed the troops constantly, resulting in the Boston massacre of 1770. Notably, the crowd had been provoking the guard posted at the customhouse. One rumor circulating in Boston even asserted that customs officials fired muskets out of the second-story windows of the customhouse into the crowd.

Maine, the third admiralty district of colonial Massachusetts, went through a very similar process of resistance to Crown authority. The only customs officials in Maine were those in the port of Falmouth (later Portland). From there they sometimes ranged up the coast to suppress smuggling and enforce the Navigation Acts. Events in Maine paralleled those in Boston. Local courts supported frivolous lawsuits against customs officials, but refused legal proceedings initiated by Crown collectors. In 1766, the people of Falmouth protested the Stamp Act by mobbing the customhouse, demanding the parcel of stamp paper, and burning it in the street. Later that year a mob rescued a cargo of smuggled West India goods seized by customs officials. The unpopularity of Falmouth's Crown officials continued to grow as their powers became more arbitrary. In one instance a crowd armed with pistols forced a customhouse officer to name an informer.[22]

Out of all the region's customhouse officers, Falmouth's citizens despised Comptroller of Customs John Malcom the most. This man had already become notorious in Rhode Island and North Carolina for his obnoxious political views and enforcement of unpopular commercial laws. Malcom proved to be just as unpopular in his native Maine as he was in other colonies. In 1773 local merchants and magistrates incited a crowd of sailors to rough up Malcom after he seized a vessel in Wiscasset, Maine. The mob broke Malcom's sword (a token of Crown authority), then tarred, feathered, and paraded him around the settlement. Malcom fled to Boston, where he suffered further abuse at the hands of another mob.[23] The lesson was not lost on his fellow customs officers.

In the spring of 1775, most of Falmouth's customs officials fled to the safety of HMS *Canceaux*, including men like Thomas Wyer, who spent much of the war at a British outpost on Penobscot Bay in eastern Maine, and later became a merchant and local official at Saint Andrews, New Brunswick, on Passamaquoddy Bay.[24]

Boston saw the most smuggling-related violence, however. The Boston crowds identified customhouse officers with royal government because they were the most obvious manifestation of Crown authority until the British army garrisoned the town. While the link between revolutionary fervor and smuggling is tenuous at best, it may be possible to link customhouse patronage with loyalism. Virtually all of Boston's customhouse officers joined the Loyalist cause in 1775 and 1776. When the British evacuated Boston in March 1776, a young Loyalist customs officer named Edward Winslow removed the royal coat of arms that hung over the entrance to Boston's customhouse. Winslow did not want the royal arms defaced by the American forces and hoped to return them to their rightful place someday. That dream proved unrealistic, but Winslow held onto the coat of arms and eventually hung them in the council chamber of New Brunswick, a Loyalist province created by the British for refugees like himself after the war. Winslow always hoped for a customhouse position himself, but like his dream of a Boston under royal rule, it never came to be.[25]

Could Loyalists be smugglers as well? Certainly Falmouth and Boston Loyalists retained their old business contacts and continued to illicitly trade with their American counterparts during the war from places like Penobscot and Passamaquoddy. After the war, too, Loyalists in New Brunswick and Nova Scotia continued to conduct illicit trade with Americans, even providing some American merchants with false shipping papers that allowed them access to forbidden British markets.[26] Unpopular customs officers in the Maritimes sometimes faced harassment similar to that in Falmouth and Boston before the war. Occasionally these attacks had ideological overtones, as when some "ill minded and disloyal person or persons" stole the royal coat of arms hanging over the door of the customhouse at Saint John, New Brunswick, in July 1814.[27]

These attacks were more likely immediate responses to unpopular taxation and the often heavy-handed methods of British Crown customs officers rather than ideological statements. Many Loyalists shared the same commercial values as the republican Americans, and smuggling was simply a means of conducting business. Lorenzo Sabine, who had been an American customs officer at Passamaquoddy and author of a two-volume biographical dictionary of Loyalists, noted the Loyalist propensity for smuggling and its seeming contradictions with their political principles:

> The Loyalists who, at the peace, removed to the present British colonies, and their children after them, smuggled almost every article of foreign origin from the frontier ports of the United States, for more than half a century, and until England relaxed her odious commercial policy. The merchant in whose counting-house I myself was bred, sold the "old Tories" and their descendants large quantities of tea, wine, spices, silks, crapes, and other articles, as part of his regular business. I have not room to relate the plans devised by sellers and buyers to elude the officers of the Crown, or the perils incurred by the latter, at times, while crossing the Bay of Fundy on their passage homeward. But I cannot forbear to remark, that, as the finding of a single box of contraband tea caused the confiscation of vessel and cargo, the smugglers kept vigilant watch with glasses, and committed the fatal herb to the sea, the instant a revenue cutter or ship of war hove in sight in a quarter to render capture probable. When a spectator of the scene, as I often was, how could I but say to myself,—"The destruction of tea in Boston, December, 1773, in principle, how like!"[28]

Loyalists were not blind followers of a royalist ideology. Canadian scholar Esther Clark Wright found that "the Loyalists were rather ordinary people subjected to an extraordinary experience." In many cases they faced the same rough frontier experience as their republican counterparts, especially in New Brunswick, where there was little British settlement before 1783.[29] One Loyalist response to New Brunswick's primitive conditions and uncertain economic conditions after the American Revolution was smuggling, a practical commercial stratagem adopted by many of their predecessors in the Bay of Fundy region.

The Bay of Fundy, as a part of the greater Atlantic economy, conformed to certain patterns, and smuggling was no exception. Throughout the seventeenth century, trade existed between the various groups surrounding the Bay of Fundy, including Indians.[30] Archaeologists studying the remains of seventeenth-century trading posts concluded that commerce with one's potential or actual enemies was "a way of life on a frontier where opportunity took precedence over political allegiance."[31]

During the eighteenth century, as the British exerted control over the area, smuggling continued as a means of ameliorating the harsh circumstances of life on a frontier. The Acadian people of what is now Nova Scotia technically fell under British control after the Treaty of Utrecht in 1713, yet they traded with whomever they pleased.[32] French influence in the Bay of Fundy endured until British forces captured Fort Beauséjour in 1755, and until then New England merchants continued to trade with their French colonial neighbors despite the law. Some of these smuggling vessels were heavily armed. The Boston smuggling sloop *Nancy and Sally* carried five swivel guns and a variety of muskets and musketoons. When a British naval vessel attempted to board the *Nancy and Sally* in June 1754, the smugglers resisted with force, and killed two Royal Navy sailors. A court convicted three of the smugglers of manslaughter, branded them on their left hands with the letter *M,* and imprisoned them for three months. Upon their release, the Royal Navy promptly impressed them.[33]

The New England settlers who came to Nova Scotia in the mid-eighteenth century, known as Planters, also smuggled in much the same way that their Massachusetts Bay relatives did. The scale was unremarkable, involving basic trade goods such as rum, wool cards, or a few gallons of molasses. The settlements surrounding the Bay of Fundy were too small to support significant trade, licit or otherwise. Furthermore, between 1713 and 1775 the region was unified under British rule. British regional domination meant that Massachusetts Bay and Nova Scotia operated under similar regulations and markets. Nonetheless, British warships occasionally patrolled the Bay of Fundy in the 1760s to suppress smuggling.

When the War of Independence broke out in 1775, new smuggling opportunities arose as governments attempted to regulate and tax trade. During the war, American timber merchants proved eager to sell masts to the Royal Navy in Halifax, and they gladly received contraband British goods that fetched high prices in Boston.[34] Loyalists at the British post at Penobscot actively participated in this contraband trade, as did various people at Passamaquoddy. An American commander described Passamaquoddy as a hotbed of smuggling and frequently reported his frustration at not being able to stop illicit trade.[35]

Soon after the end of the war in 1783, and largely due to the arrival of Loyalists, Britain created the new colony of New Brunswick on the northern shore of the Bay of Fundy. One of the first problems its administrators faced was controlling smuggling, especially at Passamaquoddy, which the Treaty of Paris in

1783 deemed the border between the United States and the remaining British North American colonies. Loyalists from Penobscot moved to Saint Andrews on the northeastern shore of Passamaquoddy Bay and quietly continued their illegal trade with American merchants. Nearby settlements also experienced an influx of contraband American goods, to the point where one Nova Scotia merchant complained in 1787 that "you can scarce enter a House, but you see an American package."[36]

Smuggling became a more important phenomenon in the region with the approach of the War of 1812, when its scope and scale became truly remarkable. Smugglers brought thousands of cattle to Nova Scotia, funneled hundreds of thousands of barrels of flour through the Maritimes, and secreted thousands of tons of gypsum across the border from New Brunswick into Maine. One New Brunswick merchant reckoned that during the War of 1812, a half million pounds sterling worth of contraband British manufactured goods went through his warehouse alone on their way to the American market. Given an exchange rate of $4.44 to £1 sterling, that amounts to a staggering $2.2 million.[37] American authorities agreed: in late 1814, Boston's customs collector estimated contraband worth some $3 million was ready to enter Maine through Halifax and Castine.[38]

The smuggling trade evolved largely as a result of a struggle between American demands for free trade and British mercantilist policies that slowly eroded in the early nineteenth century. This constantly fluctuating commercial war had consequences for the entire Atlantic community, reaching from the Caribbean sugar colonies to the Newfoundland fishing industry. On an official level, this struggle evolved as a series of trade negotiations and treaties between Britain and the United States. But at the commercial level it created greater incentives to smuggle because protective tariffs created greater incentives to engage in illicit cross-border trade.

Smuggling clearly represented a struggle over trade regulations, but what can it tell us about attitudes toward national boundaries? One answer is that the people who lived on either side of the borders imposed by the Treaty of Paris in 1783 contested them. The residents of Passamaquoddy refused to believe that their neighbors across the border were different from themselves. The American citizens of Passamaquoddy must have had great difficulty in imagining that the plantation owners of the South were more akin to themselves than the fishermen of Campobello or Grand Manan on the British North American side of the border. Borderland residents possessed an attitude that rejected the arbitrary authority of the state, an almost libertarian view that de-emphasized commercial restrictions and borders imposed by distant governments. Smuggling was the most obvious manifestation of this disregard for governmental interference in the economy. The more government forces attempted to halt unregulated trade, the more apparent it became to locals that the state was an unwelcome and alien force.

A measure of the importance government attached to the smuggling trade was the scale of the effort to halt it. The level of enforcement in the region, especially at Eastport, Maine, increased dramatically on the American side of the border. In 1807, the federal presence in Eastport consisted of an unarmed customs collector and perhaps half a dozen part-time assistants. By 1812, the federal government bolstered that presence with a new and more effective collector, a permanent U.S. deputy marshal, a fortification garrisoned by a half company of artillerists, and a revenue cutter. During the War of 1812, additional troops, up to five hundred, patrolled the area to suppress smuggling. In fact the only shots discharged in anger by the cannon of Fort Sullivan at Eastport were fired at smugglers.[39] However, the American forces at Passamaquoddy completely failed to suppress smuggling, in no small part because the local judicial system often favored the smugglers, as did customs officials and militia.

On the New Brunswick side of Passamaquoddy, officialdom mustered its strength to combat smuggling. The region's superintendent of trade and fisheries operated a cutter that occasionally captured smugglers. But the customs officers in both New Brunswick and Nova Scotia were corrupt and refused to support him. The Royal Navy sometimes interfered with smuggling, but the best tool it had to stop smuggling—impressment—was no longer in use after 1815. Nor was the authority of the Royal Navy necessarily respected; smugglers sometimes rescued vessels seized by naval units or other officials. The British imperial government as a whole did not seem to be interested in promoting colonial commerce over that of the United States, and the colonial governments were not capable of halting illegal commerce even when they acted in concert.[40]

An example of this is the effort by Nova Scotia and New Brunswick officials to control the carrying trade in gypsum after the War of 1812. Gypsum, mined at the head of the Bay of Fundy, was highly desired by American farmers as a fertilizer in the Mid-Atlantic and Upper South. Until the 1820s Nova Scotia was the foremost producer of gypsum in North America. Producers generally shipped it to Passamaquoddy, where American merchants bought it in lots of twenty to sixty tons. The plan failed in part because of American diplomatic pressure, but also because smugglers at Passamaquoddy persisted in selling gypsum to the Americans.[41] The manner in which the gypsum smugglers rejected government regulations was not subtle: it involved kidnapping government officers, shooting at provincial officials, and arming vessels with cannon and muskets. In 1820 a "plaster war" broke out between New Brunswick officials and plaster smugglers. At its height, plaster smugglers lashed together rafts of up to ten schooners and brigs for self-defense and sailed down Passamaquoddy Bay in open defiance of the official appointed to regulate the plaster trade. That official was Stephen Humbert, the same Methodist deacon and sometime smuggler who so shocked the Reverend Marsden. Despite his own experience as a smuggler, Humbert proved powerless to resist such determined opposition and could only watch as the plaster vessels made their escape.[42]

Smuggling in the Bay of Fundy eventually lessened through a combination of state intervention and economic liberalization. Small-scale smuggling persisted, but the new economic liberalism with its emphasis on free trade meant that the days of large-scale illicit trade ended in this region by the middle of the nineteenth century. Reciprocity, a trade policy whereby British colonies in North America could trade with the United States on virtually the same footing as American shippers, proved especially effective in removing the incentives to smuggle.

Because the state imposed the border in the very area where governmental authority was weakest, locals could and often did choose to ignore that border. Border populations could defy the authority of distant governments with some impunity. Passamaquoddy's isolation, low population density, cross-border marriages and connections fostered by locals, and identical frontier experiences resulted in a common rejection of bothersome commercial regulations. Border communities tolerated smuggling and extended this acceptance of illicit trade to "adventurers," smugglers from as far afield as New York City, Liverpool, England, or even Sweden and the Caribbean.

Smugglers were not usually cutthroats or pirates; generally they were ordinary merchants, farmers, and sailors seeking to augment their incomes or support their families. As Adam Smith noted in his *Wealth of Nations*, it was not the actions of smugglers that made them lawbreakers but rather the oppressive laws they evaded that made their acts criminal.[43] Public opinion often refused to associate smuggling with crime; after all, smugglers provided valuable services to the community when they brought cheap goods into it, including even the necessities of life like flour.

One unique aspect of smuggling in the Passamaquoddy region was its relative lack of violence, especially when compared with the British model. Threats were the most common form of violence. Only a scant handful of people died in smuggling-related violence, while wounds or beatings were relatively rare. There was plenty of gun play, but commonly the shots tended to be aimed at sails or ahead of a boat. Cruel atrocities were almost completely absent. One British soldier did claim that smugglers threatened to make him walk the plank, a detail that caught the attention of the authorities. The story quickly unraveled under questioning; the soldier was actually in cahoots with the smugglers and concocted the story as part of his alibi.[44]

There were many reasons to smuggle: sometimes it was a carefully calculated practice, sometimes it happened when an unusual opportunity arose, and sometimes it happened by mistake, either feigned or actual. Several factors promoted smuggling. Political control of mercantilist economies actively attempted to deny certain goods to other states, and smugglers often stepped in to provide contraband goods despite commercial laws. In effect, the political economies artificially inflated prices by regulating or taxing foreign goods; this meant that smugglers could and did often offer goods at prices below those set by law-abiding merchants. Furthermore, banking and financial systems were too crude to accommodate all merchants in the Atlantic world, especially given the perpetual shortage of specie; often merchants and mariners had to receive foreign goods in exchange for their own rather than cash. Mercantile culture, too, encouraged participants to "buy cheap and sell dear," a maxim that encouraged all manner of illicit activity, such as diluting barrels of rum, putting rocks in flour barrels, and selling short measures. Smuggling was simply a part of this mix for many merchants throughout the Atlantic world, in important ports like New York as well as isolated ones on the Maine coast.[45] But Passamaquoddy offered unusually good opportunities to both locals and those from away to engage in illicit trade because of the indeterminate border, frequent fogs, numerous secluded coves, beaches, and islands, and its placement at the interface between the mighty commercial British Empire and the rising agrarian American republic.

The lure of profit drew adventurers to Passamaquoddy, whose reputation as a smugglers' haven drew merchants such as John Clap of New York to the region. He attempted to smuggle a cargo of provisions into New Brunswick in a small fleet of eight boats and rafts, but American officials seized his goods and successfully prosecuted him.[46] Another example is Nathan Appleton, who during the War of 1812 smuggled British manufactured goods into the United

States via Saint Andrews, New Brunswick. He in turn channeled his profits into a manufacturing venture sponsored by Francis Cabot Lowell of the famous "Boston Associates," who constructed the first large textile mills in the United States.[47]

It is less easy to divine the reasons why common fishermen, farmers, and timbermen smuggled. Many undoubtedly engaged in it for profit like the adventurers; others wanted to support their families, or they found themselves trapped in unusual circumstances. Maine's sailors were notorious smugglers, stuffing their sea chests and bed sacks full of expensive cotton and packages of sugar to augment their meager wages.[48] Fishermen regularly engaged in smuggling on a small scale, trading American provisions and products like shoes to their Maritime counterparts in return for fish. This saved the American fishermen a great deal of labor, provided New Brunswick and Nova Scotia families with food and other goods at reduced prices, and had the added bonus that the practice was virtually impossible to detect. American farmers frequently drove their cattle to the border to sell in British North America, even when their own government forbade it. When government officials attempted to interfere, farmers fought back.[49] American timbermen, too, engaged in smuggling when their New Brunswick employers chose to pay them in goods rather than specie. When they attempted to cross the border back into the United States, American customs authorities seized their hard-earned British goods as contraband.[50]

In New Brunswick and Nova Scotia smugglers also came from all walks of life. Poor mariners and wealthy merchants alike engaged in illegal commerce. Moreover, British adventurers from afar came to the region to smuggle. One such adventurer was John Young, a Scottish merchant who ventured to Castine, Maine, to partake of the profitable trade with the enemy under the aegis of British troops who occupied the town during the winter of 1814–15. Apparently he was not a man for half measures. Not only did he buy smuggled goods from willing Americans, but he in turn avoided the 5 percent duty imposed by British customs officials there when he packed contraband tobacco, soap, candles, and other American goods in barrels of codfish. His justification was of ancient vintage: "We are you know creatures of imitative habits & as all around me are smuggling I am beginning to smuggle too."[51] Like their American counterparts, some Maritime smugglers used their ill-gotten gains to fund more legitimate ventures. Christopher Scott, founder of the Bank of New Brunswick, made his fortune as a smuggler "on the lines," as many referred to the border.[52]

Samuel Cunard, as a young captain of his father's coasting schooner, engaged in the Passamaquoddy smuggling trade before founding the most famous shipping line in history.[53]

Ordinary Maritimers smuggled, too. Like their American counterparts, they sought to wrest a living by farming, lumbering, or fishing, and feared taxes that had to be paid in cash. Seeking out lower prices, high-quality goods, and easy profits at the expense of the government was a rational survival strategy that often gained the acceptance or at least acquiescence of entire communities. Smuggling at Passamaquoddy quickly became something of a local tradition: one New Brunswick local who lived close to the border recalled smuggling as one of the region's most important trades, "which some are in the habit of styling Contraband—but which we call *free trade*. Our geographical position exposes us to great temptations in this respect."[54]

With the exception of John Wesley and the Methodists, and a handful of honest government officials, it is difficult to find a group that found smuggling immoral. Common people traded illegally to survive, and local traditions often condoned the practice. Merchants smuggled for profit, but even the smuggling adventurers often had a very strong strain of Christian morality, or at least liked to promote that image. In border communities the most successful smugglers topped the list of donors in constructing churches. This is most obvious in Saint Andrews, where Scottish smuggler Christopher Scott financed an elegant Presbyterian church virtually unaided by fellow parishioners. It is equally true in Lubec, Maine, where the Yankee smuggler Jabez Mowry donated liberally to the construction of that town's first schoolhouse and church.[55]

Churchly folk were just as likely to smuggle at Passamaquoddy as any. Four out of the five famously pious Baptist Tappan brothers are a dramatic example of this phenomenon. During the War of 1812 they continued their silk importation business by smuggling through Canada. Arthur Tappan, later a renowned abolitionist known for his role in the *Amistad* trial, conducted business out of Montreal for part of the war; he later introduced contraband cargoes through Castine, Maine.[56] His older brother John, who taught Arthur the mercantile trade, smuggled goods through Halifax and the Bay of Fundy.[57] Younger brother Lewis also seems to have introduced goods illegally into the United States from British North America. In 1813, he and his partner George Searle petitioned Congress for relief from the penalties incurred while importing goods into the United States through Passamaquoddy. Lewis went on to create the nation's first commercial credit-rating agency, and he was equally zealous as Arthur in promoting Abolitionism and other moral reforms.[58] The fourth brother, Charles, was involved in complex smuggling schemes known as collusive capture during the War of 1812, and he admitted as much as an elderly man.[59] Ironically, the Tappans were the primary sponsors of famed abolitionist William Lloyd Garrison.[60] The Tappans became very successful businessmen, in part because early in their careers they smuggled. Yet at the same time they were strictly moral Christians who even forbade their clerks to attend performances at theaters. Americans simply refused to perceive smuggling as a morality issue.

Did smuggling bind the region together, creating a "special relationship" between New England and the Maritimes? There is ample evidence that there were cultural sympathies between New England and the Maritimes. Adam Smith's dictum that a merchant "is not necessarily the citizen of any particular country" also hints at the tendency of commerce to diminish the importance of borders.[61] The presence of so many adventurers from distant ports indicates that smuggling was not merely a local phenomenon but part of a larger commercial pattern that encompassed the entire Atlantic basin. Smuggling thrived at Passamaquoddy and other coastal smuggling havens because it was more convenient to conduct illicit trade there than to obey the burdensome commercial laws imposed by the state. Another reason smuggling thrived at Passamaquoddy was because the border between two great commercial powers ran through it. Smuggling was closely related to the border, an invisible line between the United States and British North America that profoundly shaped the daily lives of Passamaquoddy residents. For governments, smuggling was a challenge that led to disorder, loss of revenue, and higher taxes. Smugglers and government were locked in combat, and sometimes the smugglers won.

2

"A SORT OF NEUTRALITY"

Lewis Frederick Delesdernier had delayed his report to Secretary of the Treasury Alexander Hamilton as long as possible. Hamilton demanded that the customs collectors write a detailed report outlining the boundaries and economic activities of each customs district. It proved difficult to write, in no small part because Delesdernier's district was uniquely troubled by the conflicting claims of Britain and the United States to sovereignty over the region's several islands. In point of fact, Delesdernier kept the United States customhouse on Frederick Isle, a tiny island repeatedly claimed by New Brunswick.

Another of Delesdernier's difficulties was determining exactly what Passamaquoddy was; the word meant different things to different peoples. The word *Passamaquoddy* itself is Native American and translates roughly as "place where the Pollock are" or "place where the Pollock leap entirely out of the water," a reference to the area's bountiful fishing grounds.[1] Euro-Americans generally referred to the indigenous peoples who hunted and fished local waters as the Passamaquoddy tribe. The United States Congress picked up the term in 1789 when naming customs districts, thus making it an administrative term. But the most common use of the word *Passamaquoddy* was imprecise, denoting the lands surrounding the bay and its numerous islands. Often locals shortened the term to *'Quoddy*.

The 1783 Treaty of Paris that established boundaries between the remaining British possessions in North America and the newly created United States did so in only vague terms, and the new nation and colonial power disagreed on the exact location of the borderline. The eastern shore of the bay was generally conceded to be British-held territory after 1783, and the western side was American, but both governments claimed jurisdiction over the islands in the bay. Conflicting claims resulted in legal tangles when law officers attempted to impose their authority. Delesdernier's experience of this confusion was direct. In December 1788, armed New Brunswick officials landed on the shore beneath his own home and claimed jurisdiction over the island he lived on. Delesdernier defended his house with an ax, thereby protecting hearth and home as well as the sovereignty of the United States.[2]

Because officials like Delesdernier could not discern the limits of their authority until Britain and the United States established a definite border, efforts to regulate commerce and taxation were of little avail. The most troublesome spot was Moose Island. Delesdernier described the island's inhabitants as "acting in a kind of neutrality (if the expression may be admitted)."[3] Delesdernier's apology for the term *neutrality* is in itself revealing. The collector seemed to feel that this behavior was unusual—even embarrassing—to report to the federal government in distant New York City.

Delesdernier was not the only government official troubled by the seeming lawlessness of the Passamaquoddy region. A British colonial official claimed that the region was an asylum for deserters from the British navy and army, as well as criminals and absconding debtors from both Nova Scotia and New Brunswick.[4] An American observer suggested in 1802 that the islands of Passamaquoddy were so troublesome and crime-ridden that they were best given to the British.[5] As early as 1791, a Scottish traveler thought Moose Island was inhabited by Yankee smugglers.[6]

The complex marine geography and local weather patterns proved especially advantageous to smugglers. The average tidal range at 'Quoddy is from eighteen to twenty feet. The tides did not merely rise and fall; the greater the tides, the greater the currents associated with them. Twice every day a staggering seventy billion cubic feet of water entered and exited Passamaquoddy Bay, creating rapid currents, eddies, and even whirlpools. In warmer months, the combination of warm air and cold ocean waters resulted in thick fogs that reduced visibility to a few feet and could last weeks. Currents swept even large ships onto ledges, or cliffs; currents spilled passengers from smaller boats into chill waters; fogs hid reefs and other vessels. Local smugglers boasted that fog was created to cover their actions.[7]

Prudent mariners who wanted to enter Passamaquoddy Bay picked up a pilot with local knowledge to guide them through the treacherous waters.[8] There were three channels into Passamaquoddy: the Western Passage, Head Harbor Passage (often referred to as the Ship Channel), and Letite Passage. The Western Passage was a shallow, narrow, and crooked channel between

West Quoddy Head on the American mainland and Campobello Island in New Brunswick. Only smaller craft could use this approach, such as smuggling vessels eluding pursuers. At the eastern end of Campobello lay Head Harbour Passage, a wide channel that even the largest sailing vessels could enter. The narrow Letite Passage on the eastern end of Deer Island was generally too dangerous for sail-driven or oar-propelled vessels to navigate because of its eddies, boils, and numerous rocks and ledges. Most ships used Head Harbour Passage; locals might on occasion use the other channels, but they were risky choices.

The harbor between Campobello and Eastport offered sailors a sheltered anchorage surrounded by islands, some American-held and some British. Most of the islands fell within the British jurisdiction, but the American government claimed Moose, Dudley, and Frederick islands. British-held Campobello was the largest island in the bay. Its seven-and-a-half-mile length formed a barrier between Passamaquoddy Bay and the Bay of Fundy. In 1803, about 245 people of all ages lived on Campobello, mostly fisherfolk who operated a few dozen open fishing boats and a handful of small trading schooners.[9] Campobello was ideally situated for smuggling; its proximity to both the American mainland and American-held Moose Island and its gentle cobble beaches and anchorages provided smugglers with a base to quickly introduce contraband into the United States and vice versa.

Deer Island, also on the British side of the border, was the second largest island in the bay. In 1803, about 117 people populated its shores, mostly fishermen and their families. It was a smugglers' haven as well; on still nights people on American-held Moose Island could hear smugglers loading and unloading boats on Deer Island.[10]

Moose Island was the smallest of the three major islands. While most of its settlers were Americans, New Brunswick claimed it until 1818. Because of the conflicting claims, neither government could give meaningful deeds to land there. In the meantime a few score of squatters quietly took possession, enjoying the fact that contested jurisdiction meant they paid no taxes to anyone. A Massachusetts sheriff took matters into his own hands and came to the island with an armed party. After a confrontation in which the squatters almost destroyed his boat, he finally reached an agreement whereby they received legal deeds and guarantees of a five-year tax exemption in return for their adherence to the laws of Massachusetts.[11] In 1798, the Commonwealth of Massachusetts incorporated the community as "Eastport." Even after incorporation its residents remained indifferent to the sort of improvements that marked a permanent community, such as public roads, schoolhouses, and churches. They even resented and resisted the idea of creating streets, preferring to use the beaches as rudimentary roads, climbing over rocks where necessary.[12] Despite this lack of planning, the population grew steadily from 244 in 1790 to over 500 in 1800, to more than 1,500 in 1810, and almost 2,000 in 1820. Primarily a fishing community, it increasingly became a commercial center and a notorious smugglers' den.

Passamaquoddy Bay proper lay north of Moose and Deer islands. In 1784, Loyalists founded a substantial port community known as Saint Andrews on the northern shore of the bay. Saint Andrews was the principal Loyalist community in Passamaquoddy, and besides serving as a commercial center, also served as the shire town of Charlotte County, New Brunswick. The county's jurisdiction included the islands of the bay, Grand Manan, and the entire eastern shore of Passamaquoddy Bay and the Saint Croix River. Like Eastport, Saint Andrews was a notorious smuggling port. Unlike Eastport, Saint Andrews was a well-planned community that boasted streets laid out on a grid system, a courthouse and jail, and an Anglican church.

The Saint Croix River, often known as the Schoodic, is nearly a mile wide at its mouth; it flows into the northwest corner of the bay between Saint Andrews and Robbinston. The border now runs down the middle of the channel, but for years after the American Revolution both American and New Brunswick officials debated which river was the "true" Saint Croix. The Americans claimed it lay east of the Schoodic, while British colonial officials claimed it lay to the west. Loyalist Robert Pagan of Saint Andrews finally resolved the matter in the mid-1790s when he uncovered the remains of an old French fortification dating to the early seventeenth century on an island midstream in the Saint Croix. The ruins proved that the Saint Croix was the border as intended by the 1783 Treaty of Paris.[13]

The Saint Croix's head of navigation lay about ten miles upstream from its mouth; settlements formed there on both banks. On the American side lay Calais, and on the New Brunswick bank lay Saint Stephen, barely a hundred yards away. Shipping could not go beyond this point, but rafts of timber floated down from the forests upstream to the sawmills at the falls that lay between the two communities. Here, too, the border proved awkward. For example, the New Brunswick assembly refused to grant a license to operate a ferry from Saint Stephen to Calais because it lacked the powers to permit an international voyage.[14] Nonetheless, boats constantly crossed between the two communities, which shared churches, schools, and employment at saw mills and wharves.

Although it was not always obvious to visitors, several different groups occupied the Passamaquoddy landscape. The first was the Passamaquoddy Nation, the original inhabitants of the region. The second were British colonists who arrived before 1775. The Loyalists, the largest group of settlers, arrived very suddenly in large groups in 1783 and 1784. On the American side of the border a steady trickle of Yankee fishermen, timbermen, and merchants developed a community on Moose Island and along the west shore of the Saint Croix.

The Passamaquoddy Nation was separated from later settlers by race, religion, and language. Numbering in the several hundreds, the Passamaquoddy maintained their traditional lifestyle as best they could in the face of white invasion. They were in many ways a marine people; observers noted their abilities to navigate the area's rough waters, especially when hunting porpoise. The Passamaquoddy suffered directly from the 1783 Treaty of Paris in that Loyalist settlers displaced the native community. These troubles peaked in 1784, when the Passamaquoddy captured and held a Loyalist surveyor encroaching on their lands. The surveyor soon escaped, and the tensions eased.[15]

Correctly perceiving their perilous situation on a border between aggressive Loyalist and American settlers, the Passamaquoddy pursued a cautious diplomacy with both New Brunswick and Massachusetts officials. The result was that whites perceived the Passamaquoddy as essentially neutral and therefore worth courting on occasion. For example, both sides sought Indian depositions in the 1790s when a commission met to determine the location of the "true" Saint Croix River. The Passamaquoddy seem to have steered clear of smuggling. However, there is some evidence that they may have sold canoes to smugglers or even acted as guides to smugglers who used Indian trails and canoe routes to bring smuggled goods away from Passamaquoddy.[16]

White settlers largely shunned the Passamaquoddy. American veterans who fought alongside the Passamaquoddy in the Revolution, such as John Allan and Lewis Delesdernier, did advocate for them, as did David Owen of Campobello, who took a paternal interest in their affairs. Other borderland residents had more difficulty, such as Moose Island merchant Nathaniel Goddard, who recorded several scuffles with Indians who came to his store.[17] Furthermore, whites on both sides plundered valuable timber from Indian lands.[18]

If the Passamaquoddy people were distinct and separate from the people who arrived later in the region, they were also the reason the first English-speaking settlers came to the region. Fur traders came first, followed by fishermen, lured by the bountiful fisheries. A settlement emerged on Campobello in the early 1770s because the wealthy Owen family received this island as a land grant from Nova Scotia colonial authorities. Most of these early settlers were English, Irish, Welsh, and Scottish, but a few were Yankees from New England. During the Revolution some sided with the British, others sided with the Americans, and some remained neutral or left the region. A few early settlers remained at Passamaquoddy after the War of Independence, but the arrival of the Loyalist refugees and American settlers quickly subsumed them.

New Brunswick's Loyalist refugees were a diverse group that included Germans, Scots, Irish, southerners, Quakers, New Englanders, New Yorkers, and blacks, both enslaved and free. Many were former members of the British military, while others were civilians. The Loyalists arrived en masse in late 1783 and 1784; several thousand settled on the eastern shore and islands in the bay. Many were members of the "Penobscot Association," both civilian and veteran Loyalists who had collected in eastern Maine during the latter phase of the Revolution. Saint Andrews was their main settlement, planned on a rigid grid system by military engineers as a commercial center and regional port.

Settlers on the American side arrived more slowly. A few veterans, such as John Allan and Delesdernier, moved to Passamaquoddy immediately after the Revolution. In the 1780s, fishermen from Cape Ann and other Massachusetts fishing communities settled on Moose Island. Small communities began to develop along the western shores of the bay and banks of the Saint Croix by 1790, primarily focused on the timber trade. While many of these settlers were veterans of the American Revolution, they were not pursuing a political or ideological goal in settling the region; rather, they hoped to prosper. Land speculators divided the land into lots, fisherman pursued shoals of fish, and timbermen worked the woods. John Faxon, a Continental Army veteran, moved to Grand Manan island and initially got along very well with its Loyalist proprietor, took an oath of loyalty to the British Crown, and just as easily moved back across the border when better opportunities presented themselves.[19] Nathaniel Goddard, Moose Island's first merchant, sold goods to anyone for payment up-front, including Indians, Loyalists, and criminals. He also slept with a loaded musket in his store to protect his merchandise.[20]

The harshness of the conditions at Passamaquoddy and the identical nature of the extraction economy tended to suppress the differences between the peoples on both sides of the border. Passamaquoddy and white, Loyalist and republican, all found accommodation more advantageous than confrontation. Trade was the obvious manifestation of this accommodation, the most remarkable example of this being Benedict Arnold's occasional appearances in the early 1790s. Arnold's presence drew a variety of reactions from the American population. One soldier who had fought under Arnold in the Continental Army burst into tears of anguish when he saw his old commander near Campobello. Others reacted more negatively, especially those who had suffered in his raid on New London, Connecticut, after he defected to the British.[21]

There are numerous examples of family and other social ties that spanned the border. Lewis Delesdernier himself had kin in Nova Scotia.[22] John Brewer, a local postmaster, militia officer, and innkeeper who also engaged in shipbuilding and the timber trade, married a daughter of Nehemiah Marks, a prominent Loyalist who helped found nearby Saint Stephen, just across the border in New Brunswick. This action, combined with his close dealings with New Brunswick merchants and his occasional smuggling ventures, ensured the enmity of some Americans who viewed him as a traitor, both to the United States and to the Commonwealth of Massachusetts.[23] Men such as the merchant Joseph Porter from New Hampshire easily crossed the border with few qualms. Arriving at Passamaquoddy in 1786, he moved into New Brunswick around 1795 after marrying another daughter of Nehemiah Marks, a prominent Loyalist. Despite some concerns about whether he was actually a British subject or not, he eventually became a magistrate and a representative to the provincial assembly.[24] Cross-border marriages were frequent, both among the better-off merchants and poor fishermen. Eastport's vital records list dozens of cross-border marriages in the first decade of the nineteenth century.[25] Cross-border friendships are harder to trace. But clearly merchants developed commercial relationships that built cross-border trust. The creation of Masonic lodges and churches with transnational memberships in the nineteenth century indicates a community that spanned the border, among both local leaders and ordinary folk.[26]

Strangers to the region reported no difference in the appearance of Passamaquoddy's white population; they dressed alike, spoke alike, ate alike, and worked alike. Even the vernacular architecture was identical.[27] The similarity created considerable confusion about who belonged on which side of the border; occasionally it turned out that an American citizen served in New

Brunswick's provincial assembly, or a New Brunswicker held office in Maine, even though he never renounced his British citizenship.[28] Their aspirations and experiences were similar, too. Settlers came to Passamaquoddy seeking economic opportunity. Daily life was a fierce struggle in which settlers attempted to farm the land or more likely extract timber or fish from the forests and coastal waters; few had the time to reflect on the political nature of their communities. Moose Island's settlers knew this fact well, stating, "The fate of first settlers, in a new Country, is well known, to work hard, and fare hard."[29] Frontier hardships consumed much of their energy, leaving little time for ideological concerns. When at their ease, both Loyalist and American settlers were far more likely to engage in hard drinking than political discourse.[30]

People also came to Passamaquoddy because it offered refuge from conflict, personal failure, or criminal conduct. New Brunswick's Loyalists were all refugees from the American Revolution. Many colonials came to Eastport fleeing debt prosecutions; Americans fled to New Brunswick for the same reason.[31] Others fled bad marriages, like Colonel George Peck of Rhode Island, who, despite his Revolutionary War service fighting the British, fled to Campobello when his marriage failed.[32]

Whether seeking a bright future or fleeing a dark past, settlers on both sides of the border faced similar challenges and conditions. As noted by one observer, a new settler

> fixes upon a spot for his house.—Takes his axe and cuts down Fir Trees which he afterwards junks to twenty or six & twenty feet length, dovetails them at the four corners of his Cottage, which made up of these logs and well stuffed in the seams with moss serves for his House.—A cellar is built underground in the same manner to preserve his potatoes and thus in one year's time has something to live upon.—A pig is next wanted and a cow.—The cow feeds in the Woods with a Bell round her neck to discover where she is.—And the Pigs are often two or three months away & come home frequently in Autumn full fed & fit to kill.

Personal possessions were few, as were other amenities:

> "The breakfast and supper of a Labourer is Fish, Potatoes and Tea sweetened with Molasses—his Dinner Pork & Potatoes.—His Bed a Blanket upon the floor.—Custom makes his sleep easy—all Payments are made in Barter.—There is no Specie in the Bay.—Dried Fish is the Common Truck at 12/6 a Quintal upon an average.—Fish are not so plenty as for-

merly, so that now the land begins to be cultivated: for a Fisherman will never cultivate.—He is like an Indian in that respect."

The one difference from other areas was that this observer went on to assume that "smuggling will naturally take place," a phenomenon he did not seem to find offensive.[33]

Ordinary settlers did not have to rely on the goodwill of wealthy patrons or landlords and usually did not have to display deference to those who considered themselves socially superior.[34] This is not especially surprising in the post-Revolutionary United States, but it is somewhat surprising in New Brunswick, where the Loyalist leadership openly espoused an elitist political worldview.[35] The island of Campobello offers further evidence of how poorly British-style deference worked on the frontier.

The island's proprietor was David Owen, a member of the Welsh gentry, educated at Cambridge, and a sometime tutor to future British prime minister William Pitt the Younger. When he arrived on Campobello to reassert his family's claims to the island, he faced opposition from Loyalists who thought they had a right to the land because of a provincial grant and from pre-Loyalists such as the Wilson family who claimed ownership through continued possession and improvement. Owen easily swept aside the Loyalist claims, but the courts found in favor of the squatter Wilson family.[36]

Undaunted, Owen attempted to establish his superiority when he expressed his contempt for New Brunswick officials, defied other Charlotte County magistrates, and displayed his disdain for Loyalist settlers. Owen even considered himself above trade regulations. Royal Navy officers accused him of taking steps "in favor of the smugglers," and he rented wharves and warehouses to American smugglers.[37]

Owen ran his island like a feudal estate, leasing out plots of land rather than selling them. Owen's relationship with his tenants was often violent rather than deferential. Angry tenants assaulted Owen numerous times, sometimes in his own house. Servants betrayed him, tenants in arrears burned outbuildings, and Owen in turn physically attacked, swore at, and used legal proceedings against his opponents. Deference played little role in everyday life at Passamaquoddy in part because most settlers possessed frontier ideas of equality that had little to do with American revolutionary ideology. Like their American counterparts, Loyalists preferred to work on their own lands, eschewing wage labor and tenantry in favor of working on their own farms.[38]

British observers found New Brunswickers' lack of deference deeply troubling. For example, one British military officer complained of his colonial escort at Passamaquoddy, claiming the manners of his boatmen savored of American equality, joining in his conversations and refusing to carry his portmanteaus from the boat to his lodgings. Observers found that even Loyalist offspring behaved in a "Yankee" manner. Like the United States, poor New Brunswickers felt no compulsion to observe deference because the availability of opportunities and land elsewhere fostered independence.[39]

'Quoddy was a resource frontier, where the extraction of staple goods such as fish and timber dominated daily lives. The region's settlers were reliant on distant markets for their economic well-being. Agrarian self-sufficiency was impossible due to the region's poor farming conditions, and external markets were absolutely vital to raise the money required to buy essentials like flour, molasses, rum, and other goods. Many sought to engage in wage labor to load ships, mill timber, or construct buildings, returning to their scratch farms and fishing boats when there was no demand for their labor. Weaving, making lime, stitching shoes, or setting themselves up as small-scale traders were also common activities. Trade was a natural and everyday occurrence; smuggling was a pragmatic response to bothersome trade regulations that interfered with family economies.[40] This opportunism meant that when smugglers offered high wages to pull their oars or move their contraband, locals jumped at the opportunity and asked few questions.

Three groups dominated the region's economy on both sides of the border: fishermen, timbermen, and merchants. All had unique relationships with smuggling. Fishermen had their boats, timbermen notoriously worked the woods on both sides of the border, and merchants by their very nature engaged in trade, even if it was illicit.

In the 1780s and 1790s, fishing was the most common vocation pursued by settlers, especially on the islands. An 1800 census of Moose Island reveals that 83 percent of the heads of household were fishermen, and only one individual was listed as a "farmer."[41] Moose Island's fishermen had a few cleared acres—generally less than ten—and some cows. Fishermen were noted for their poverty. A Loyalist wrote in 1784, "The people, as a Body, will ever be *poor* and *miserable*—From my own observation at Passamaquoddy, I am persuaded that a coast calculated for fishing is so far from being a benefit, that it really is a *curse* to the Inhabitants. Who ever knew a Fisherman Thrive?"[42]

New Brunswick fishermen tended to sell their catch to American merchants because they consistently provided not only better prices but also higher-quality provisions at lower cost than colonial merchants.[43] American fishermen took advantage of this by loading their vessels with provisions and swapping them for a New Brunswick fisherman's catch. This illicit form of trade was mutually advantageous and proved very difficult to uncover. Fishermen were an ideal smuggling population; they lived on the border, had an intimate knowledge of local waters, had access to boats, and suffered a grinding poverty that compelled them to augment their living any way they could. British colonial officials described Passamaquoddy's fishermen as a "lawless rabble" and complained of their extensive violations of sovereignty and smuggling.[44] Furthermore, by the 1790s Passamaquoddy fishermen usually fished at night, using torches to draw shoals of herring to their nets.[45] This provided them with the perfect excuse to be on the water after dark—which also happened to be the best time to engage in smuggling. Fishermen were as unconcerned with ideology or national borders as the fish they caught. They came to Passamaquoddy Bay in pursuit of fish, crossing and recrossing the border at will. Their worldview was essentially local and libertarian.

When opportunities arose, fishermen eagerly abandoned their boats for timber camps. Timber prices rose dramatically in 1807 and 1808, causing many fishermen to go up the Saint Croix and work in the woods.[46] Timbermen were poor and like many fishermen lived in perpetual debt to merchants. External observers in both Maine and New Brunswick thought that timbermen were little more than shiftless, drunken banditti.[47] They had little respect for authority, and often stripped Crown forests and Indian lands of their valuable trees.[48] Timbermen, too, were smugglers, often not from choice but because colonial merchants paid them in British manufactured goods. When they crossed the border, American customs officials sometimes seized these goods as contraband.[49]

Passamaquoddy's merchants were the most significant component of the borderland population in terms of smuggling. Merchants were the vital link with the outside world. They understood markets and profit, and they owned the wharves, warehouses, and ships that made smuggling possible. Like the less wealthy borderland population, the region's merchants engaged in varied mercantile pursuits; few merchants could afford to specialize in any one activity. Many of these merchants came to Passamaquoddy specifically because they wanted to engage in smuggling. Three groups of merchants dominated local commerce, both licit and illicit: Scots, Loyalists, and Yankees.

Lowland Scots held a large amount of economic influence within the

British Empire. Keenly competitive and clannish, they were often detested by non-Scots.[50] They may also have been unpopular because of their success. Scots merchants dominated both Halifax and Saint John and initiated the true capitalist institutions in the region, such as banks, insurance, and steamships. Many of the foremost commercial figures in Charlotte County were Scots, including Robert Pagan, the McMasters family, and Christopher Scott. They controlled the county's courts and the region's most advanced and productive dam and sawmill complex at Saint Stephen. All of Charlotte County's Scottish merchants were well-known smugglers or colluded with them, including Colin Campbell, a corrupt customs officer.[51]

Foremost among the Scots was Robert Pagan of Saint Andrews. Pagan emigrated to America in 1768, establishing himself at Falmouth, Massachusetts. The Revolution forced him to flee; Pagan chose to remain as close to the American market as possible. First he established himself at the British post at Penobscot. While there, Pagan smuggled British goods into British territory by arranging for the sham capture of his vessels.[52] When the British evacuated that post, Pagan settled in what became Saint Andrews. Many of Pagan's activities were illicit in some manner; he plundered Crown timber reserves, illegally imported American timber, sold fish to American merchants contrary to the law, and actively violated Jefferson's embargo.[53] Even in shipbuilding, Pagan and other Scots smuggled American ironware and Scottish copper fittings to complete the vessels.[54]

Loyalist merchants participated in all the illicit economic activities that the Scots did and engaged in illicit trade in the West Indies as well. One important difference is that Loyalist merchants did not have the narrow ethnic viewpoint of the Scots. Instead, Loyalist merchants sought to reconstruct the old trade patterns that existed before 1775, especially the West Indies connection. Rather than compete or innovate, Loyalist merchants often looked to government for bounties or trade privileges.

Since aggressive American merchants successfully shut out Maritime merchants from the West Indies trade, New Brunswick and Nova Scotian traders found themselves in a secondary role. Loyalist merchants sold their fish and timber to Americans who carried it to the West Indies. Christopher Hatch was the most prominent Loyalist merchant at Passamaquoddy. Originally from Boston, Hatch served with Loyalist forces during the War of Independence, after which he established himself as a merchant on Campobello before moving to Saint Andrews.[55] Hatch never fully committed himself to commerce. He retained an interest in military matters, serving as a colonel in the militia, and was one of Charlotte County's foremost magistrates, as well as an occasional member of the assembly. Given his powerful political position as both a justice and a militia officer, it is not surprising that no one pointed an accusing finger at him. So many of Charlotte County's leaders participated in smuggling that the chances of one of them upsetting the widespread illicit trade that benefited them all appear slim.

American merchants were aggressive and forward-looking like the Scots but without ties to specific ports. American merchants actively and aggressively sought new markets, even if those markets were closed to legal trade. American smugglers could claim that the Revolution freed them to pursue the wealth that guaranteed democracy.[56] Practical aspects of commerce also encouraged borderland merchants to engage in illicit trade, the foremost of which was the region's perpetual shortage of specie and credit.

The smuggling merchants made up the overwhelming majority of the local political machinery, including the judiciary. As early as 1796, a New Brunswick customs officer found contraband tea and liquor in the homes, warehouses, and other outbuildings belonging to the leading figures and magistrates on Grand Manan, Indian Island, and Campobello.[57] Most of the American magistrates at Passamaquoddy also engaged in smuggling to some degree. Somehow these individuals rationalized their borderland experience, permitting them to simultaneously defraud the state and organize banquets celebrating their patriotism.

Economic opportunism bridged the temporal world to the supernatural. Many frontier settlers believed in what has been termed a "nocturnal" or supernatural economy.[58] Many mariners and settlers were superstitious. Seamen sometimes reported sighting sea monsters. Freeman Smith of Lubec, an experienced whaleman, reported a sea serpent with a body six feet in diameter and a head that stood fifteen feet above the water.[59] Passamaquoddy's fishermen believed in witches and nailed horseshoes to the masts of their boats for protection from them.[60] More commonly, settlers fantasized that treasure lay at their very feet. Passamaquoddy had its own incidents, such as when a boy reportedly found a large gold nugget on a beach at Eastport.[61] Campobello residents reportedly wasted much of their time digging for Captain Kidd's treasure; Money Cove on Grand Manan was also rumored to have buried pirate treasure.[62]

Passamaquoddy had a uniquely nocturnal economy as well, both legitimate and illicit. Fishermen frequently fished at night, a legal and legitimate practice, using torches to attract fish to their nets. Smugglers operated at night in direct contravention of both American and British laws that forbade loading or unloading vessels of any size after sunset. During peak smuggling times, a man might make several weeks' wages in one night; the highest amount recorded was $47, paid in cash.[63] Unfortunately, there is no recorded response of wives and children to tired husbands and fathers returning at dawn after a night spent transporting contraband goods across the border. Perhaps smugglers explained the unexpected appearance of cash or goods in supernatural terms, probably with tongue in cheek.

Aside from superstition, Passamaquoddy's settlers had a vibrant and often unusual spiritual life. Generally the settlers were Christians, although at least one Eastport fisherman appears to have been a sun worshipper.[64] Virtually all settlers were Protestant, but when established religion failed to ease their spiritual needs, they opted for an evangelicalism that transcended borders, thereby reinforcing attitudes that tolerated activities such as smuggling.

To the followers of more established denominations, such as Congregationalists and Anglicans, the emotional religious experience of the evangelicals appeared chaotic. The emotional excesses, the lack of a trained clergy, the spontaneous meetings in fields and barns during the week that sometimes ran late into the night challenged the established order, both in the newly created United States and in Britain's remaining North American colonies.[65] Radical evangelicalism prevailed because it was more in tune with the primitive conditions settlers faced, and it reinforced the cooperative work ethic of the settlers and confirmed their suspicion of hierarchy and authority.

Maritime evangelicals such as Henry Alline had a profound impact on the Maine frontier. His parents moved from Rhode Island, where he was born, to Nova Scotia in the 1760s. During the Revolution, he had a dramatic conversion experience and became a popular and influential preacher in Nova Scotia and northern New England. Alline emphasized an otherworldliness that undermined ideas of deference and loyalty to the state. His message resonated with American and Loyalist borderland residents because they could recognize him and other lay preachers as people very much like themselves.[66]

Many settlers associated established churches, such as the Anglican Church in New Brunswick, with those in power who wished to oppress them. Campobello's proprietor was also an Anglican minister; the squatters whom he so detested were Baptists. Another example is George Leonard, a devout Anglican whose perpetual antismuggling campaigns mirrored that faith's demands for social order. Anglican clergy like the elderly and ailing Rev. Samuel Andrews of Saint Andrews had a difficult time gaining converts among ordinary settlers. There may have been a generational element to this trend as well. The Lloyd family of Deer Island were Anglican, but their daughter Fanny found herself attracted to the evangelical Baptist faith spread by itinerant preachers. Outraged by Fanny's response to what he considered ill-educated and vulgar preachers, Fanny's father cast her out of his household.[67]

Even other mainstream faiths such as Catholicism and Methodism undermined government influence in this borderland. Father Romagné reported the presence of a few Catholics among the settlers, too, notably the crypto-Catholic Dunn family of Saint Andrews. The Dunns were an influential family of officeholders in Charlotte County. Their secret adherence to Catholicism is especially interesting because British officeholders were required to abjure papal authority.[68] Saint Stephen's Methodist minister, former British soldier Duncan McColl, served a decidedly transnational parish and strove to lessen conflict. When the War of 1812 broke out, he reportedly told his parishioners that having christened, married, and buried them, he was not going to let them fight one another.[69]

Much of Moose Island's populace adhered to Allinite religious principles, and at least two Baptist preachers from the Maritimes took up residence there. James Murphy was a Nova Scotian of Loyalist parentage who spread the Allinite version of Baptist faith in eastern Maine in the 1790s and founded a church in Eastport by 1800. Murphy was also typical of radical evangelicals in that he refused to write a formal sermon, believing that "if the preacher was sent by God he would be taught what to say."[70] This sort of statement verified the suspicions of Anglican clergy like the Reverend Andrews, who thought Baptist preachers ill educated.[71] Murphy's unfortunate death further reflects the rowdy and nongenteel nature of Allinite preachers. He had an argument with his brother-in-law, who violently threw him to the ground; he died within a few hours.[72]

Gilbert Harris was another Maritime Baptist who crossed the border. In his case, he fled New Brunswick for Eastport after he illegally married a couple in 1811 (only Anglican priests were allowed to officiate over marriages at that time). Harris's defiance of the law represented the borderland rejection of state authority in all matters, including spiritual, as well as how Passamaquoddy could shelter those hiding from the law.[73]

Religion, economics, and the frontier experience thus drew Passamaquoddy's population together despite their ideological differences, encouraging cooperation even if it meant smuggling. This region was not unique in that; other areas of North America also experienced a reconciliation of sorts.[74] For the ordinary settlers, this was largely a pragmatic consideration that ensured survival, an outgrowth of the frontier's egalitarian communalism. The justifications for smuggling are as diverse as the people who participated in illicit trade. Participants in the "dark trade" made excuses for their behavior, acting in ways that sometimes appear hypocritical, devious, or even traitorous. Examining these contradictions reveals that everyday life brought borderland peoples into conflict with social ideals, national ideologies, and the power of the state. These struggles existed throughout North America, but the presence of the border meant that Passamaquoddy's settlers had unusual stresses and opportunities that brought these contradictions to the fore.

3

"A COMMERCE OF MERE STONE"

Almost three decades of tension between British customs officials and smugglers at Passamaquoddy Bay came to a head in June 1807, when His Majesty's schooner *Porgey* arrived to eliminate the thriving smuggling trade. Advance warning had been given; Lt. James Flintoph printed an advertisement in the *Royal Gazette* with his intentions: "to discourage and punish all those concerned in illicit traffic."[1] True to his word, Flintoph sailed for Passamaquoddy and seized American vessels engaged in the plaster trade. Locals reported that Flintoph "fired his guns promiscuously, and in every direction, even among houses." One shot reportedly rolled between innocent children.[2] Flintoph's crew fired cannon, impressed sailors into naval service, and beat or threatened to shoot mariners who resisted. When one smuggling merchant did not obey a midshipmen's orders promptly enough, the young officer damned him and ordered him into the *Porgey*'s boat. In the ensuing quarrel, the midshipman knocked the smuggler down, put a pistol to his breast, and told him if he did not immediately comply, he would "blow him thro."[3]

A few weeks later, the *Porgey* returned and seized two more American vessels with additional violence and gunfire, despite the protests of the American customs collector, Lewis Delesdernier.[4] Upon the collector boarding the *Porgey* to demand an explanation, its commander swore at Delesdernier, shouting that he would fire as often as he wanted at whatever he wanted, and ordered him off the schooner. Little wonder that borderland residents considered Flintoph insane.

One of the vessels Flintoph seized was the American schooner *Harmony*, which had illegally loaded one hundred tons of plaster directly from a British vessel. The seizure was a comic opera, in which British sailors ordered one of *Harmony*'s American crew into their boat. The crewmember, probably fearing impressment, refused. Four sailors grabbed him to put him into the boat, but he held fast to the schooner's boom. The British sailors pulled with all their strength, but did not break his hold; they then beat him with the flat of their swords and pricked him with the points until he finally let go.[5] The *Harmony* case went to trial, and the judge handling the case had to contend with the fact that while its hull was in British waters, its anchor lay in American mud near Green Island.[6] But British officials claimed the island was in New Brunswick. The island itself was scarcely more than a rock, but despite its tiny size, an American smuggling merchant named Pope built a wharf and store on the island.[7] Furthermore, New Brunswick's chief customhouse officers testified that they always considered the island American territory. Flintoph found his seizures quickly became the source of a diplomatic squabble between the United States and Britain, as well as an ugly power struggle between New Brunswick's customs officers and George Leonard, the region's superintendent of trade and fisheries. Flintoph's acts were not madness, but it did prove to be a rash decision that ended his career.

The *Porgey* incidents were the culmination of almost three decades of efforts by Leonard to stop smuggling and seize control of all the islands in Passamaquoddy Bay. It was also the peak of his efforts to embarrass colonial officials who countenanced illicit trade. To fully understand these events, it is necessary to compare the economic policies of the United States and Britain after the American Revolution and see how the respective nations' customs officers often subverted those commercial policies for their own gain.

The general American impulse until 1816 was to regulate and tax trade as little and as conveniently as possible. This was in accord with the principles set forth in Adam Smith's *Wealth of Nations*, a work that had a profound effect on early American policymakers such as James Madison, Alexander Hamilton, and Albert Gallatin. American regulations were relatively simple and inexpensive, a fact noted with envy by New Brunswick inhabitants such as David Owen of Campobello.[8] The American system was also less violent than the British. For example, a Treasury Department circular issued by Alexander Hamilton to revenue cutter captains in 1791 enjoined them to act with "a cool and temperate perseverance in their duty, by address & moderation rather than by vehemence or violence," a principle completely at odds with the actions of British officers like the commander of the *Porgey*.[9]

The British at least in theory clung to mercantilism, a system that demanded a high degree of regulation and taxation as outlined in a body of legislation known as the Navigation Acts. These laws excluded American shipping from colonial ports and restricted colonial merchants from trading directly with other nations like Spain, a fact that caused considerable grumbling among the province's elite, essentially forcing them to smuggle Iberian wine and fruit from the United States because it was so much cheaper than importing through Britain.[10] The Navigation Acts should have protected New Brunswick's shipping, especially with the West Indies, which provided a market for the province's timber. But the British imperial government, locked in a series of wars with France, sacrificed ideology and Saint John's promising West India trade for more pragmatic concerns.[11] Britain needed American agricultural goods to supply its valuable and strategic Caribbean possessions. Jay's Treaty of 1794 allowed American ships to trade with British colonies in the Caribbean. American vessels rapidly displaced New Brunswick ships in the West Indies trade. This, too, forced New Brunswick merchants to engage in an illegal trade with the United States to acquire rum, molasses, and sugar. Often these transactions took place at the border, or "on the lines" as they called it, at Passamaquoddy.[12] Furthermore, Jay's Treaty opened American trade with the East Indies as well. New Brunswickers and Nova Scotians soon developed a taste for the much cheaper tea American merchants offered.[13]

Defenders of mercantilism were vitriolic in denouncing smugglers, especially if they were Americans. Ideologues, such as Nova Scotia's vice-admiralty judge, Dr. Alexander Croke, claimed while prosecuting a smuggler that every deviation from the Navigation Acts was a "nail driven into the Coffin of the British empire."[14] One of mercantilism's last great champions was Lord Sheffield, a man with a deep suspicion of American commerce. Sheffield's vision matched well with the economic aspirations of New Brunswick's Loyalist leadership; they even went so far as to hang a portrait of him in their legislative chamber.[15]

In practice, however, New Brunswick's Loyalists eagerly engaged in illicit trade with the United States, including many of the legislators who voted funds for the portrait of Sheffield.[16] New Brunswick's customhouse condoned or even promoted smuggling, while the region's superintendent of trade and fisheries condemned and actively attempted to suppress it. American smugglers eager to provide British North America with contraband goods and corrupt American customs officials on the border who gladly undermined British commercial restrictions exacerbated the problem of illicit trade. Furthermore, American officials protested loudly every time colonial officials attempted to suppress smuggling on the border. Loyalist officials very quickly found that overzealous enforcement embroiled them in international incidents that drew rebukes from the Colonial Office, creating a further disincentive to enforce commercial laws.

From its creation as a separate colony in 1784, New Brunswick experienced difficulties trying to adhere to mercantilist principles. Within days of his arrival in the colony, Lt. Governor Thomas Carleton posted a printed proclamation that forbade illicit and illegal trade with the United States.[17] But the struggling province could not provide itself with basic commodities like flour, which had to be imported from the United States. Recognizing this reality, Carleton authorized licensed British vessels to import American foodstuffs. The system proved open to abuse; American tobacco and other contraband entered along with the needed flour.[18]

By 1786, New Brunswick officials cracked down on smuggling at the border in two separate incidents, one aimed at a Loyalist and the other at American shipping entering what they claimed to be British waters. In April, a court convicted Gillam Butler of Campobello of violating British commercial laws. Not only had Butler attempted to import American whale oil as British, but he had attempted to do so in an American-built vessel for which he obtained false British papers. The judge made an example of Butler by fining him £500 and sentencing him to three months in prison, an unusually harsh sentence.[19] In June, George Leonard, acting on a temporary commission as a customs officer, launched a customs raid at Passamaquoddy. Without warning, he seized two American vessels and drove a third onto shore in its effort to escape him.[20] Carleton persuaded a reluctant Leonard to release the vessels because he wanted to avoid a confrontation with the United States and Colonial Office officials.[21] Leonard seems to have been further disappointed when the customs commissioners did not grant him a permanent customs commission. Instead Governor Carleton found him a more demanding and less remunerative position, that of superintendent of trade and fisheries. In this capacity Leonard once again had a mandate to prosecute those engaged in illegal trade with the United States. He also used his position as an opportunity to criticize New Brunswick's customs establishment for its laxness.[22]

Leonard was not the only official who used violent methods to curb smuggling at Passamaquoddy. Richard Batchelor, an Englishman who served as New Brunswick's surveyor and searcher of customs from 1790 to 1793 became very unpopular for his violent methods. For example, at midnight on August 13, 1791, at Portland Parish (across the harbor from Saint John proper),

Batchelor bludgeoned a dog to death with the butt of his pistol before beating down the door of suspected smuggler William Comely. During the ensuing fracas, Batchelor ordered his assistant to blow Comely's brains out.[23] A few weeks later, Batchelor broke into a house on Campobello looking for contraband goods from the United States. The island's headstrong proprietor, David Owen, ordered Batchelor arrested. Batchelor resisted, escaped, and apparently assaulted Owen himself with a knife.[24] Owen pressed charges against Batchelor for breaking open stores, stealing one of his boats, and resisting two men who attempted to recover it. Owen noted, "This fellow has occasioned almost a civil war" and that the official was re-creating the sort of hostility against Crown officials that ignited revolution in Massachusetts in the 1770s.[25]

Undaunted, in July 1792, Batchelor seized a vessel for smuggling at the head of the Bay of Fundy. A crowd subsequently rescued the vessel, and troops had to be called in twice before the vessel arrived safely at Saint John.[26] By 1793, the unpopular official tendered his resignation and returned to England for alleged ill health.[27]

Batchelor's replacement as searcher was Colin Campbell, a Scots Loyalist who had served as the deputy customs collector at Saint Andrews. In late 1795, he seized the American vessel *Mary* for bringing corn to a gristmill on the New Brunswick side of the Saint Croix River. The American owners rescued it from his assistants, and Campbell had to call in militia to recover it. Local magistrates complained that Campbell was destroying the goodwill they had built with their American neighbors.[28] Governor Carleton agreed and ordered the *Mary* returned to her American owners, who later sued the searcher.[29]

In 1796, Campbell struck back at his critics when he testified that some of Charlotte County's most prominent men, including several magistrates, were involved in smuggling tea, wine, and brandy from the United States and that they hid them in "houses, warehouses, and other outhouses" on various islands throughout Passamaquoddy.[30] Later that year another violent incident took place at Passamaquoddy. Campbell seized an American vessel for smuggling and placed armed guards on board the boat, which was anchored off Grand Manan Island. On the night of October 21, the guards shot and killed an American smuggler during an effort to rescue the vessel. The guards responsible faced only a cursory trial, but after this incident Campbell's tactics changed.[31]

After 1796, Campbell became more interested in the timber trade than in acting as surveyor and searcher. By this time he was one of several Charlotte

County notables reported for plundering the King's forests.[32] Perhaps Collector of Customs William Wanton, Governor Carleton, or some other individual encouraged him to modify his ways. His apostasy was clear by 1805, when his involvement in the illicit plaster trade became known. Campbell thus made the transition from law enforcer to smuggler.

Most New Brunswick's customs officials, like their counterparts in the rest of British North America, proved extremely tolerant of illicit trade. In this they closely resembled the behavior of Crown customs officers in the thirteen American Colonies before the Revolution. Locally appointed colonial customs officers were lax, and Crown customs collectors appointed from Britain were unpopular due to their venality, corruption, or inflexibility.[33] One problem was that the entire customs hierarchy existed outside of the colonial government's direct authority—almost "a state-within-a-state" that was connected with, but basically independent of, other officials within the colony.[34]

Crown customs officials viewed their posts as patrimonial, an office they owned based on their loyalty to the king, and being so far from the king's authority, they quite naturally pursued personal agendas. In cooperating with smugglers, customs officers avoided a great deal of trouble, profited from official and unofficial remuneration, and gained the esteem and friendship of colonial merchants without loss of self-respect, social standing, or even much risk of censure from the customs commissioners in distant London. Public profession of loyalty to the king and the widely held conviction that the growth of trade was better served by disregarding the unreasonable restrictions embodied in the Navigation Acts sufficed to earn these officials positions of respect within the colony.[35]

Customhouse officials' interests degenerated from those of the Crown to more local concerns due to their great distance from London and the fact that their pay was based on fees collected directly for their services.[36] While the imperial duties or taxes on imported goods went to the Crown, customs officers performed a number of other regulatory duties for which they charged a small sum. Law decreed that a table of these fees be posted prominently in the customhouse, but they seldom were, and customs officials drew up fee structures that greatly exceeded the official ones or invented new fees for services that should have been free.[37] The sum of fees customs officers collected at 'Quoddy exceeded even that of the much larger port of Saint John.[38] Half of those fees went straight into the local official's pocket, while the other half went to the colony's top two customhouse officials. While the fees damaged legitimate trade, smugglers gladly paid the inflated fees so long as customs officials were not overly diligent in enforcing the Navigation Acts. New Brunswick's customs officials were what one study termed "creoles": imperial officials who fell under the sway of colonial influences that undermined the Navigation Acts. In contrast to the creoles were the "schematists," customs officers who attempted to enforce the laws more rigidly and reported frequently to England."[39]

What were the reasons for Campbell's conversion to creole behavior? Economic incentives surely played a role, but they do not seem to be the sole reason he abandoned his duties as surveyor and searcher.[40] There must have been social pressures, too, as his fellow Charlotte County magistrates and merchants (Scotsmen like himself) sought accommodations with their counterparts in Washington County, Maine, including commercial connections. Lawsuits, censure from other Crown officials, and lack of support by the customs commissioners further persuaded him to turn a blind eye to smuggling and adopt the profitable and painless creole mode of officeholding.

In so doing, Campbell conformed with the behavior of the other customs officials at Passamaquoddy as well as his superiors at Saint John. There was considerable peer pressure to do so. The deputy customs collector at Saint Andrews, John Dunn, was known as a "man proverbially kind, liberal, and hospitable," who actively colluded with American officials to create a thriving smuggling trade on the border.[41] Thomas Henderson, the other deputy collector in the area, also comes down in local memory as an affable character. He made few or no seizures, and even took in a plaster merchant as a boarder.[42] Henderson largely kept out of the official record, making him the perfect creole official: honored, rewarded, and mostly invisible.[43] Campbell had also noted that Henderson engaged in smuggling in the 1790s, begging the question of how he became customs officer.[44]

All of Passamaquoddy's officials took their cues from the colony's leading customs official, William Wanton, based in the province's leading port city, Saint John. A popular man in that city's social circles, Wanton maintained an epicurean lifestyle on the emoluments of his office. Knowing that the province relied on trade, Wanton spent little effort suppressing smuggling. Instead, he quietly collected his fees from shipmasters and merchants who were eager to pay them so long as he ignored their illicit trade. Wanton regarded his position as collector as a sinecure, a reward for their personal loyalty to the monarch. Wanton's malfeasance proved extremely profitable; in his final year in office alone he garnered over £5,500 in fees.[45] As with creole customs officers in colonial Massachusetts, merchants honored and rewarded Wanton for his laxity.

In opposition to the creoles were "schematists," officeholders who constantly submitted reports and suggestions for improving the customs service, thereby creating a reputation for diligence that ingratiated them with the customs commissioners.[46] Foremost among New Brunswick's schematists was Superintendent of Trade and Fisheries George Leonard. From the late 1780s to the eve of the War of 1812, Leonard launched a personal campaign to eradicate smuggling in the Maritime Provinces. Repeated charges of corruption against the Saint John customhouse were an important part of this campaign.

Leonard's hatred of Americans and bitter memories of the War of Independence fueled his zealous enforcement of the Navigation Acts. He was the most zealous of the New Brunswick Loyalists, a man who refused to temper his loyalty with "either caution or business acumen" and who professed to believe that "the War of the American Revolution was still being fought on New Brunswick soil."[47] His dogmatism blinded him to the fact that imperial authorities were more interested in maintaining amicable commercial relations with the United States than in rigidly enforcing commercial laws.[48]

Leonard's efforts as a schematist, including his reports and recommendations to the customs commissioners, and even trips to England in 1787 and 1797, seem to have paid off. In 1796 the customs commissioners extended his commission to include all of New Brunswick, Nova Scotia, and what is now known as Prince Edward Island. In 1800 they granted him an annual subsidy to operate the small patrol vessel *Union*, carrying two small cannon and commanded by his son Charles.[49] In 1801 the commissioners made him a preventative officer with broad powers to seize vessels and property engaged in contraband trade. In 1810 they gave him a more substantial grant to operate a larger revenue cutter capable of patrolling the Bay of Fundy year-round. The ship was virtually a miniature naval vessel, armed with eight 12-pounder carronades and a crew of twenty-five.[50]

Leonard's strict enforcement of the Navigation Acts made him enemies. Nova Scotia's governor complained that Leonard's actions "have entangled us in constant Disputes and Broils with the United States" and that he interfered with Nova Scotia's customs officers.[51] As early as 1798, an anonymous letter to Lord Portland mocked him as "an illiterate, silly, contemptible fellow" who was "even ignorant and weak enough to suppose that he has the right to control the customs house."[52] The issue became uglier after 1800, when a highly profitable but completely illegal trade in gypsum sprang up at Passamaquoddy. This trade infuriated Leonard not only for its obvious illegality but also because his old nemeses in the Saint John customhouse became rich from the illicit plaster trade at Campobello.[53] By 1802, Leonard embarked on a campaign to harass and embarrass New Brunswick's customs officers even as he attempted to eradicate smuggling at Passamaquoddy.

Why should plaster, this "commerce of mere stone" as David Owen put it, be such a widely smuggled item?[54] The answer lies in the needs of American agriculture. Plaster, usually known as plaister or plaister paris, is now better known as gypsum. In the eighteenth and early nineteenth centuries, plaster was the first chemical fertilizer, a miracle substance that when ground up and scattered over fields substantially increased harvests, especially of wheat. Farmers in the American wheat-raising heartland in Pennsylvania, Maryland, and Virginia demanded huge amounts of plaster, but the only known North American source lay at the head of the Bay of Fundy in Nova Scotia and New Brunswick.

Gypsum is a soft rock found close to the surface or even exposed on banks and hillsides. Farmers blasted the plaster loose and transported it by the cartload to small vessels, where it was dumped into their holds, still in loose, rocky form. The vessel then delivered the gypsum to Passamaquoddy, where it was either lightered ashore in small vessels and dumped into piles on shore, or transferred directly to an American vessel, either by small boats or actually coming alongside, preferably under cover of night. Once in America, the shippers delivered the gypsum in its raw state, and finally at the retail level it was smashed into smaller lumps in a stamping mill and ground into a fine powder in a common gristmill, placed in casks or barrels, and delivered to farmers for fertilizer or builders for plaster. Experts deemed six to eight bushels of plaster sufficient to fertilize an acre of wheat.[55]

Getting plaster into the United States offered few difficulties, even if the trade was illegal. Colonial customs administrators largely ignored the smaller coasting craft engaged in the plaster trade, except to extract heavy fees from those engaged in it. American custom regulations allowed plaster in American bottoms to enter duty-free, but charged British vessels carrying plaster into the United States $1 per ton, a penalty that essentially excluded British-flagged vessels from exporting directly to American markets in New York. The trick then was to somehow get the plaster into an American vessel. Passamaquoddy's uncertain boundary, fogs, and accommodating customs officers made it the ideal place to illicitly transfer the plaster from British vessels into American ones. The trade grew rapidly: in 1794, about 100 tons passed through Passamaquoddy; by 1802, about 13,000. That same year the *Boston Gazette* began to regularly report the current price of plaster on a per ton basis, an indication of the growing importance of plaster to the American market.

The colonial mariners who transported the plaster were the neighbors and kinsmen, and in some cases the same persons, who quarried it. This was somewhat unusual; generally cargo producers and ship owners were not the same individuals, but the low unit value of plaster, combined with high freight rates—generally higher than the value of the plaster itself—encouraged ship ownership by the plaster producers. The vessels they operated were primarily small schooners of around forty tons burthen, operated by a master and a few deckhands. This upset the merchants of Saint John, who wanted to see the plaster carried in their larger vessels directly to market in New York and Philadelphia.[56] The small schooners went back and forth from the Minas Basin to Passamaquoddy several times a year as convenient. Once at Passamaquoddy, they generally anchored in the waters between Moose Island and Campobello, deposited their ship's paperwork with the customhouse officer there, and arranged to sell and transfer their cargo either to the American shore, especially Allan's or Rice's Islands, or directly into an American vessel.[57]

At least some Saint John merchants participated in this trade, especially smaller merchants like Stephen Humbert, the Methodist deacon and occasional smuggler. Between 1802 and 1809, Humbert exported at least 1,844 tons of plaster. During the same period he imported at least 2,673 barrels of American flour into the colony. Humbert sent his vessels to Philadelphia, New York, or more usually Boston from two to seven times a year up until 1810, at which time his American trade suddenly stopped.[58] Like many plaster traders, Humbert augmented this trade by picking up contraband such as Souchong and Bohea tea.[59]

The American mariners who brought the plaster to market in New York, Philadelphia, and the Chesapeake were small operators too. Generally they worked through agents on Moose Island who took a commission for providing them with cargoes of plaster. Merely transporting the plaster was moderately profitable, running anywhere up to $4 a ton depending on where it was transported. Earning could be augmented by transporting British contraband goods carefully concealed beneath the plaster, especially textiles and tinware.

Leonard concluded that the plaster was paid for "principally, if not altogether, by Teas and coarse cottons imported from the East Indies by the Americans, adulterated brandies, and other spirits, coarse shoes and Boots, and other articles, principally the manufactures of the United States, received in return for the Plaister and Grindstones. These contraband articles, thus received, are afterwards easily distributed by boats and small craft thro' every part of this Province, and also thro' that valuable and populous part of the Province of Nova Scotia lying upon the Bay of Fundy."[60] He also complained that illicit trade drained specie from the colonies into the United States.[61]

A number of merchants on both sides of the border specialized in the plaster trade. On Campobello, Christopher Hatch owned a wharf at Snug Cove, the primary spot for landing gypsum before transporting it across the border. Eastport especially prospered from the trade because it was safely out of the reach of George Leonard but very handy to the border and Snug Cove. By 1803 a growing number of merchants set themselves up in the plaster trade, building warehouses and wharves to facilitate the trade.[62] Among them were Jabez Mowry and the firm of Dana, Wheeler, & Bartlett. Eastport plaster merchant and smuggler Josiah Dana seems to have sealed his cross-border connection with marriage; he married Mary Dewolf of Horton, Nova Scotia, in the heart of the gypsum producing region.[63]

Among the New Brunswick merchants were the firm of Andrews and Campbell of Campobello. Notably, the senior partner was Israel Andrews, who lived in the same household as Thomas Henderson, the British customs officer who turned a blind eye to the smuggling trade at Passamaquoddy.[64] His junior partner, Colin Campbell Jr., was the son of the region's surveyor and searcher of customs. Clearly, these two had little to fear from the local customs authorities. Andrews and Campbell arranged for American provisions, gunpowder, sails, iron, tea, brandy, wine, and gin to be sent to Passamaquoddy in return for their plaster, timber, and fish. The partnership moved a large amount of plaster. In July 1805, this firm alone had five hundred tons of plaster on hand and daily purchased more.[65]

Passamaquoddy's plaster trade was possible because American customs officers at the border were just as corrupt as New Brunswick's. Lewis Frederick Delesdernier served as the first United States customs collector at Passamaquoddy, a post he held until 1810. Like his counterparts in New Brunswick, Delesdernier tolerated and even promoted illegal trade at the border. In part this may have been because of his cross-border connections. Delesdernier was one of the few Nova Scotians who had joined the American cause in the War of Independence. While he had to flee the province, many relatives remained under British jurisdiction.[66] Delesdernier saw himself as a facilitator of trade, and largely ignored cumbersome regulations. Delesdernier's sloth also played a role; he was barely literate and was often away from his office for days at a time while he conducted personal business at Saint Andrews, on the other side of the border.[67] Delesdernier's great triumph was convincing Congress to open his port to foreign trade. Together with his old Revolutionary War commander John Allan, they argued that legalizing trade with New Brunswick would lessen the local sympathy for smuggling and produce more income for the federal government from duties and tariffs.[68] Congress agreed and opened Delesdernier's district to foreign shipping in 1802.

Another problem remained, however. Federal statutes banned foreign vessels under thirty tons from entering American ports, a regulation difficult to enforce at Passamaquoddy due to the border. Delesdernier seem to have largely ignored this last regulation. Small boats, especially fishing vessels from Campobello and other islands on the New Brunswick side of the border, regularly appeared at Eastport's wharves. Indeed, these small vessels were almost indistinguishable from their American counterparts, customs authorities often sympathized with the owners of these small boats, and the effort to distinguish them from American vessels would have required enormous effort. Furthermore, prosecution would have cost more than the money recouped from their seizure. There was simply no incentive to harass people involved in what was local business, even if it did cross the border.

Delesdernier's mode of accommodation permitted British ships to anchor alongside American vessels and transship their cargoes of plaster directly into American holds.[69] This saved the labor of depositing the cargo on either the American shore or wharves, and then reloading the plaster onto an American vessel. But it also violated the principle that foreign cargoes come under customhouse scrutiny, whether they be inbound or outbound. But plaster entered the United States duty free, so Delesdernier did not defraud the U.S. government in so doing. However, Delesdernier clearly broke American commercial regulations when he permitted American coasting vessels to perform "international" voyages, even if that voyage consisted of a few hundred yards across the harbor into British waters, and there exchange cargoes of American produce, especially flour, for foreign cargoes. His actions did not go unnoticed. The British admiral in command of the Halifax station reported that

Delesdernier "appears to be an agent for smuggling teas and East India goods into our colonies."[70] But Delesdernier was not acting alone; in fact, he was acting in concert with John Dunn, the long-standing British customs official at Passamaquoddy. As the presiding customs officers in the region, Dunn and Delesdernier worked out a compromise whereby they deemed a portion of the harbor between Campobello, New Brunswick, and Moose Island, Maine, as "neutral waters" where American and British vessels could exchange cargoes unmolested by customs officials from either side.

The neutral zone arrangement played on a peculiarity for mariners coming to 'Quoddy. Often it was not clear what jurisdiction their vessel lay in. There were some rough guidelines that could be used, such as lining up a well-known chimney on a distinctive house and so on, but in fog or at night these aids proved useless. A ship could drop anchor in what appeared to be one jurisdiction, but a dropping tide or a changing wind might swing the vessel across the invisible border. In other words, one's anchor might be securely in British mud, but tidal currents carried the hull into American waters, or vice versa, as in the *Harmony* case. This question came to court: Were vessels in the jurisdiction of its anchor or of its hull? Generally it was conceded that a vessel was in the jurisdiction of where its anchor lay. This worked to the advantage of smugglers, who could craftily cross the border by easing out a little more scope on their anchor cable.[71] Dunn and Delesdernier twisted the difficulty in placing the borderline to facilitate the plaster trade. The neutral zone agreement ensured a steady flow of fees for both and permitted the trade to be conducted in broad daylight.

This smuggling was a gross affront to Leonard, who hatched a scheme to stop smuggling and remove his opponents in the Saint John customhouse. Remembering the problems he created by seizing American vessels in 1786, he moved to provoke a crisis that would oblige the imperial government to intervene. If all went well, the British imperial government would claim possession of all the islands in Passamaquoddy Bay and the customs commissioners would replace Collector Wanton with his friend Edward Winslow. Leonard wanted to create a scandal, and he succeeded when the cutter *Union* seized the American sloop *Falmouth* on October 24, 1805. The pretext for taking the vessel was that the *Falmouth* violated British commercial laws that forbade American vessels to trade while within New Brunswick waters.

The seizure on the surface appears to be routine. As recently as 1803, Leonard successfully prosecuted two American vessels engaged in the plaster trade.[72] But the *Falmouth* case became a difficult one for Leonard. First, the American captain proved especially able to defend his case in court. Second, New Brunswick's customs establishment opposed his rigid enforcement of the Navigation Acts. Third, the possession of the islands in Passamaquoddy Bay was still indeterminate, and the matter drew the attention of officials in Washington and London.

In January 1806, the *Falmouth* case went on trial before William Botsford, New Brunswick's vice-admiralty court judge. Ebenezer Lock, the master of the *Falmouth*, and his lawyers put up a skillful defense. They contended that the sloop was in American waters at the time of seizure and that Delesdernier gave him permission to proceed to what was termed a "neutral area" where it was customary for American vessels to take on cargoes of plaster directly from British vessels.

This defense was problematic because both Britain and the United States claimed jurisdiction over the waters in which the *Falmouth* anchored. Diplomats had yet to decide which nation should possess Moose, Dudley, Allan, and Pope's Folly islands. American citizens lived on and claimed all the islands as part of Massachusetts, but New Brunswick officials claimed them as well. Furthermore, the "neutral zone" the *Falmouth* lay in was an unofficial construction made in 1799 between Delesdernier and his New Brunswick counterpart from Saint Andrews, deputy customs collector Dunn.[73]

The prosecution countered with its own arguments. Foremost among these was the point that the *Falmouth* lay in British waters because all of the islands in Passamaquoddy Bay were part of New Brunswick according to the 1783 Treaty of Paris. The prosecution also attacked the idea that local customs officers could create a neutral zone on their own authority. The defense contested the allegations of British sovereignty over all the islands in Passamaquoddy Bay, and brought forth New Brunswick's customs collector and comptroller as witnesses to attest to the validity of the "neutral zone." They even brought Delesdernier to Saint John to testify.

Leonard in turn brought some damning evidence against the customhouse authorities, including the fact that the agent for the *Falmouth*'s cargo of gypsum was the customs surveyor and searcher, Colin Campbell; the owner of the cargo was Campbell's son. By extension this was a direct assault on corruption in the Saint John customhouse.[74] Leonard put them in a very difficult spot by making them come forward and testify in the *Falmouth* case.

Judge William Botsford found against the *Falmouth* and ordered the cargo condemned, but refused to fine the owners or captain, because they were engaged in a trade that had been tolerated for so long. Botsford also found that all the islands in the bay were within New Brunswick's jurisdiction and that the customs authorities had indeed exceeded their authority in creating a neutral zone. However, the judge also condemned Leonard for his conduct in bringing unfounded charges against the owners of the vessel. Botsford probably sought to avoid controversy by censuring both sides, but the mixed results of the trial only hardened the rivalry between Leonard and New Brunswick's customhouse establishment.

Leonard complained bitterly to all who would listen about the *Falmouth* incident and the opposition of the customs authorities to his cutter. To further his cause, he published a pamphlet detailing the matter and sent a copy to imperial officials, noting that New Brunswick's customs officers allowed the illicit plaster trade "from motives I fear not altogether honorable."[75] Displeased by the judge's verdict on the *Falmouth*, Leonard published an advertisement in the *New Brunswick Royal Gazette* that despite his respect for Botsford, he would continue to pursue smugglers at Passamaquoddy. However, by early 1806 diplomatic pressure built for Leonard to ease his anti-smuggling campaign. At the request of Anthony Merry, Britain's minister to the United States, New Brunswick's lieutenant governor ordered Leonard to abstain from seizing any more U.S. vessels at Passamaquoddy.[76] Leonard complied but continued his campaign from afar, informing Merry that the "evils" in Passamaquoddy Bay had greatly increased since the lieutenant governor's order.[77] By September Leonard reported that the illicit trade on the lines had become worse than ever, and American smugglers were becoming bolder. In October he called for an investigation into the activities of the deputy collector at Passamaquoddy.[78] In 1807 the feuding went before the House of Assembly, with both the customhouse officers and Leonard claiming the proceeds of fourteen barrels of contraband rum seized by the superintendent.[79]

The Saint John customhouse reacted to accusations of corruption with the blandest of denials. Collector Wanton and Comptroller Robert Parker responded, "Where countries border on each other, it is utterly impossible to put an effectual stop to illicit intercourse between the Inhabitants on each side." They thought that Leonard exaggerated the scale of smuggling at Passamaquoddy, and they were astonished at Leonard's accusations, but items manufactured in India did find their way into New Brunswick from the United States.[80]

The *Falmouth* incident, the abuses by customs officials, and their creole attitudes display some of the less flattering aspects of Loyalist and colonial society. New Brunswick's colonial population, like its Nova Scotia counterpart, had a double standard when it came to government. As Neil MacKinnon observed about the Loyalist experience in Nova Scotia, "If the government was obliged to be honest and conscientious towards them, it did not mean that they in turn had to be honest and conscientious towards the government."[81] This pragmatic, even hypocritical, colonial attitude toward the state seemed to grow in power with distance from the imperial core in London. Far from embracing mercantilist dogma, New Brunswick's customs officers viewed their posts as lifelong sinecures. The lure of illicit trade transcended Loyalist ideology. Sometimes these underlying contradictions between officeholding and corruption became a public struggle between creoles and schematists, as with the *Falmouth* case.

The aftershocks of the *Falmouth* case continued to impact the border for years. Because he was ordered not to interfere at Passamaquoddy, he had to conduct his war on smuggling by proxy. Leonard found a sympathetic ear in Lieutenant Flintoph of the Royal Navy. It was at Leonard's urging that the officer posted his warning to 'Quoddy's plaster traders in the *Royal Gazette*, and it was Leonard who urged him to seize vessels engaged in smuggling. Thus the *Falmouth* case of 1805 led directly to the *Porgey* incident of 1807 and explains why Saint John's customs officers moved to actively embarrass Leonard and thwart his efforts to use Flintoph as a proxy by testifying in the *Harmony* case that Green island lay in American territory.

The little Royal Navy schooner *Porgey* set off another minor diplomatic squabble, but it was the aggression of another British naval ship that really altered the cross-border relationship at Passamaquoddy. In June, the same month *Porgey* struck a blow against the plaster trade, HMS *Leopard* made an unprovoked attack on the American frigate *Chesapeake*. It looked like Britain and the United States were going to war, and border regions such as Passamaquoddy threatened to become battlegrounds.

4

"THE RASCALS OF PASSAMAQUODDY"

The trial of the New Brunswick sloop *Industry* in the United States federal court system reveals some of the difficulties American officials at Passamaquoddy had when enforcing Jefferson's embargo. David Way, captain of the forty-seven-ton *Industry*, left Eastport on March 18, 1808, with the stated intention of sailing for Halifax. But instead of proceeding to Nova Scotia, Way hovered just outside of the United States' jurisdiction, loading the *Industry* with Virginia superfine flour and other contraband from small boats within plain sight of American customs officials. On March 28, the *Industry* drifted into American jurisdiction, and Collector Lewis Delesdernier seized the vessel. However, federal law made no provision for arresting people involved in breaking the embargo, only the vessel and cargo, thus leaving Way free to act as he pleased. Fearful that Way might attempt to rescue the vessel, the collector sent the *Industry* to another port for safekeeping.[1]

When the case came to trial, a question put to customs inspector John Swett revealed some of the problems Delesdernier had in stopping smuggling during the embargo. The United States district attorney asked, "Have you found difficulty in preventing the running of goods across to the British line—in executing the Embargo laws?" Swett responded, "Yes: a great deal—we have been fired at—people have come over from the other side."[2] Delesdernier, usually tolerant, even supportive of smuggling, suddenly found himself in the very awkward position of attempting to stop all commercial intercourse with New Brunswick. In 1808, Delesdernier brought approximately fifty cases to trial, more than he had initiated in the entire period between 1789 and 1807.[3]

United States v. the Sloop Industry was a struggle in which the defense attorney pitted his evidence against that of Maine's U.S. district attorney. Witnesses disagreed on events; some probably tried to distort the facts. John Kendall, the owner of the warehouse where the flour was stored, swore he saw no boats from the American shore approach the *Industry*. Yet Phineas Nevers, a witness for the prosecution, swore Kendall had personally assisted in the smuggling. The defense countered by questioning that witness's credibility. The defense's attorney, an Eastport lawyer named Jonathan D. Weston, was well known for his sympathy with smugglers.[4]

A closer look at the sources reveals something else: *Industry* was a smuggler twice over. The *Industry* contained not only American contraband but also items forbidden by British commercial regulations, such as trunks of tea. Tea could not be legally exported during the embargo, nor could tea from the United States legally enter New Brunswick, because the East India Company held a legal monopoly on all tea sales in the British empire. The *Industry*'s owner, Stephen Humbert of Saint John, knowingly violated the laws of both the United States and the British Empire.

The embargo brought out multiple reactions from the borderland populace. Some, such as Delesdernier and his supporters, attempted to enforce the embargo. Many seized on the embargo as a windfall, an opportunity to make money. For colonial Maritimers, breaking Jefferson's embargo was a profitable patriotic chore that promised to bring a new degree of wealth to New Brunswick and Nova Scotia. Others played both sides, taking every opportunity presented during the embargo to make money. Examples of these include the smuggler who turned informant against the *Industry* and even some of Delesdernier's customhouse employees, who aided and abetted embargo violators. The embargo thus divided Passamaquoddy society, creating tensions between neighbors. Adventurers from as far away as Britain and New York compounded these tensions when they incited further resistance by taking advantage of borderland opportunism and smuggling expertise.

Jefferson's embargo was the result of increasing diplomatic tensions between the United States and Great Britain. Aggressive American commercial policies were at odds with Britain's naval strategy during the war against Napoleon. The issue of impressment, whereby British naval vessels removed seamen from American ships was an especially sensitive one. The issue came to a head when Rear Admiral Berkeley—the same officer who had sent the *Porgey* into Passamaquoddy Bay in 1807—gave orders for the recovery of British naval deserters to the commander of HMS *Leopard*. The captain of the *Leopard* stopped the American frigate *Chesapeake* off the coast of Virginia and demanded permission to search that vessel for British deserters. When the captain of *Chesapeake* refused to comply, *Shannon* fired into the unprepared American warship, quickly overwhelmed it, and removed the suspected deserters.

The *Chesapeake* incident sparked a vociferous anti-British movement in the United States. Many people called for war, Congress began a program of expanding the military and building coastal fortifications, and the British envoy departed Washington. Even at Passamaquoddy, citizens prepared for war. In Eastport, written pleas for federal defenses were answered with promises to construct a small fort. In Saint Andrews, militia units drilled in preparation for war.[5]

President Thomas Jefferson could have asked Congress for a declaration of war and undoubtedly would have received it. Yet he did not. Under the influence of Secretary of State James Madison, Jefferson chose a different route. Late in 1807, Jefferson asked Congress for a complete embargo on overseas shipping. Congress forbade American vessels to depart for foreign markets, and foreign vessels could not bring American cargoes away from the United States.

Jefferson gambled on Britain's need for American agricultural produce, especially flour. British North America, the West Indies, including a whole host of colonies recently captured from Napoleon and his allies, and even British armies operating on the Iberian Peninsula relied on American provisions produced in the Mid-Atlantic states and Upper South.[6] Jefferson hoped that this embargo would force Britain to negotiate with the United States without having to resort to war.[7] Congress complied with Jefferson's wishes and on December 22 passed the Embargo Act, which was followed by supplementary embargo legislation and various enforcement acts that gave federal officials a wide range of powers.

Jefferson's embargo ultimately failed to achieve its diplomatic ends and created an economic crisis and political problems that affected all sectors of society. Seaports suffered huge unemployment and a near cessation of all economic activity. Farmers lost the lucrative overseas markets for their produce, which declined drastically in price; land speculators could not afford to sell land on credit to frontiersmen; sailors found themselves unemployed. Intricate credit networks collapsed throughout the nation. Resistance to the embargo sprang up across the country, especially in the form of exporting American goods illegally to British colonies. This happened in every American port and along the borders with British North America and Spanish Florida. With more resistance to the embargo came increasingly draconian laws to enforce it. President Jefferson and Congress authorized the use of the militia, the regular military, and naval units to enforce civil laws.

At Passamaquoddy the embargo was often termed the "Flour War," a reference to the most common form of contraband smuggled. A conservative estimate by locals placed the quantity of smuggled flour at 150,000 barrels, the quantity brought legitimately to the border by coastal vessels.[8] Under the earlier versions of the embargo, coasting vessels could legitimately bring the flour to Moose Island; it only became illegal when it crossed the border.

Almost as soon as Congress authorized the embargo in 1807, smugglers flocked to the border with shiploads of flour, salt beef, and naval stores such as turpentine and tar. In the spring of 1808 it looked like the adventurers flocking to the bay would overwhelm Delesdernier and his supporters. The British government at the imperial and colonial level aided embargo breakers, making the embargo all but unenforceable at Passamaquoddy. Only the timely arrival of American military and naval units prevented the complete collapse of federal authority in the area. Smugglers continued their efforts, however, using increasingly violent methods. By autumn, Delesdernier's authority vanished as his subordinates betrayed him.

The quick reaction of smugglers to the news of the embargo put federal customs collectors on the defensive. By February 1808, the Treasury Department indicated its concern that it would be difficult to enforce the embargo at Passamaquoddy. Secretary of the Treasury Albert Gallatin wrote to Delesdernier and asked him to watch both warehouses and boats suspected of attempting illegal exportation. He also authorized hiring more customs inspectors and two or three boats armed with swivel guns and muskets. In addition, Gallatin ordered the revenue cutter *New Hampshire* to Passamaquoddy.[9]

Matters became worse in March. Gallatin warned Delesdernier that many embargo violators from Boston and New York were headed to Passamaquoddy with vast quantities of flour and other American goods intended to be smuggled into New Brunswick and Nova Scotia and to markets as far away as Jamaica and Demerara.[10] The Boston customs collector warned that vessels were loaded daily for Eastport with flour, beef, pork, and other contraband; on March 22 he reported that two vessels loaded with 1,400 barrels of flour had departed his port bound for Passamaquoddy.[11]

By the end of March, Delesdernier had hired numerous inspectors to assist him. In addition, he had engaged a number of boats to patrol around Moose

Island every night.[12] In early April, the captain of the revenue cutter *New Hampshire* reported that Delesdernier's vigilance had defeated attempts to evade the embargo, but his assessment was overly optimistic.[13] In mid-April, Gallatin received alarming reports from ports as far south as Baltimore that vessels were heading to Eastport, some loaded with more than 1,500 barrels of flour.[14] Gallatin ordered Delesdernier to place all flour, provisions, lumber, and other American goods under lock and key immediately and, if necessary, to remove them to a safe place where they could be guarded. He also ordered Delesdernier to impound any goods not voluntarily placed under his control; he was to hire inspectors, boatmen, and other revenue officers without regard to expense. Any person who wanted to remove their property from federal control was to pay bonds worth twice the value of the goods as a security that the goods would not be exported illegally.[15]

The situation deteriorated to the point where Washington sent troops and naval vessels to the border. At the end of April, the secretary of war wrote to Delesdernier that he was sending troops to Passamaquoddy to assist him. This must have been welcome news indeed for the collector, who complained that there were upwards of a hundred vessels in the harbor, and he found it impossible to execute the laws. A mob threatened to burn his house, and he feared that unless troops arrived soon, he would have to flee Eastport.[16]

Smugglers took advantage of every opportunity to frustrate Delesdernier. They used their knowledge of the area's fogs and currents to advantage, but on occasion they found federal officials pursuing them. Sometimes they fired muskets at their pursuers, although no fatalities are recorded. Apparently they fired as a warning, aiming at sails to deter pursuers. At the same time, Delesdernier forbade his men to fire if the smuggling vessel had already crossed the boundary line.[17] Embargo violators also knew that if they jettisoned their contraband cargo, they could not be tried. The smuggling boatmen frequently threw the barrels of provisions into the bay when pursued, knowing full well that customs employees would stop to recover the contraband.[18]

Delesdernier faced both adventurers from away and local smugglers in his efforts to enforce the embargo. Adventurers were usually young traders on the make, willing to take risks and thrilling in the intrigues smuggling required.[19] John Clap of New York was one such adventurer. On April 29 he landed a variety of goods on Allan Island, and that night attempted to smuggle them across the nearby border "in eight different boats, vessels, & rafts."[20] Adventurers came for fast money, and they were willing to pay locals very well to help them, as much as $1 per barrel of flour. One local man reportedly made $47 in twenty-four hours simply by rowing flour across the harbor, and he was paid in hard coin.[21] Delesdernier's assistants received only $2 per day to enforce the law and only after waiting months for a disbursement from the Treasury.

Despite the risks, locals leaped at the opportunity the easy money and worried little about the law. For example, when Robert Little stood on a hill on the American side of the Saint Croix River in May 1808, he told William Sherman he would pay $53 to get fifty-three barrels of tar across to the New Brunswick side of the river. Sherman never asked if it was legal, nor did Little warn of any consequences.[22]

Breaking the embargo was too profitable for locals to resist, especially those with little money such as Jonathan Leavitt, a fisherman described as "poor as a man can be, not worth five dollars." Leavitt had the misfortune to get caught smuggling and had difficulty paying his $75 fine.[23] Fishermen did most of the manual labor associated with smuggling, including loading barrels into boats and actually rowing them across the border. Solomon Mabee, a Loyalist who moved from Saint Andrews to Eastport in 1795, used his cross-border connections, his knowledge as a local fisherman, and his personal boat to smuggle flour across the lines. Federal officials caught him on one such trip with contraband flour in his boat, and prosecuted him to the full extent of the law, a fine of $1,075 plus legal costs. Claiming poverty, old age, illness, and the fact that it was "two barrels flour only," the elderly fisherman begged Gallatin for reprieve from the crushing fine and was fully supported by local worthies in so doing.[24] He was, in fact, about to be committed to jail for his debt to the United States.[25] Comparing Mabee's piteous petition with his court records reveals some troubling discrepancies. He was indicted on two counts of smuggling, once on May 17 and again on May 20. The first time federal officials apprehended him with a whaleboat laden with ten barrels of flour, ten boxes of candles, and ten boxes of soap; the second time they caught him in a different boat laden with five barrels of flour. Mabee lied to Gallatin and was probably well accustomed to smuggling. Nonetheless, President Madison fully remitted his fine in early 1809.[26]

The Johnson family also violated the embargo repeatedly. Authorities caught both Paul and Paul Jr. smuggling in May, as was a Thomas Johnson. Notably, Paul Sr. was a fisherman who owned a wharf and thus was ideally situated to take advantage of smuggling opportunities.[27] Delesdernier apparently was an easy touch; Paul Sr. borrowed money from the collector to pay his fines; Delesdernier had to sue him in local courts to recover it.[28]

On occasion smugglers also introduced contraband into the United States. Officials found a cask of rum and a cask of sugar in Stephen Bruce's cellar in Eastport.[29] Faced with a $400 fine, Bruce pleaded insanity and poverty. Like Mabee, President Madison pardoned him, too.[30] Some vessels that brought provisions to the region returned with contraband. Customs officers in New York discovered British textiles and sixty tons of plaster on board the schooner *Hiram* when it returned from 'Quoddy.[31] Baltimore authorities claimed plaster came into the country after being exchanged for flour at Passamaquoddy.[32]

Some locals stepped forward to enforce the embargo. For example, Eastport resident Joseph Livermore joined the crew of the revenue cutter *New Hampshire* as second mate.[33] During the embargo Delesdernier poured over $17,000 in payroll into the community, an enormous sum of money in 1808.[34] One newspaper claimed that between smuggling and the $2 per day Delesdernier paid them, the region's "poor people had suddenly become rich."[35] But others chose to forego federal employment. It proved especially difficult to recruit a U.S. deputy marshal for Passamaquoddy. Delesdernier recommended two men for the position before finding a third man who finally accepted the post in August, his neighbor William Coney.[36] Notably, the two men who posted bonds for his service as deputy marshal, Samuel Tuttle and Jabez Mowry, were both notorious smugglers.[37] Coney, who also served in the customhouse, was clearly a weak reed who had the appearance of honesty but worked closely with Eastport's smuggling merchants.

Like Coney, the men Delesdernier hired as guards often allied themselves with the smugglers. One observer found that the collector received into his service "persons whose habits rendered them needy, and who had never been trustworthy; and thus, undoubtedly, yielding to the temptation which beset them, they were paid by both sides." Popular accounts claimed that all but three such guards took bribes. But even those three were rumored to assist friends involved in smuggling by going to sleep on duty. While guards received $2 per day from Delesdernier to watch over the contraband goods stockpiled in Eastport, the smugglers paid them fifty cents for every barrel of flour they took away. The temptation was too much for the guards, and the piles of contraband goods quietly melted away at night or during foggy days.[38]

May was the worst month for embargo violations in terms of violence and quantities smuggled. Royal Navy officers noted that the flour smugglers were becoming increasingly violent, and they wounded some customs officers with harpoons and other sharp instruments.[39] In the first week of May alone, Delesdernier reported that 19,000 barrels of flour, 2,700 barrels of salted pork and beef, 1,700 barrels of bread, 3,059 barrels of naval stores, 4,500 bushels of corn, and unknown quantities of butter, lard, and other goods landed in the district. When these goods arrived at Passamaquoddy, Delesdernier promptly impounded them and took all the keys to the warehouses in his district into his personal custody. Even the owners of the warehouses could not enter their buildings unaccompanied by a customs officer.[40] Most of this smuggled flour found its way to the West Indies. For example, in late June 1808, a reported 15,000 barrels of flour arrived from Passamaquoddy at Port Spain, Trinidad, a quantity sufficient to drop its price by a full third.[41] By 1808, Passamaquoddy supplied Demerara with large quantities of timber and provisions to support its slave plantation economy.[42]

These measures did not stop embargo violators, a fact that came to the attention of President Jefferson. He wrote to Gallatin, "I hope you will spare no pains or expence to bring the rascals of Passamaquoddy to justice," and asked him to cooperate with the secretaries of the navy and army to bring the border under control.[43] By the end of May, armed sentries stood guard at the door of every warehouse, and customs guards looked over piles of flour barrels on the beaches.

Delesdernier faced a huge problem in obeying orders from Washington because many, if not most, of his underlings cooperated with the smugglers. If necessary, the smugglers tied up and confined the guards as a ruse to cover the latter's cooperation. An example of this occurred on May 27, when four men allegedly assaulted customs officer Thomas Pettigrove Jr. at Schoodic Falls while he was guarding several hundred barrels of flour, tar, and other goods. Pettigrove claimed they captured him at the wharf he guarded and confined him for six hours while they transported the goods across the Saint Croix River and into British territory; however, the only sure fact in the case was that the flour disappeared across the border. But usually such stratagems were unnecessary. Smugglers easily bribed men like William Sherman of Schoodic Falls. A federal grand jury indicted him, but Maine's federal district attorney refused to pursue the case, probably because Sherman had fled to New Brunswick.[44]

Happily for the collector, the promised troops arrived in June, an artillery unit commanded by Captain Moses Swett. He moved to squash resistance to the embargo, which he considered an act of rebellion, and blamed Delesdernier for not enforcing its provisions more vigorously from the outset. But his unit's effectiveness was severely hampered by desertion, much of it instigated by smugglers who bribed sentries with liquor and cash. More than a dozen soldiers deserted by the end of the month.[45]

Swett's unit arrived on board the USS *Wasp*, which lingered a few days to pursue smugglers, capturing fourteen boats in one night.[46] The American government also sent two gunboats at Passamaquoddy, No. *42* and No. *43*. Just across the harbor, British war vessels such as HMS *Squirrel* and *Plumper* anchored directly on the boundary line to keep an eye on the American military and naval presence.[47]

The border and Passamaquoddy's fogs offered special problems for the naval forces sent there. The commander of one gunboat complained of the fog in a letter to the secretary of the navy:

> In consequence of the extraordinary fogs, which have completely enclosed us since our arrival in these boats, it is, at times, utterly impossible to designate the exact boundary line of the United States. I have been extremely particular in my orders to the officers of the guard, relative to encroachments on the dominions of Gt. Britain, but yet it frequently happens that when one imagines himself within a few yards of shore, he may, in consequence of the tides and eddies, which run with remarkable velocity and *from every point* of the compass, be some miles out. About three weeks since, a boat was sent from [Gunboat] No. *42*, with orders to return in fifteen minutes, and altho' the officer of the boat exerted utmost of his abilities to obey his instructions, he was nearly sixteen hours absent, before he was able to find his vessel.[48]

British diplomats were quick to protest American naval incursions into British waters, as when a gunboat seized a boat laden with flour off Deer Island.[49]

By the end of June, Eastport was an armed camp. The federal government built a battery and blockhouse on a bluff overlooking the town. The calls and challenges of sentries and musket fire broke the night silence.[50] Newspaper editors questioned Jefferson's use of military force against civilians and described the situation in Passamaquoddy:

> Come with me, sir, to yonder eminence that overlooks the union—cast your eyes eastward—do you see that vessel—that battery—those armed men—it is the *Wasp* sloop of war—she is stationed there in conjunction with the soldiers—for what? To attack our enemies? No such thing. All the energies of Mr. Jefferson are exhausted against our citizens. These warlike preparations are intended to prevent our merchants from selling their produce to those who would purchase.[51]

But it was not only the military who were armed. Many smugglers openly carried arms in the streets. The impression is one of a community suddenly swamped with armed men, walking the streets, skulking about hidden coves, all waiting for nightfall or a heavy fog to continue their illicit trade.[52] The New Brunswick brig *Isabella* armed itself with six cannon and anchored within fifty yards of Indian Island to protect itself. The crew sensed trouble was brewing, especially fearing seizure by the USS *Wasp*. Meanwhile, smugglers loaded it with contraband provisions from both the American and British shores in boats and canoes. One of *Isabella*'s crew described the rush to load contraband "taken on board in the course of seven or eight days at all Hours, morning, noon and night—that the Indian canoes brought some two and three Barrels at a time, the Brig's boat brought ten or twelve barrels of salted provisions some biscuit and two Barrels of Flour each time. That the Brig's Boat went two or three times to Moose Island for Provisions." For such hazardous and strenuous duty, the crew demanded a raise from $12 per month to $20, and even then the captain described them as being in a state of mutiny.[53]

Despite military support, the smugglers continued to trouble Delesdernier, who complained of the "nefarious schemes of miscreant Individuals having no motive but illicit gain." These adventurers bombarded Delesdernier with arguments and pleas to permit them to land their cargoes, undoubtedly so that they could be smuggled across the border at an appropriate moment. Frequently the meetings between Delesdernier and merchants turned into shouting matches. At least one New York merchant threatened to sue him.[54] The gunboat commander reported, "There are nearly a hundred merchants and adventurers with immense quantities of flour etc., who do not hesitate to bribe sentinels for the purpose of smuggling their property."[55] Newspaper reports indicated that smuggling continued unabated, and that under cover of every fog, hundreds of barrels a day found their way across to the British side.[56]

Even when confronted with military might, locals vigorously defended themselves. The region's local history cites one example when the American military commander, the captain of the USS *Wasp*, and Delesdernier together confronted Samuel Wheeler, a local merchant and suspected smuggler. The federal officers demanded the merchant place his goods under federal custody. The man refused to comply. Despite the threats, the merchant knew that he had as yet violated no law, and stated to the federal officers: "Gentlemen, I am here on my own soil, in defence of my own property, and—as you have seen fit to conduct—of my personal honor. Heed me, then, when I say, as I now do, that no man, be he who he may, touches a barrel of this flour except at the peril of his life. I have said: now take care of yourselves."[57] While this is an uncorroborated anecdote, it touches on the difficulties of enforcing an embargo in a nation where property rights were sacrosanct. According to the story, the federal officers withdrew, perplexed by the smuggler's self-righteous determination and bluster.

The success of the American smugglers was only possible because New Brunswick merchants and British officials acted to undermine Jefferson's embargo. The embargo and subsequent commercial restrictions benefited New Brunswick and Nova Scotia. New Brunswick, already experiencing economic resurgence by 1807 due to increased British demand for ship timber, witnessed a revival of its moribund West Indies trade. With the American competition gone, New Brunswick merchants seized the opportunity to revive their flagging trade, especially with the West Indies.[58] The colony's exports to the West Indies increased 150 percent over those of 1807. Saint Andrews, a busy timber port in 1807, became even busier in 1808: between March 1 and August 1, 1808, twenty-two brigs, fifteen ships, and numerous schooners and sloops entered the port.[59] The embargo compounded the port's prosperity by providing a steady source of cheap American labor to work in the forests and on the ships involved in the timber trade.

Loyalist merchants such as Robert Pagan and James McMaster established stores on Indian Island, as close to the border as possible in order to take advantage of the smuggling trade.[60] They eagerly participated in the contraband provision trade and cooperated with adventurers and local American merchants to bring tens of thousands of barrels of flour, provisions, and naval stores across the border. Some American merchants such as Divie Bethune of New York attempted to send clerks to set up shop in Saint Andrews, but even the lax colonial authorities had to object, albeit somewhat apologetically.[61] During the embargo, these merchants bought flour and other commodities at low prices from a glutted American market and sold them at high prices in the West Indies. Flour worth $6.50 at Eastport fetched $12.50 on Indian Island, New Brunswick, and up to $40.00 per barrel in West Indian markets.[62]

The British imperial and colonial governments also moved to undermine the embargo and did so with surprising speed. A royal directive dated April 11, 1808, ordered British naval vessels to not interrupt neutral vessels loaded with provisions, timber, and other enumerated goods that were sailing to British colonies in the West Indies or South America, "notwithstanding such vessels may not have regular clearances and documents on board."[63] This order encouraged American shippers, the primary providers of provisions and timber to the West Indies, to break the embargo. A further incentive permitted those same neutral vessels to take cargoes away from those same colonies.

Colonial administrators gladly complied with Colonial Office orders to open trade to embargo breakers. New Brunswick's political leadership concluded that it was their "duty" to subvert the embargo and correctly predicted the embargo would benefit their colony's economy.[64] The colony's agent in London predicted a wave of American immigrants to the province, and claimed to "applaud Jefferson very much as an Englishman, and especially as a New Brunswick agent and planter for the measure of the Embargo."[65] Nova Scotia's lieutenant governor even opened small ports in the Bay of Fundy like Digby to the previously banned American trade.[66] A Nova Scotian merchant concluded to an American friend, "Your Embargo may ruin your own merchants, and many others; but if it is continued, will make the fortunes of the traders in this province" (*Portland Gazette* June 20, 1808).

New Brunswick officials deemed Saint Andrews, Indian and Marvell Island, and other places in Passamaquoddy Bay "places of deposit," where smuggling craft would find an asylum and the proprietor was at liberty to sell to whomever they pleased or reship them in British bottoms to a British market. This plan supplied the Royal Navy with vital naval stores like tar, pitch, turpentine, and rosin, while British North America and the West Indies received American tobacco, provisions, and other articles, all transported on New Brunswick vessels once smugglers brought the contraband across the border. The British customs inspector on Indian Island was especially blithe in considering the mountains of provisions that appeared at night on the small island. According to local tradition, as he strode along the beach crowded with barrels of contraband, he playfully told the smugglers: "Just clear away a path for me to walk through, so that I will not break my legs, and that will do!"[67]

The Royal Navy worked to subvert the embargo, too. British warships anchored directly on the border to enforce Crown jurisdiction. Contraband flour barrels crowded the decks of British warships, which sometimes escorted smuggling vessels out of the bay to prevent interference by American patrol vessels.[68] Smugglers used the presence of British warships to their own advantage. For example, when sailors from the USS *Wasp* seized a British vessel loaded with American contraband, smuggling merchants appealed to the commander of HMS *Squirrel* for protection. He complied by ordering HM's schooner *Porgey* to escort the vessels and their contraband cargoes as far east as Nova Scotia.[69] Samuel Bucknam, an Eastport merchant who moved to New Brunswick just before the embargo, was lucky enough to have the assistance of HMS *Cleopatra* in getting two shiploads of provisions and other supplies out of Passamaquoddy Bay and to Barbados, where they undoubtedly commanded a high price. But the consequence of his actions was that he could not return to the United States for fear of legal action against him.[70]

The imperial government also sought to undermine the embargo by reviving its old claim to Moose Island. Alarmed by the presence of American troops and fortifications on the island, British military and naval authorities sent a stiff note to the American commander demanding his withdrawal from what they considered to be part of New Brunswick. The American commander declined, but sent the message on to Washington, where President Jefferson personally drafted a response that asserted American claims to Eastport and Moose Island. For the time being, the British had to accept the American presence, but that did not mean they had to cooperate with the embargo.[71]

With the blessing of Loyalist merchants and British officials, English merchants like Richard Hasluck of Birmingham, England, moved to Passamaquoddy to engage in illicit trade. Hasluck was an adventurer, an ambitious young merchant who operated as an agent for English hardware merchants Alexander Walker Sr. and his brother, Thomas H. Hasluck.[72] His job was to bring British hardware into the lucrative but often closed American market and procure an American cargo destined for the West Indies in return. Hasluck had a large store in Saint Andrews, where he conducted both legal and illicit trade. During the embargo he sometimes used Swedish-flagged vessels, an early instance of using neutral-flagged vessels in the Passamaquoddy smuggling trade.[73]

He was not an especially successful smuggler; American authorities interfered with his operations several times. The first of these occasions was on the night of April 5, 1808, when customs officials caught Hasluck attempting to illegally export 135 kegs of butter across the St. Croix River.[74] Nonetheless, Hasluck continued his operations into the summer and autumn of 1808.

Hasluck was not alone. Many smugglers remained at 'Quoddy and developed new tricks to subvert the forces arrayed against them, such as plying the commander of American gunboat No. 43 with drink. The young officer quickly succumbed, to the point that he did not appear on deck for weeks at a time and suffered delirium tremens. The officer's alcoholism neutralized his ability to pursue smugglers and resulted in his dismissal from the service.[75] Another tactic was to involve British naval units stationed at Passamaquoddy. Smugglers sought to convince Royal Navy officers that American officials enforcing the embargo violated British sovereignty when pursuing smugglers.[76]

Undaunted by previous failures, Hasluck continued to engage in the illicit exportation of American foodstuffs. By October he expressed his frustration that vast quantities of provisions lay at Passamaquoddy for lack of ships to take them away.[77] Finally he found a ship and loaded it with a large quantity of American flour at Snug Cove, Campobello, within sight of American customs officers at Eastport. The customs officers must already have suspected the vessel *Eliza* was carrying contraband, but somebody whom Hasluck referred to as "a notorious b____d" informed Delesdernier of the ship's illicit cargo.[78] While the vessel was in British waters, the collector could do nothing, but the *Eliza* strayed into American waters almost immediately after raising anchor. Passamaquoddy's fierce tides almost swept the vessel on some rocks, and the captain brought his vessel to anchor. An American customs officer immediately boarded the vessel, soon followed by sailors from U.S. Navy gunboat No. 43, which anchored alongside the *Eliza*.

Probably alerted by Hasluck, the captain of a nearby Royal Navy vessel demanded that the commander of the gunboat immediately release the *Eliza*, but the brash American lieutenant replied "that he had possession of her and nothing but bloodshed and hard fighting should take her from him."[79] The Royal Navy officer responded by moving his ship to within a few hundred feet from where the *Eliza* lay. The situation was extremely tense; in the aftermath of the *Chesapeake* incident, American naval officers were anxious to assert their fighting ability. Fortunately, Delesdernier and Captain Swett intervened and agreed to return the *Eliza*, thereby defusing the crisis.[80]

Averting a crisis with the *Eliza* was Delesdernier's last success. Within a few days his own assistants betrayed him. The crew of a customhouse boat conspired with a sentry guarding contraband goods in a warehouse. The sentry and the boat's crew took forty barrels of naval stores and a bale of cotton and delivered it to a British vessel anchored in Snug Cove, just a short row across the harbor from Eastport. The master of the vessel paid them in cash and with 170 pounds of coffee. Delesdernier soon found out about the missing goods and was able to recover some of them, and the next day he initiated proceedings in the local court against his own men. Nathaniel Sevey, the man in charge of the revenue boat, posted a bond of $400 for his appearance in court. But sentry Stephen H. Kankey was too poor to post bond, and so was sent to the county jail in Machias. He soon escaped the old wooden jail and never faced trial.[81] Ultimately the federal government dismissed Delesdernier for the malfeasance of his subordinates. Despite Gallatin's protests that he was a zealous and active enforcer of the embargo, President Jefferson had considered removing him from office as early as May.[82]

By November, Delesdernier's local influence completely collapsed. A symptom of his weakening influence in the community was an assault made by Aaron Olmstead, a local blacksmith and trader. Federal court records reveal that on November 17, 1808, Olmstead did "beat bruise wound insult & ill treat" Delesdernier's son, Lewis Jr., with "cruel heavy & grievous blows."[83] Lewis Jr. was a customs inspector. Like so many other customs collectors at the end of Jefferson's embargo, Delesdernier found himself less able to enforce the laws as community attitudes hardened against federal interference in their everyday livelihoods.

The collapse of Delesdernier's authority, the rise of violent smuggling in the region, and the activities of the smuggling adventurers are personified in the experience of John McMaster. He was the most troublesome of the adventurers at Passamaquoddy and in some respects best reflects Adam Smith's model. McMaster was the only adventurer who can be associated with a smuggling-related murder. It is impossible to pin down McMaster's nationality; true to Smith's dictum, he was one of those smugglers who changed their nationality at will. McMaster also delighted in defying state authority, what Smith termed "hair-breadth escapes." McMaster also suffered the fate Smith prescribed for smugglers: bankruptcy due to government prosecution.[84]

McMaster arrived at Passamaquoddy during Jefferson's embargo. He was a slippery character; in various documents he claimed to reside in Castine, Buckstown, and Eastport in Maine; Boston, Massachusetts; and Halifax, Nova Scotia. He may have had connections with the McMaster family of Saint Andrews, New Brunswick, which had branches in Halifax and Augusta, Maine. In the spring of 1808, customs officials found McMaster illegally exporting flour and confiscated the cargo. Undeterred, McMaster ordered a shipload of American flour to be delivered to him at Passamaquoddy in the autumn of 1808, but Delesdernier refused to permit McMaster to unload the vessel and forced him to store the flour in a warehouse guarded by federal officers on remote Isle au Haut, almost one hundred miles west of Passamaquoddy.

McMaster's reaction to this setback was to plot to free his flour and get it to market in Nova Scotia. McMaster easily recruited a crew at Passamaquoddy to repossess his impounded flour on Isle au Haut.[85] Nor did these men balk at the armaments on board his schooner *Peggy*, which included muskets, blunderbusses, and cutlasses. The *Peggy* sailed to Isle au Haut, and on a dark night the crew landed and attacked the guards at the warehouse holding his flour. One guard died in the gun battle, and one of the *Peggy*'s crew suffered a severe wound. The smugglers threw the guard's body into the ocean, hoping to conceal their murder. The smugglers succeeded in carrying off McMaster's flour, but a revenue cutter pursued the *Peggy* and captured the smuggling vessel without resistance. Authorities put *Peggy*'s crew in the Castine jail, but a mob broke most of them out. The court released the remainder for lack of evidence.[86]

Federal prosecutors uncovered McMaster's connection with the *Peggy* incident and tried him in Maine's federal district court in September 1809. A jury found him guilty of breaking the embargo laws and fined him $10,000.[87] Unable to pay this staggering sum, McMaster went to the Lincoln County jail in Wiscasset for debt. He remained there for years, initially chained and confined to a cell, but later was given the liberties granted to other debtors. He petitioned Congress on several occasions for release. Congress ignored his pleas, and McMaster was still confined in Wiscasset when a drunken sailor murdered him in August 1815.[88]

McMaster's violence and persistence even after being caught reflects his own ruthlessness. His ability to recruit what amounted to a gang of mercenaries at Passamaquoddy also indicates that the region had truly become a refuge for the lawless.[89] McMaster's punishment also displays the determination of the American government to suppress smuggling.

While violence was not unknown at Passamaquoddy before 1808, murder, beatings, and other violent crimes dramatically increased during 1808 as the stakes became higher. With specie and banknotes flooding into the region, robberies became more common. Even store robberies, heretofore unknown, began to occur. Richard Hasluck was a victim of a robbery when thieves robbed the messenger carrying the $2,700 he intended to use to pay for the cargo of the *Eliza*. Hasluck posted a reward of $500, apparently without success.[90] Hasluck was a victim of the very lawlessness that customs officers accused adventurers of bringing to Passamaquoddy.

Another violent incident indicates how smuggling could be a slippery slope into more violent crime. The schooner *Mark* arrived at Passamaquoddy from nearby Addison, Maine, in the late autumn of 1808. One night the crew hoisted anchor and permitted the vessel to drift into British waters. Despite the fact that the vessel had no official papers, New Brunswick customs authorities allowed the vessel's owner to sell the vessel, acting under the Crown order that permitted the entry of American vessels despite irregularities in their documentation. New Brunswick customs authorities also permitted the vessel to load a cargo and clear for Demerara in South America. The owners must not have realized what desperadoes the crew were; on the return trip they threw the owner's agent overboard and sold the vessel in Cuba for their own profit. On their return to Eastport, word soon leaked out, and federal authorities arrested the men and placed them in irons in the fort. Passamaquoddy's U.S. deputy marshal called their actions "the most atrocious and barbarous that has occurred in this country."[91]

Happily for Delesdernier, President Jefferson repealed the embargo laws in March 1809. After receiving the news, he immediately rowed across the border to inform David Owen on Campobello Island. According to the magistrate, the good news brought Delesdernier "great happiness and peace of mind."[92] When full trade relations were reestablished with Britain on June 10, 1809, residents from both sides of the boundary joined to celebrate at Eastport; undoubtedly, Delesdernier was among their number. At noon the cannon of Fort Sullivan and the local militia company fired celebratory salutes, after which some fifty notables gathered for a dinner. Sixteen toasts, each punctuated by the discharge of a cannon, followed the meal. There were obligatory toasts to the American president and the British king, and a waggish toast to "The American Fair—We prefer Commerce to Non-Intercourse." But the most relevant toast was "May the 'Harmony of Social Intercourse' remain uninterrupted between the Inhabitants of both sides of the Saint Croix." Borderland residents here expressed their continuing hope that the border would not divide them but bring a mutual prosperity.[93]

5

"THE PURSUIT OF IGNOMINIOUS GAIN"

Passamaquoddy became one of the great smuggling centers of the Atlantic world in the first decades of the nineteenth century, ranking with regions like Saint Mary's, on the Georgia–Spanish Florida border, and Heligoland in the Baltic.[1] By 1811, Passamaquoddy's new American customs collector, Lemuel Trescott, reported that

> there never was a greater quantity Plaister carried to the westward in one year than there has been this so far.—This Plaister, the greater part of it, has been either taken from British vessels in our waters in the night time, or taken on board in the British waters, in either case the Americans goes immediately to sea after obtaining their cargoes to avoid the British Cutter on one side and the American on the other.—I have done all in my power to check this growing evil, but when it is considered that this Plaister on the British side brings only 4$ the ton, it is worth 8$ in our waters and when it is seen this District has in it men of enterprise in pursuit of gain, and well versed in eluding the officers of the Custom House, add to this, there now in this place not less by estimation than one hundred Merchants from New York and other places, after Plaister to lade their vessels I fear it will be impossible to check the unlawful intercourse.[2]

The collector noted several changes in the trade. First, it was now both larger and more surreptitious, occurring at night. Second, he noted the powerful market forces that drove the trade, 100 percent profit for merely crossing the invisible boundary line between the United States and British North America. This provided plenty of incentive for smugglers from as far away as New York City and Philadelphia. Passamaquoddy's smuggling trade was big business, with a reach that extended at least as far as the mid-Atlantic states.

British officials, too, showed concern. In 1812 a panel of commissioners arrived in New Brunswick and reported that the international border remained a problem in suppressing smuggling:

> It is at this middle channel, or supposed line of boundary, that contraband goods are exchanged for fish and plaister of Paris, from coasting vessels moored alongside of the vessels of the United States; and the interchange is effected with most perfect security, from the immediate vicinity of Moose Island, the place of refuge in the event of interruption. Upon this island there are most extensive establishments, stored with American produce, on purpose to be smuggled into the British provinces. A most respectable merchant stated in evidence that he had seen at Moose-Island last spring warehouses larger than any at Saint John's, filled with articles acknowledged to be for the Bay of Fundy.[3]

British concerns were a little different. They were more concerned with the actual boundary line and the fact that the center of this trade was Moose Island, over which Britain still claimed jurisdiction. Again, smuggling's impact was more than local. It extended beyond New Brunswick to the Fundy shore of Nova Scotia, to towns like Yarmouth, Digby, Annapolis, and Windsor.

Both reports indicate that between the embargo and the War of 1812, smuggling continued on a massive scale at Passamaquoddy. Two forces perpetuated the smuggling trade. The first was government use of commerce as a diplomatic weapon. The British and American governments attempted to punish each other by alternately opening and closing trade. The second factor was the continued growth of the illicit plaster trade and the reciprocal provisions trade in spite of, and often because of, government trade restrictions. While government intervention was erratic, merchants consistently pursued trade, but were often forced to peripheral regions like Passamaquoddy to do so. The result is that Passamaquoddy became an international smuggling entrepôt, a true haven for free traders. The region enjoyed a measure of prosperity as a result, but also suffered an increase in violent crime.

The American government, now led by President James Madison, continued to attempt to use trade as a weapon against Britain. After Jefferson's disastrous embargo, less sweeping trade restrictions aimed at Britain and its colonies followed under the Non-Intercourse Act, which was in force from August 1809 to May 1810, and the Non-Importation Act, sometimes known as Macon's Bill No. 2, which was in effect from February 1811. These laws faced the same problem the embargo did: a popular lack of support that resulted in massive smuggling all along the border with British North America. President Madison was particularly enraged by American citizens subverting the law, and he complained to Congress, "The practice of smuggling, which is odious everywhere, and particularly criminal in free governments, where, the laws being made by all for the good of all, a fraud is committed on every individual as well as on the state, attains its utmost guilt when it blends with a pursuit of ignominious gain a treacherous subserviency, in the transgressors, to a foreign policy adverse to that of their own country."[4] For Madison, smuggling was a betrayal of republican virtue, but this founder had already lost touch with a new generation who pursued profit unfettered by the revolutionary generation's sense of republicanism.[5]

The Non-Intercourse Act of 1809 replaced Jefferson's embargo and allowed foreign trade except with Britain and France in an effort to wring concessions out of those warring nations. The measure had some initial success, but when officials in London refused to rescind the offensive measures that permitted British warships to harass American shipping, President Madison invoked a "Non-Intercourse Law" and barred trade with Britain and its colonies effective August 9, 1809. Congress allowed that law to lapse on May 1, 1810, but within days attempted another effort at peaceful coercion through commercial restrictions.[6] Known as Macon's Bill No. 2, this measure restored commerce with Britain and France if they stopped interfering with American seaborne commerce. The French dictator Napoleon quickly promised to do so, but Britain refused, and on February 2, 1811, the American government once again stopped all commerce with Britain and its colonies. This measure remained in force until early 1812, when Congress passed a complete embargo on American shipping in preparation for its declaration of war on Britain in June.

The British imperial government had long enacted a number of policies meant to subvert the American commercial restrictions. This was essentially an extension of the commercial tactics they used to undermine Napoleon's continental system.[7] In 1807, the British opened colonial ports to American shipping provided they carried only certain enumerated goods that the British empire needed. These goods included timber, shingles, livestock, flour, and other foodstuffs and "naval stores," which included pitch, tar, and turpentine. In return, the American vessels could fill their holds with plaster, grindstones, and any colonial produce except ship timber, as well as British manufactured goods or West Indian products like molasses or sugar.[8]

However, imperial authorities revoked this measure effective September 15, 1809, making trade between British North America and the United States illegal on both sides of the border. The British government reacted to Macon's Bill No. 2 in October 1811 by opening selected ports to American trade, including Halifax, Nova Scotia, and Saint John and Saint Andrews, New Brunswick. The impact was immediate: in 1811, New Brunswick doubled both its imports and exports to the West Indies, largely at the expense of American trade restrictions.[9]

Thus when the United States closed trade with Britain and its colonies, Britain opened its markets to American shipping and vice versa. Government trade policies fluctuated wildly in these years, and ship masters could never be sure when entering an American port with British cargo or a colonial port with American goods whether customs authorities would seize their ship. These measures created enormous problems for American merchants and British merchants, both of whom were anxious for trade to resume.

The result was that smuggling at Passamaquoddy steadily grew after 1809, in defiance of both British and American policies. Trade restrictions brought a measure of wealth to 'Quoddy. New Brunswick's provincial secretary claimed, "The late American embargo has given a spring to the commerce, and thereby extended the improvements to an incredible degree. The banks of the Saint Croix (formerly Scoudiac) which in 1796, were on both sides deserts, *now* exhibit uncommon scenes of enterprize—industry & activity."[10]

Plaster remained at the heart of this smuggling trade. The embargo had also taught merchants the profitability and ease of smuggling provisions at 'Quoddy. Hand in hand with plaster and provisions was a new trade in British manufactured goods, a highly valuable trade that drew yet more adventurers to the border.

By 1812, an estimated 50,000 tons of plaster crossed the border annually, employing some 10,000 tons of shipping.[11] The amount of shipping involved was itself significant, for transporting gypsum, or "the carrying trade" in the parlance of the times, was worth as much as the material itself.[12] Plaster bought at $4.00 per ton in Eastport was worth $1.25 more in Boston and yet more in Baltimore and Philadelphia. As an example, in late June 1811, the small American coasting schooner *Amphibious* took on board ninety tons of plaster at $4.00 per ton. Six weeks later the plaster sold at Philadelphia for $13.00 per ton, providing a nice profit for the cargo's owners.[13] Often the plastermen conducted these transfers at night, in contravention of both American and

British laws, but the dark partially cloaked their illicit activities. Ideally, the two vessels moored alongside one another and transferred their cargo from hold to hold. If that was not possible, the crew transferred the cargo in small boats. Working in the dark was far more dangerous than during the day; injuries and drownings were common.[14]

Officials on both sides of the border complained about the plaster trade. Colonials complained that it was "most ruinous" and that it was "the means of corrupting the morals of the diggers & carriers. It is a cloak for smugglers, and it takes off the Farmer from improving and raising grain."[15] For American authorities the problem was not the plaster itself but that smugglers hid British manufactured goods underneath the plaster to introduce them into the forbidden American market. Newspapers lampooned merchant tailors and dry-goods merchants from Baltimore, Philadelphia, and New York rushing off to Boston where they claimed to buy plaster when, in fact, they were buying smuggled goods.[16] In 1811, Secretary of the Treasury Albert Gallatin issued a circular to all customs collectors in the nation warning them to be especially vigilant when dealing with vessels from Passamaquoddy and even more so with those carrying plaster.[17] He also suggested to Congress that no vessel be allowed to proceed there without permission from the president.[18]

Like plaster, the scale of the illicit provisions trade was considerable. Flour, especially Virginia superfine, was in high demand in the Maritime Provinces. Like plaster, flour increased significantly in value as soon as it crossed the border. Recognizing their mutual needs, and well accustomed to smuggling flour after the embargo, American and colonial merchants happily traded Virginia flour for Nova Scotia plaster. Colonial merchants like Simeon Perkins of Liverpool, Nova Scotia, even went so far as to send his son-in-law to live at Eastport to coordinate trade with New York merchants.[19]

The problem was that sometimes the British government, both imperial and provincial, allowed this trade and sometimes it did not. In the spring of 1811, New Brunswick's executive council recommended that customs officers allow American salted provisions into the province for six months because of shortages, provided the Royal Navy agreed. Yet, a year later, that same body denied a request from the official charged with feeding the British garrison to buy five hundred barrels of salt pork at 'Quoddy, even if it saved the government £500. The council denied the request, "as there does not appear to exist such an emergency as to justify a suspension of the Law of Trade."[20]

Faced with these inconsistencies, merchants simply persisted in trading, even those who should have known better. For example, in late September 1811, George Barclay of Nova Scotia attempted to smuggle 459 barrels of flour, 222 barrels of bread, 96 barrels of pitch and tar, and 5 barrels of pork into New Brunswick, citing the need for provisions in the province. While certainly a large quantity to smuggle, the case was unremarkable except for the fact that George's father was Thomas Barclay, the British consul at New York and former boundary commissioner who helped determine the border running through 'Quoddy's waters in the 1790s. Notably, the whole scheme was underwritten by the consul.[21]

Not all of these provisions were destined for the Maritime Provinces. Colonial merchants re-exported the provisions to Newfoundland, the West Indies, and the Iberian Peninsula. New Brunswick merchants exported some 17,792 barrels of American flour exported from Saint Andrews during the second quarter of 1812, during an American embargo that theoretically should have stopped all intercourse.[22] Many of these foodstuffs found their way to the British garrison at Halifax; Jabez Mowry is known to have sent over $50,000 worth of provisions to Halifax in 1812.[23]

Sometimes these provisions crossed the border on the hoof rather than in barrels. Lubec, originally the mainland component of Eastport, became a separate town in 1811 and proved particularly convenient for cattle smuggling because whole herds could be driven to the narrow channel that separated that community from Campobello. At slack low tide, when the channel was narrowest and the tidal currents momentarily halted, cattle drivers could simply urge their herds across the mud flats and narrow strip of water in less than five minutes. In early September 1810, William Bodfish of Kennebec County drove thirty-six oxen and two steers across the channel in just such a manner and received $1,200 for the herd.[24]

The trade in British manufactured goods may have been the most troublesome, in no small part because these goods were of far greater value than staples like flour or gypsum. British merchants like Richard Hasluck continued smuggling, encouraged by the depressed prices of Birmingham manufactures and the conversely inflated price of British manufactured goods in the United States. American merchants eagerly bought up British manufactured goods, but uncertain of when trade was legal, many shipped their goods to British North American ports such as Montreal, Halifax, and Saint John. Once in British North America, the goods could be sent to the American market on short notice if legal trade opened again, or they could be smuggled across the border at places like Passamaquoddy. New York merchants Jabez Harrison and David Smith Jr. did so and anxiously petitioned Congress for permission to bring British hardware from Saint John across the border, but to no avail. Harrison alone had $40,000 worth of goods in Saint John warehouses, costing him considerable storage fees and no end of worry.[25]

James Colles of New York City is representative of the American adventurers who flocked to 'Quoddy before the War of 1812 broke out. Colles was a clerk for New York merchant Hugh Kennedy Toler, an aggressive entrepreneur who engaged in importing British manufactured goods such as textiles from Liverpool.[26] Like other New York merchants, Toler had British goods delivered to New Brunswick. Once his goods arrived there, Toler could either import them legally or smuggle them into the United States if Congress banned trade with Britain. To that end, Toler sent Colles to Passamaquoddy in the spring of 1812 to bring goods stored in Saint Andrews and Saint John into the United States.

Colles's extensive correspondence reveals a man at home in the Loyalist salons of Saint John, where he was familiar with the influential Wetmore family. His easy interaction with Loyalists was no doubt aided by his own Federalist politics. Colles also moved among an elite circle in New York, including the Roosevelt family. He lived at a fashionable Manhattan address—42 Pearl Street—and drank his tea from custom-ordered monogrammed china from Canton. Colles was an ambitious young man, full of self-confidence, tightly bonded with his social peers, accustomed to a life of privilege, yet unceasing in his pursuit of wealth.[27] At the same time, Colles was quite capable of haggling on the docks of a rough-and-tumble frontier town like Eastport in order to move British manufactured goods across the border. He hired experienced smugglers such as one Captain Osgood to bring contraband goods concealed under a load of plaster to New York City.[28]

By the time the War of 1812 broke out, a steady stream of British manufactured goods illicitly entered the United States through Passamaquoddy. The fact drew the attention of American newspaper editors, one of whom archly noted, "At the very eastern boundary of the State, so lately a howling wilderness, are also produced fine broadcloths, cutlery, &c. equal to the best English, and in large quantities."[29] Smugglers had made a mockery of President Madison's Non-Intercourse efforts.

Both governments responded to the reinvigorated smuggling trade with increased enforcement methods. The American government attempted to crack down on the border by replacing Delesdernier with a more effective collector and posting a revenue cutter to the area. The British government dispatched the Royal Navy to patrol the area more aggressively and sent a commission to investigate the smuggling trade. Both governments largely failed to stem the rising tide of smuggling.

After Jefferson's embargo, the American government removed Delesdernier from office and instituted legal proceedings against the collector that led to his financial ruin. His replacement was Lemuel Trescott, who had previously served as the collector of nearby Machias. Trescott was a Continental Army veteran made famous by a successful attack on a Loyalist outpost on Long Island in 1780. He probably owed his appointment to fellow veteran Henry Dearborn, the secretary of war under Thomas Jefferson. After the war he became a merchant in the Passamaquoddy area and was active in the Order of the Cincinnati and the Freemasons. Similarly to Delesdernier, Trescott was a local booster; he was involved in early attempts to establish a bank at Eastport and took an active interest in civic affairs. Like Delesdernier, he facilitated local trade as much as possible.

Trescott was undoubtedly more subtle than his predecessor, and Delesdernier's old neutral zone approach was no longer viable anyway. Trescott's method of accommodating the plaster trade allowed him to assume the appearance of vigilance while actually facilitating the trade. His system required that the plastermen land their cargo, and then he went through the motions of seizing it. Court-appointed appraisers, usually plaster merchants and smugglers themselves, deliberately undervalued the gypsum at about 25 percent of its real worth. The owners of the plaster then put up a bond for the value of the plaster, or even twice its appraised value, upon which he released the seized goods. Even if the court condemned the bonds, the owners still realized a profit; Trescott received a proportion of the plaster's value as a reward, and the appraisers received a per diem from the government for their work and probably a commission from the cargo's owners as well.[30] By his own account, during 1812 Trescott seized a staggering 2,684 tons of plaster on beaches, wharves, and vessels at Passamaquoddy; the entire amount entered the United States under this bonding ploy.[31]

The bonding ploy required the full cooperation of local smuggling merchants. Men like Jabez Mowry acted as agents on behalf of outsiders who came to the region to buy plaster. Mowry was a major player in the plaster trade; he had wharves and warehouses on both Campobello and Eastport, and owned about one-quarter of the plaster seized in 1812. Solomon Rice of Eastport claimed to own about one-fifth of all the plaster seized that same year, but approximately two-thirds of the seizures occurred on his beach or the island he owned right next to the boundary. They often acted as plaster appraisers or as sham informants who could thus claim a large proportion of the proceeds of any federally seized plaster. They also received a small commission for conducting their deals and profited from providing wharfage and other services to plaster traders.

Like any racket, there were those who tried to cheat the system. In late 1811, Capt. Abel Staples of the Boston sloop *Marietta* slipped across the border and landed a cargo at Harbor de Lute on Campobello. When it reentered American waters, Trescott had the vessel seized. In court Staples swore that he did not know that he unloaded in British territory. Trescott would have none of it and vigorously prosecuted the case.[32] Another way to elude the collector was to bring plaster to Passamaquoddy in an American vessel. The vessel's paperwork declared that it had a "quantity of plaster" aboard, a purposely vague description of perhaps a few hundred pounds that accompanied a cargo of provisions or naval stores. On arrival the ship off-loaded the foodstuffs and other cargo, topped off its load of plaster, often two hundred tons or more, and immediately sailed for Boston or New York to avoid both British and American customs authorities. On arrival the vessel's paperwork appeared correct—it still had "a quantity" of plaster on board. Trescott estimated that 75 percent of all plaster brought into the United States thus evaded his detection. Trescott made it very clear to his superiors that any plaster that entered the country without his permission in the form of a clearance certificate could be seized as contraband.[33] Trescott's old friend Henry Dearborn, now the customs collector at Boston, accepted his report uncritically and forwarded it to Washington. With Dearborn firmly on his side, Trescott had little to fear from further investigation.[34]

Trescott's racket demanded some vigilance on his part, and so he could rightfully complain to the Treasury Department that he needed more support to control the border. Specifically, Trescott wanted a revenue cutter assigned to Passamaquoddy. The vessel ostensibly would suppress smuggling, but it also gave Trescott more muscle to pursue his own agenda.

The mere presence of a cutter forced those engaged in illicit trade to work much harder and carefully than they normally would have. Cutters maximized their utility by sending out smaller craft to patrol. For instance, in August 1811, the American revenue cutter *New Hampshire*'s boat approached more than a dozen vessels anchored off West Quoddy Head. When the anchored vessels realized who was approaching, they immediately got under way. Despite this precipitous flight, the cutter's boat boarded and seized three coasting schooners with a total of 210 tons of gypsum.[35] An anonymous letter dated June 30, 1812, indicates the game of cat-and-mouse played between smugglers and revenue cutters. Unsigned, addressed to a New York City merchant and smuggler conducting business on the border, the letter concludes: "Look out for the Revenue Cutter at East Port. LOOK OUT."[36]

But cutters were only as effective as their crews, especially their captains, who were not always effective in fighting smuggling. This was especially true of Hopley Yeaton, captain of the cutter *New Hampshire* from 1803 to 1811. Yeaton is a significant historical figure in that he was the first commissioned officer in the United States Revenue Cutter service, the "father of the United States Coast Guard." Yeaton became acquainted with Passamaquoddy while captain of the *New Hampshire*, and he moved there in 1800. A fisherman himself, Yeaton seems to have acted with restraint and forbearance when dealing with local mariners. In fact, he may have been too tolerant during the embargo, and the federal government dismissed him about the same time it did Delesdernier. He retired to his farm at Eastport, where he died in 1812.[37]

William P. Adams, who replaced Yeaton as captain of the *New Hampshire*, offered a vivid contrast. He was a former naval officer, and it showed in his imperious attitude. Even his superiors considered him too haughty for the position; one told Gallatin, "He is not possessed of the discretion requisite for the command of a Revenue Cutter."[38] It is possible, however, that his main fault was too much vigilance in enforcing the letter of the law. In August 1811, his vessel seized five vessels loaded with four hundred tons of plaster in the space of a few days.[39] Adams's unpopularity and arrogance soon caught up with him: the federal government removed him from command in 1812, despite his appeals to the press.[40] One wonders if Trescott had a hand in his dismissal and desired someone more pliable in his stead.

Happily for Trescott, the federal government in 1812 bought a cutter designated exclusively for Passamaquoddy, a sloop armed with six cannon.[41] But it was not easy finding an appropriate commander for the new patrol vessel. The recommendation for one candidate even noted the applicant's smuggling past.[42] Collector Trescott did well not to forward that application to the Treasury Department, for within weeks the applicant stood accused of plaster smuggling.[43] Trescott instead had a neighbor and former customhouse employee take command of the vessel, Daniel Elliot of Machias. Elliot had few connections outside of Trescott, making him a reliable subordinate who could be relied upon to do as ordered. The collector extended his web of patronage when he handpicked the rest of the crew as well. They were almost all locals, knowledgeable of the region's tides, currents, and fogs.[44]

The British also attempted to tighten control of the border. They gave George Leonard a new and more powerful cutter and sent a commission from London to investigate smuggling. In late 1807 the customs commissioners gave him more funding to operate a larger revenue cutter capable of patrolling the Bay of Fundy year-round. With a refit in 1810, the vessel became a miniature naval vessel, armed with eight 12-pounder carronades and a crew of twenty-five.[45] The *Hunter* made a few seizures at Passamaquoddy, such as the schooner *Encouragement* at Snug Cove, Campobello, with a cargo of tea in August 1811.[46] But the *Hunter* was expensive to operate, customs authorities opposed Leonard's decisions at every opportunity, and colonial authorities frequently sent the *Hunter* on missions far away from contentious Passamaquoddy. Smugglers further hindered the cutter's operations by accusing its commander of using it to smuggle.[47]

More important than cutters was the arrival of a commission from London to investigate smuggling in New Brunswick and neighboring colonies. It looked like the imperial government had finally awoken from its slumber and intended to seriously reform New Brunswick's customs establishment. The commission made some startling discoveries. It found that in 1810, smugglers brought into New Brunswick nearly all the tea, three-quarters of the wine, nine-tenths of spirits such as gin, seven-eighths of all soap and candles, most of the indigo, starch, mustard, tobacco, and East India textiles, and all of the nankeens, sailcloth, cordage, and anchors.[48] They also found that Eastport's warehouses were larger than any in New Brunswick and that smugglers conducted more business there in one day than honest traders conducted at Saint John in two months. American merchants from Boston, New York, and other ports established those warehouses expressly for the smuggling trade and employed some one hundred vessels in it. American contraband from Passamaquoddy supplied not only the needs of New Brunswick but also small ports like Digby, Annapolis, and Windsor on Nova Scotia's Fundy shore. The commissioners estimated that the Maritime Provinces imported £30,000–40,000 worth of American goods per year, equivalent to the colony's legitimate trade (roughly $175,000).[49]

The commissioners made a number of recommendations concerning the lack of vigilance among New Brunswick's customs officers. They suggested that Saint John's customs collector, William Wanton, retire, along with Colin Campbell, the surveyor and searcher. By this time Wanton was a frail old man who seldom personally attended to customhouse business. But he drew emoluments of almost £1,000 per year, a sum rivaling that of a colonial lieutenant governor. Somehow he resisted pressure to retire and remained in office until his death in 1816. Campbell, too, managed to cling to office until 1816, when the slow acting customs commissioners finally removed him from office.[50]

The commissioners also singled out John Dunn at Saint Andrews as not possessing the requisite zeal and vigilance expected of customs officers.[51] George Leonard had long complained about Dunn, and the commission confirmed that he was liberally lining his own pockets without taking in any income for the Crown.[52] As deputy collector he earned £602 in fees in 1810, without collecting even one penny for the king's revenue in either duties or seizures.[53] Dunn's creole leniency with smugglers made him a popular man; an American smuggler who had dinner with Dunn at Saint Andrews found him "a very open warm hearted Irishman."[54] Like Collector Wanton in Saint John, or his American counterparts Delesdernier and Trescott, Dunn was remembered by a local historian as a "man proverbially kind, liberal, and hospitable."[55]

The commission made a few other suggestions, none of which promised to seriously curtail smuggling. They recommended a "preventative officer" take station on Campobello to oversee the plaster trade, but the customs board did not act to do so. They also recommended that Leonard's position as superintendent of trade and fisheries be abolished. This was apparently acted upon, punishing Leonard for his vigilance, while his corrupt nemeses in the Saint John customhouse remained. The one remaining recommendation they made was that the Royal Navy send some vessels to suppress illicit trade. But that, too, was doomed to failure.

The Royal Navy's role in suppressing smuggling was neither significant nor enthusiastic, serving as an occasional ally rather than as an integral part of antismuggling efforts.[56] Its greatest impact was that if a British naval vessel was nearby, both American citizens and British subjects stayed off the water, for fear of being impressed into the Royal Navy.[57] But Royal Navy officers were not eager to pursue smugglers, they disliked taking orders from customs officials, and they noted the fate of the commander of the *Porgey* when he attempted to stop the plaster trade in 1806.[58] Clearly a young commander could get himself into a great deal of trouble when chasing smugglers; even the great Nelson found himself subject to irritating lawsuits when enforcing the Navigation Acts.

Nonetheless, when New Brunswick's new military administrator asked for the help of the Royal Navy in suppressing smuggling in the Bay of Fundy in July 1811, the region's naval commander complied. Admiral Warren sent a small schooner, HMS *Cuttle*, commanded by Lt. William L. Patterson, to patrol the area.[59] Patterson had some success, as when he seized the Nova Scotia schooner *Boyne*. While the *Boyne*'s clearance, signed by acting naval officer John Dunn, listed only eight barrels of flour and sea stores consisting of one and a part barrels of pork, bread, and small stores, the actual cargo was two kegs of gin, three rolls of tobacco, two bags of raisins, one barrel of biscuit, one barrel of pork, and eight barrels of flour. Clearly that was more "sea stores" than the schooner's crew of three could possibly need. Patterson also seized the *Sally*, a Nantucket vessel that he found in British waters off Campobello, but such small seizures barely put a dent into the smuggling trade.[60] Why were Royal Navy officers so timid?

One reason was that colonial vice-admiralty courts were not very supportive of their seizures; they condemned only about 25 percent of American vessels seized by the Royal Navy.[61] Furthermore, American merchants at Passamaquoddy encouraged sailors to desert, on one occasion inciting a nearly successful mutiny. On July 4, 1809, a mutiny broke out on HMS *Columbine* as it lay at anchor between Campobello and Eastport. So many sailors and marines jumped ship that the captain, George Hills, could not move his ship. In the struggle to escape, some stole the ship's boats, while others simply jumped in the water and swam away. Some drowned, others escaped, and loyal crewmembers shot others as they fled. The captain himself shot the ringleader and placed more than twenty men in irons. When the captain impressed locals to operate his vessel, they encouraged further desertion. Most frustrating of all for Hills was that many of the deserters had taken refuge in Eastport under American jurisdiction, just a few hundred yards away. He asked Eastport's magistrates to return the men; the selectmen replied that the deserters had already departed. When the *Columbine* got to Halifax, the Royal Navy flogged several of the mutineers with three hundred to five hundred lashes, ordered others transported to Australia, and hanged six men. Their corpses hung at the mouth of Halifax harbor, a public warning that the authority of the Royal Navy was not to be taken lightly.[62]

The *Columbine* mutiny highlights the growing violence in the region, some of it associated with smuggling, some of it with the growing military presence in the region. Conditions began to deteriorate as early as 1808, when three British deserters shot and killed a man on their way to Dipper Harbour. A civilian court ordered two of the men hanged.[63] Ironically, that unit had just arrived in that province to defend it. In 1809 there was a serious jailbreak in Saint Andrews as well as the attempted mutiny on HMS *Columbine*.[64] In 1810, the customs collector at Digby, Nova Scotia, reported violent resistance by smugglers; it seems likely this matter was exacerbated by that port's illicit trade with 'Quoddy. Troops remained at Digby some six months.[65] Some crime was directly related to the plaster trade. In 1812, David Owen of Campobello posted advertisements in newspapers complaining that plaster traders stole wood, ballast, and spars from Campobello.[66] His complaint may have initiated a local mariner's assault on him in his own bed one night. Campobello's proprietor fended off the attack and raised the "hue and cry" against his assailant, who fled to Moose Island, within sight of Owen's home but beyond his legal reach.[67]

On the American side, too, violence became more prevalent, the most troubling of which was piracy. Two Eastport men actually turned to piracy during the embargo, murdering the supercargo on board their vessel. These would-be pirates spent many months incarcerated in Fort Sullivan but escaped the gallows on a technicality.[68] In late 1810, a schooner bound from Eastport for Ireland faced a mutiny and piracy by two of its passengers.[69] Eastport's reputation became so bad that when some rowdy Irish sailors arrived from the border in Castine in May 1812, local magistrates assumed they had stolen the boat after killing its owners. No evidence could be found, however, so the court merely ordered the men out of town.[70]

Robberies became more common at Eastport. William Priest and John Hutchins broke into at least two stores each before authorities apprehended them in early 1811.[71] Facing several years in the state prison, Priest escaped the Machias jail with some other prisoners and lit out for the border, only to be rounded up by a posse at Eastport.[72]

But the most heinous crime was the shooting of a deputy attempting to apprehend a gang of counterfeiters. Minting false coins was a potentially lucrative business, given the number of strangers in the area freely spending silver coins. In early 1811, counterfeiters shot and killed a Washington County deputy who had stumbled across them. A posse moved quickly to apprehend them; at least one counterfeiter made a daring escape attempt when he leaped from a second-story window and ran away before recapture near the border.[73] One made it to Grand Manan, New Brunswick, only to starve to death. Another made his way to Granville, Nova Scotia, and eventually hanged himself.[74] A court sentenced one of those who did not escape to life imprisonment at hard labor; the man who killed the deputy was hanged.[75]

Crime became endemic at Passamaquoddy between the embargo and the War of 1812. The region suffered from anomie, a disruption of cohesion and order due to its rapid growth, sudden prosperity, and dependence on illicit trade. Part of the blame can be laid upon the inconsistency of government trade policies, which essentially made criminals out of merchants who simply wanted to trade. By 1812, those trade policies had clearly failed, and war between Britain and the United States was fast approaching. The American government girded itself for war with yet another embargo, a ninety-day effort to clear the seas of American shipping so that the Royal Navy could not capture it after Congress declared war.

Trescott postponed in closing the port during the ninety-day embargo, claiming he had not received official word, which was delayed by a washed-out bridge. Of course, he knew through unofficial channels about the embargo. Meanwhile, his port hummed with activity as shipping hurriedly cleared out, until at last he ran out of official papers for them, thus preventing further departures until an official circular that closed the port finally reached him.[76]

Shortly after that, news of the declaration of war reached Passamaquoddy. On June 25, a U.S. government courier roused Trescott out of bed to inform him. The collector's reaction, and that of Passamaquoddy's residents in general, was to attempt to see to the safety of the community through accommodation. The morning after the news arrived, Eastport residents gathered in a meeting and unanimously agreed to preserve a good understanding with the inhabitants of New Brunswick and to discourage all depredations on the property of each other. Toward that end, they formed a committee of safety, with Trescott as its chairman. This committee drafted a letter assuring their New Brunswick counterparts of their peaceful intentions. They sent it to Robert Pagan in Saint Andrews, who in turn forwarded it to the lieutenant governor in Fredericton. In the meantime, a number of Eastport's inhabitants fled for fear of attack by the Royal Navy and sought safety in Portland, Portsmouth, and Boston. Merchants removed their merchandise, and many goods from Indian Island were smuggled across the border in the confusion.[77] Borderland residents soon discovered, however, that even war could not stop the region's smuggling trade.

6

"ULMER WAS A RASCAL"

Smuggling certainly conjures images of stealthy boat landings at night, and on the chilly evening of February 24, 1813, the New Brunswick sloop *Polly* was doing just that. The smuggling vessel approached a beach on American-held Moose Island, its cargo some forty-two bales, trunks, and cases of British manufactured goods worth an estimated $40,000. Elaborate plans had been laid by the smuggler in charge of the goods, the wealthy young New Yorker James Colles. His plan included a complex scheme hatched with Eastport's most notorious smuggler, Jabez Mowry, and the American customs collector, Lemuel Trescott. Thus far, the plan worked well; Mowry had the goods loaded on board the *Polly* at Saint Andrews, and the vessel ran down to Kendall's Cove on Moose Island, where a party of men gathered to swiftly unload the contraband in small boats. Colles himself was on board to oversee the operation.

But as the *Polly* approached shore and anchored, the plan began to unravel. A party of six American soldiers lay in wait in the bushes. The local American military commander, Colonel George Ulmer, had learned of the *Polly*'s smuggling plan and arranged an ambush. The soldiers charged the smugglers on the beach, seized one of the row boats, and used it to board the *Polly*. The sergeant in charge questioned Colles about his intentions, but on receiving what they deemed as evasive answers, the soldiers seized the *Polly* and sailed for the town landing in Eastport. Colles was probably relieved when Deputy Collector William Coney boarded the sloop within minutes of the seizure. He questioned the sergeant's authority to seize the vessel and called the soldier's actions illegal. Coney claimed he had jurisdiction over the vessel and seized it in the name of the United States in an attempt to avoid a potentially embarrassing situation.[1] But after Coney took the sloop to the customhouse wharf, a dozen soldiers again took control of the sloop, for Colonel Ulmer rightly suspected Eastport's customs authorities were crooked. When customs authorities attempted to remove the *Polly*'s valuable cargo to a warehouse, it reaffirmed his suspicions, and he ordered the goods taken to the blockhouse in Fort Sullivan, safe from civilian control. Colles's carefully laid plans had gone terribly wrong.[2]

The original plan called for Colles to land the contraband and have Coney seize the goods, acting on a sham tip from Jabez Mowry. This worked to Colles's advantage because it brought the goods into the American market via an auction process that smugglers easily manipulated.[3] Ulmer's intervention proved awkward, but the game was not finished yet. Trescott and Coney complained to federal court officials about Ulmer's interference in what they saw as customhouse affairs.[4] Ulmer in turn charged the customhouse officers with colluding to facilitate smuggling. Ultimately the federal district court favored Trescott's version of events, condemned the goods, and auctioned them for roughly $100,000. Trescott and Mowry each received $25,000 as their share of the seizure, with Mowry immediately remitting his share to Colles.[5] Despite the court costs, Colles recovered the goods, sold them in an American market starved for British manufactures, and still made a profit. It was to be but one of many bitter defeats for Ulmer in his war against smuggling at Passamaquoddy.

The battle of wills between smugglers and crooked customs officers such as Colles and Trescott on one side and the American military led by Ulmer on the other was part of a larger struggle over illicit trade at Passamaquoddy. While largely a bloodless struggle, it did have its casualties. Foremost among these was Ulmer himself; the reward for his vigilance against 'Quoddy's smugglers was to be dismissal from the service under conditions highly embarrassing to himself.[6]

Colles's method of smuggling at Eastport was to cooperate as closely as possible with American customs officials. He used his social acumen and promised financial remuneration for the officials' time and trouble. He smuggled goods from New Brunswick into Eastport and then informed against his own cargo. The officials seized the goods with Colles's permission, and auctioned them off after an uncontested court hearing. He arranged to have the goods underappraised by at least 50 percent, apparently by providing the appraisers with a good meal, as "a good dinner has a great tendency to soften men's hearts."[7] Because of the false appraisal, Colles bought back the goods at a fraction of their true value, pocketed 25 percent of the proceeds of the auction as the informant, and acquired customhouse certification that the goods had legally entered the United States. In the meantime, his employer petitioned Maine's federal district court for remission of the seizure entirely.[8] While this was a convoluted and expensive way of conducting business, high wartime prices ensured a sizeable profit.

A variety of local merchants assisted Colles, including Mowry in Eastport, Nehemiah Merritt in Saint John, Robert Pagan in Saint Andrews, and Edward Blackford in Halifax. Colles sometimes stayed in their homes, received mail at their offices, borrowed money from them, and undoubtedly paid to store his contraband in their warehouses. These were business transactions, but there was a social element to them as well, a recognition that despite their various nationalities and degrees of wealth, they pursued similar goals. Face-to-face transactions, kinship and marriage links, and socialization remained an important part of conducting business, especially when conducting intricate smuggling deals.[9] Adventurers like Colles who came to Passamaquoddy depended on the sympathy and cooperation of locals to evade commercial restrictions.

The officials charged with pursuing smugglers had very little sympathy from locals. Ulmer possessed none of the social skills of Colles and faced the antipathy of the borderland population. In the autumn of 1812, alarmed by the massive smuggling occurring at Passamaquoddy, the War Department belatedly assigned a regiment of one-year volunteers under Ulmer to guard what was termed the "Eastern Frontier." The War Department instructed him that his primary mission was to suppress smuggling. He faced a number of adventurers and enemy aliens who thronged Eastport's crooked streets, many of them smugglers openly wearing arms. Ulmer estimated that almost two hundred people in Eastport were involved in supplying the British with provisions.[10]

Was Ulmer exaggerating? Were the region's inhabitants truly traitors? Certainly other observers claimed the region was rife with treason on both sides of the border. Some Americans suspected that John Brewer of Robbinston, Maine, was a traitor, despite his commission in the Massachusetts militia and his position as a federal postmaster.[11] The American sheriff of Washington County, who also held a commission as a general in the Massachusetts militia, allegedly made such traitorous statements during after-dinner toasts at Saint Andrews that he offended even English observers, who thought he should have displayed more loyalty to his nation.[12]

Conditions were little better on the British side of the border. British regulars placed little reliance on Charlotte County's militia; one officer estimated less than half were reliable, and even Grand Manan's militia commander doubted the loyalty of his own men.[13] There is some evidence of treasonous activity by Aaron Rogers, a nearly illiterate American who had moved from Maine across the border in 1809. He claimed that the province's ordinary settlers were "for the States which I believe is true republikins the other party is strong for king Gorge witch they consist of old Torys and Scotch men." Rogers encouraged Maine's militia commander to invade, claiming that the colony's poor would rise up and assist the American forces.[14]

But most borderland residents were not traitors. They probably considered themselves neutrals who wanted nothing to do with the war. Foremost among these were "enemy aliens," British subjects who lived in American communities and United States citizens who lived in New Brunswick. The U.S. State Department ordered that all "enemy aliens" register with deputy marshals to prevent any mischief such as espionage; similar provisions were made in the Maritime Provinces, where officials reminded local magistrates to keep a sharp lookout for strangers and foreigners.[15] Thus when an American from Eastport arrived in Nova Scotia offering to sell contraband provisions, local authorities quickly reported it.[16]

Eastport, the commercial center of Passamaquoddy and the site of Ulmer's headquarters, offers the most vivid examples of tolerance for enemy aliens. Some thirty-five heads of households registered as enemy aliens; with their families the number was at least 208 out of a total population of approximately 1,200, more than one in six inhabitants (see appendix B). Yet the numbers are more dramatic than that, for many so-called enemy aliens did not register for fear of persecution. Ethel Olmstead, a merchant and captain of Eastport's militia artillery company, was an enemy alien. He begged a correspondent not to reveal his true nationality, as "I am an Englishman & would be delt with roughly should some people in this country hear of it."[17] Olmstead was not alone in serving in the Massachusetts militia; at least four others in Eastport served in local militia companies as well (see appendix B). Moreover, these militia units had a reputation for permitting smuggling to proceed unmolested.[18]

Like Olmstead, other enemy aliens took advantage of their ambiguous status to conduct illicit trade. Thomas H. Woodward invested everything he had in a scheme to bring flour from Baltimore to Eastport in two schooners, and even traveled to Maryland to oversee the matter. Posing as an American, he purchased approximately 1,200 barrels of flour that he planned to sell at Halifax. Sadly for Woodward, the Royal Navy captured his two American-flagged schooners and burned them, despite his protests that he was a British subject and that the flour was destined for colonial markets.[19]

Ulmer faced more problems than just smugglers and enemy aliens. Supply routes to Passamaquoddy were tenuous at best, and the Royal Navy and privateers from Maritime ports controlled the ocean approaches to Passamaquoddy. On at least one occasion the master of a vessel destined to Eastport with supplies for Ulmer instead simply sailed for New Brunswick and sold the provisions to the British.[20] His troops largely consisted of old men and young boys with little equipment and no uniforms, and his officers bickered among themselves. Provisions were scarce and expensive for Ulmer but abundant for smugglers willing to pay inflated rates. The local contractor who supplied Ulmer's regiment was a prominent local smuggler, Jonathan Bartlett. Ulmer accused Bartlett of informing the British about the quantity of provisions he supplied Ulmer and of giving the American soldiers spoiled flour and substandard meat, the salted pork mostly pig heads, the salt beef including internal organs.[21]

Despite these obstacles Ulmer attempted to perform his duty. He required all enemy aliens to register with him and take an oath of loyalty or face trial for treason. All persons crossing the border required a pass from him; his officers examined all mail going to New Brunswick. His actions resulted in a substantial reduction in smuggling, but deeply offended the borderland community. Local merchants and magistrates, adventurers, conspired against Ulmer, and even threatened to tar and feather him.[22] Smugglers used tactics learned during the embargo, such as bribing soldiers who guarded impounded contraband with both liquor and money. Local officials harassed the troops. When one of Ulmer's soldiers shot and wounded a smuggler, Sheriff Cooper arrested the soldier and sent him to jail at Castine to await trial for attempted murder.[23] Merchants and customs officers engaged in a letter-writing campaign against Ulmer, especially after the *Polly* incident.[24]

The corruption of Collector Trescott and his assistant Coney especially vexed Ulmer. The collector revived the old bonding ploy used for plaster smuggling, but now he applied it to introducing British manufactured goods such as textiles or tinware. The system required that Trescott seize goods that smugglers themselves informed against, and locally appointed assessors again valued the goods at only 10 percent of their true market value.[25] The system actually encouraged smugglers to inform against themselves because they could recover the informant's share of the proceeds.[26] Furthermore, if the smuggler successfully defended his case, he recovered the bonds; if that failed, he could always petition the district judge. These petitions reveal who the real owners of the contraband were, such as Charles Bird of Philadelphia and Lewis Tappan of New York City.[27] Collector Trescott's motivations in permitting bonding seem to have been twofold. First, it got both the contraband and its claimants out of his district, saving him considerable time, effort, and worry about rescues or storing the illicit goods. Second, he stood to make a great deal of money. In the case of the schooner *Fortune*, Trescott's share of a seizure worth roughly $100,000 was $25,000. But it seems likely that as the transaction was all carefully prearranged, he probably only received a fraction of that, just as the informant, Jabez Mowry, immediately remitted his $25,000 share to Colles.[28] Ulmer was aware of this ploy and did his best to have seized goods transported to Portland and appraised fairly.[29]

Faced against smugglers like the suave Colles and corrupt customs officers like the canny Trescott, Ulmer stood little chance. But even against unsophisticated smugglers, he could do little. While Ulmer clearly possessed zeal and a sense of duty, somehow everything he did served to embarrass him. For example, on March 20, 1813, smugglers took nine barrels of tobacco from Josiah Little's wharf in Eastport, and one of Ulmer's patrol boats pursued. But the soldiers were unable to seize the craft when a nearby British vessel opened fire on them. Nonetheless, an officer identified the smugglers, and Ulmer ordered his troops to keep an eye out for them.[30] A few days later, soldiers at the small post in Robbinston observed the smugglers trying to cross back into the United States. The soldiers captured the smugglers and the boat they were in, but within minutes the prisoners rose up and took their guards prisoner.[31] Not only did the smugglers turn the table on their captors, but they handed them over to the British garrison at Saint Andrews.

The British commander discovered one had only recently emigrated from New Brunswick to the United States. He was, in fact, a British subject bearing arms against his king. The British officer therefore brought him to trial for treason.[32]

But greater embarrassments yet awaited the unfortunate colonel. The masterstroke against Ulmer was a piece of legal trickery made possible by the remoteness of Fort Sullivan. The federal government failed to supply Ulmer's troops adequately, and thus he went into personal debt to buy them provisions. In mid-March 1813, several merchants pressed Ulmer to pay his debts. When he failed to pay, they had him incarcerated for debt in the Washington County jail at Machias. Ulmer remained there for a few weeks until he persuaded local justices that it was illegal to prevent a military officer from performing his duties during wartime. When Ulmer returned to Fort Sullivan, he found the garrison in chaos. He attempted to reestablish order through a draconian decree that banned civilians from Fort Sullivan, strictly prohibited all cross-border traffic, and forbade civilian officials to arrest his troops. In effect he declared martial law.[33] But Ulmer's power to control the region was slipping away; even his command over the soldiers was rapidly eroding. He took to drinking too much, further diminishing the confidence of his officers and men. Matters came to a head during a Fourth of July celebration in 1813, when both soldiers and officers may have drunk too much, and Ulmer's troops and locals clashed in a riot.[34]

Local residents celebrated Independence Day by forming a procession that wound its way to Eastport's sole schoolhouse. Some of the troops disrupted the proceedings by celebrating the holiday in their own manner and shooting their muskets in the air, thereby halting the event in the schoolhouse. When the locals continued their parade, soldiers gathered to shout insults and hurl pieces of brick, broken kettles, and stones at them. Determined to continue, the locals proceeded to an inn to drink toasts and fire salutes from the local militia artillery company's cannon. One hundred soldiers surrounded the inn and terrified the locals within when they threw rocks and gravel at the windows, seized the militia cannon and fired it, and even threatened to throw it over a cliff. Ulmer ordered the soldiers to stop, and when they continued to fire their guns, he ordered cannons to be charged with grape shot pointed at them. He told them if fired again he would have the field pieces discharged at them. Having thus warned them, he turned and left, and almost immediately his troops began to fire their guns again. The soldiers manning the cannon refused to fire on their comrades, and the rioting continued into the night, culminating in the burning of figures in effigy.[35]

Ulmer's own officers turned on him as well. Capt. Sherman Leland, a local attorney who joined the Volunteers for one year, abruptly left Ulmer's unit when he acquired a regular commission in the Thirty-fourth U.S. Infantry. Leland then began recruiting troops away from his former regiment, taking away not only his former commander's men but their equipment as well. Leland had a grudge against Ulmer. According to one soldier, Leland complained openly about his former commander and told him that he believed that Ulmer had taken bribes from smugglers to pay private debts, adding that he thought that the region's commander would soon remove the colonel from his post, and that "*Ulmer was a Rascal.*"[36]

With some fellow officers, Leland complained to the district commander about Ulmer's conduct. In August 1813, the region's commander relieved Ulmer of his command and placed him under arrest. A military court of inquiry held in May 1814 found Ulmer innocent of any criminal charges, but the damage was already done: the War Department disbanded his regiment entirely in December 1813.[37] Leland eventually succeeded Ulmer as the commander of Fort Sullivan and reduced antismuggling operations to a minimum.

With Ulmer gone and active collusion with the port's customs officers, Eastport continued to be a smuggler's haven for the remainder of the war. One of the most favored methods was to use neutral-flagged vessels, especially Spanish and Swedish, to introduce British manufactured goods into the American market. Because the United States was not at war with Spain or Sweden, trade was legal with those nations. If a ship flew a neutral Swedish flag, its cargo was neutral, too, even if it obviously originated in Britain, a policy known as "free ships—free goods." Swedish merchants, often Americans who became naturalized Swedish subjects at Saint Bartholomews in the West Indies, bought cargoes of British manufactured goods in Halifax and Saint John. Under the "free ships—free goods" policy, those British manufactured goods now became Swedish and therefore could freely enter the United States. Eastport residents were quick to adopt this mode of smuggling, and the town's foremost attorney acquired a commission as Swedish vice-consul to expedite matters.[38] New Brunswick merchants also used this ruse. When the British captured Eastport in 1814, they found Swedes Johan Nymann and Andros Armidson had made Moose Island their smuggling base.[39]

Spanish smugglers also engaged in the illicit neutral trade. The best-documented instance is Constantino Llufrio, a Spanish Floridian who had also engaged in illicit trade at Amelia Island between American Georgia and Spanish Florida, another borderland where smuggling was rife. During the war, Llufrio made his way to Saint John, New Brunswick, where he learned of the potential profits to be had at Passamaquoddy.[40] Llufrio capitalized on his neutrality by shipping high-value British manufactured items like textiles to Eastport from Saint John. At least once he posed as the owner of goods, while they actually belonged to a British merchant who was attempting to avoid their seizure by American privateers.[41] Besides Llufrio, fellow Spaniards Joze Deganttes and J. De Sola operated at 'Quoddy, too.[42]

Another way to abuse neutral rights was for an American vessel to file clearance papers for a neutral port, but then sail for Halifax, Saint John, or Passamaquoddy. The schooner *Rebecca* sailed with a cargo of 570 barrels of flour from New York with a stated destination of neutral Cadiz, Spain. When American privateersmen boarded the vessel far off course near Grand Manan, they suspected it was smuggling flour to New Brunswick despite the captain's excuse that he deviated from his course because of a bad leak. Actually, the captain had opened a leak prepared for just such instances. The privateersmen worked hard trying to pump the vessel out, but gave up after twenty minutes. The privateersmen left the vessel to its original crew, convinced that the vessel would sink. The canny captain quickly repaired the leak and shaped his course for Saint John, which was his original destination the whole time.[43]

The use of licenses furnished by the British became another form of deception. The British military was reliant on American provisions and encouraged American merchants to ship flour to destinations such as Saint John or Halifax. An example is a license issued to James Congdon, an Eastport smuggler by the military governor of New Brunswick, that permitted him to import provisions or naval stores into the province for four months. Unfortunately for Congdon, this license fell into the hands of American federal authorities.[44]

British licenses could be problematic for smugglers. If American officials, privateersmen, or naval units found an American ship with such a license, they would seize the vessel and send it back to the United States for trial. Early in 1813, the Supreme Court ruled that such licenses were grounds for seizure.[45] Congress reinforced that ruling by outlawing licenses. Masters of merchant vessels concealed their licenses when boarded by armed vessels until they determined the nationality of the boarding party. If the boarders were British, it was important to produce the papers; if American, they had to be kept concealed. An example is the case of the American schooner *Joanna*, captured by the New Brunswick privateer *Dart* in June 1813. The *Joanna*'s papers stated that the vessel was sailing for Eastport with a cargo of corn. Captain Alexander Newcomb of the *Joanna* claimed he really intended to sail for Halifax, but filed a clearance with American customs officers in order to deceive any American privateers or warships that chanced to board his vessel. At first Newcomb thought the *Dart* was an American privateer and concealed his license. When he found out it was a colonial vessel, he rowed over to his captor in a small boat and presented his license to sail to Halifax. But Captain John Harris of the *Dart* said "he did not care for it, that it was good for nothing," and threatened to sink Newcomb's dinghy if he did not leave.[46] Newcomb responded with threatening language as well, and Harris sent him ashore.[47]

The license trade was a ticklish business. American naval officers often pretended to be British officers, and sometimes British naval officers and privateersmen did not accept the licenses and sent the vessel into a British port as a prize.[48] There the colonial vice-admiralty court system had to sort out the complicated details and determine the true intent of American merchants. Happily, the vice-admiralty courts were often sympathetic to license holders and released them after adjudication. A typical example of this is the case of the American schooner *Lucy*, captured by HMS *Martin* off West Quoddy Light in March 1813. The captain of the *Martin* sent the *Lucy* to Saint John, but when the schooner's captain produced a British license, the court released the vessel.[49]

If deception via neutral ships or licenses failed, smugglers could turn to other methods that relied on manipulating the legal system to their own benefit in a phenomenon known as "collusive capture." In a collusive capture, merchants arranged for a privateer to conduct a prearranged sham capture of an enemy vessel. A number of collusive capture cases went to the U.S. Supreme Court, all of them concerning small privateers operating in the waters of Passamaquoddy, especially around Grand Manan. These collusive captures were often so blatant as to insult the intelligence of the courts. For example, virtually all privateers operated on a shares system whereby the crew received a portion of the proceeds from captured vessels. But on board privateers that conducted collusive captures, the crews received wages rather than shares. Typically the privateers involved in sham captures were also very small; sometimes they were mere open boats. Collusive captures and other misdeeds became such an infamous practice that President Madison revoked the commissions of all privateers carrying crews of less than twenty.[50]

Madison's suspicions were well founded, as an incident involving the sloop *Venture* indicates. American troops captured the *Venture* when it entered American waters within the range of Fort Sullivan's cannon. The battery fired on the sloop and crippled it, and American soldiers boarded the vessel and took it to the town landing. Slowly the American commander unraveled a collusive capture plot. The *Venture* was waiting for the small American privateer named the *Mary* to capture it. But the presence of HMS *Martin* off Campobello prevented the sham capture from taking place.

Meanwhile, the *Mary* skulked about, waiting for an appropriate moment to make a sham capture of the *Venture* and its rich cargo. The *Venture* was indeed a smuggling vessel, loaded with a valuable cargo of British manufactured goods valued at $100,000 to $200,000. Had the plan gone well, the goods would have entered the country not only legally but at a considerably lower tariff rate than was otherwise possible. However, the presence of the Royal Navy prevented the privateer from venturing out, and the strong currents of the bay brought the vessel within range of Fort Sullivan's guns, and so their plan unravelled.[51]

Virtually everything about the *Mary* was suspicious. It was the only American privateer commissioned in the Passamaquoddy district during the entire war. The vessel was tiny, a mere six tons. Its captain, one Noah Edgecomb, was a former customhouse inspector at the Passamaquoddy district who was sure to have known the best way to smuggle goods into the country. The two merchants who gave bonds for the *Mary* were two Eastport merchants, Jabez Mowry and Benjamin Bucknam, both notorious smugglers who previously had been outspoken opponents of privateering. To cap off the farcical nature of the scheme, the *Mary*'s captain had even bought his gunpowder from colonial merchants in Saint Andrews.[52]

The story did not end there. Maine's federal district court awarded Capt. Leland thousands of dollars for capturing the *Venture*. Although he had used the fort's cannon and soldiers under his command to take custody, Leland alone received the "informer's part" of the proceeds of the *Venture*'s cargo. He promptly resigned his commission after receiving the funds. He next appeared in Dorchester, Massachusetts, where he made a patriotic Independence Day speech in which he concluded, "None but a servile wretch would sell his country's honor for gold." This seems a curious conclusion from an individual who had profited so handsomely during his command of Fort Sullivan.[53]

Leland's seizure in the *Venture* case was a deviation from the norm after Ulmer left Eastport. An anonymous report to the secretary of war indicated the garrison showed an almost complete indifference and disregard to illicit trade and that illegal trade flourished under the guns of the fort. Sentinels stationed on the wharves ignored the passing and repassing of passengers from one shore to the other. The officers at the fort, many of them recruited locally, made a point of keeping up a good understanding with their friends on the other side. Some claimed they needed to retain a friendly understanding if they ever wanted to cross the border after they left the service. Others claimed that if they acted too severely, the British would destroy the town.⁵⁴

The secretary of war believed his anonymous informant, and within a few weeks he ordered the old garrison to march to Vermont and a new one to replace it. The new garrison, a part of the Fortieth Infantry, had no local connections. The officers of the Fortieth fully realized their predecessors had winked at smuggling, and its commander was determined to suppress it. But after firing on a smuggling vessel with the fort's cannon, the local community ostracized him and his officers, cutting them off from society and other comforts of Eastport. For its last few weeks in Eastport, the garrison was under a virtual siege. It lifted only when a British fleet anchored off the port on July 11, 1814, and demanded the fort's surrender, which the American commander did without firing a shot.⁵⁵ The occupation lasted until June 1818, long after the war ended. For three years after hostilities ceased, a British garrison remained, waiting for international arbitration to once and for all determine that Moose Island lay within American territory.

The British garrison was considerably larger than its American counterpart, but nonetheless it faced problems controlling smuggling. The British commander usually ignored smuggling, an approach that made it considerably easier to govern the populace and provided the garrison with smuggled American provisions. One of the first acts of the British commander was to open Moose Island to the licensed provisions trade.⁵⁶

With British occupation, some people left Eastport while others remained. British troops captured Collector Trescott when he attempted to flee with his customhouse records, but released him after a few days. He moved to nearby Lubec and observed the smuggling trade on occupied Moose Island from there without actively moving against it. His assistant Coney chose to remain, in part because newspapers claimed that he had "been in the British interest some time, and was in the habit of giving every facility to smugglers."⁵⁷ He even took a loyalty oath to the British Crown, but contrary to rumor he never served as a British customs officer in the occupied territory.

Others moved to Lubec as well, notably Jabez Mowry and some of the town's other smuggling merchants. They possessed a unique problem in that they had deposited bonds with Collector Trescott to cover their illicit trade. The British claimed these bonds as war prizes, but the American federal government acted on these bonds, too. With both governments suing them for the bonds, the merchants found themselves in a hard spot. On one occasion a party of British soldiers searched Lubec for the bond holders in a post-midnight raid. One of the smugglers evaded detection by hiding in an oven.[58]

Of all the smugglers, Mowry reveled in these hair-breadth escapes the most. On one occasion, he evaded a U.S. deputy marshal who attempted to serve him papers by crossing to Campobello in the fog, apparently with the collusion of Collector Trescott.[59] Mowry proved equally adept at dodging British officials. He even dressed in women's clothing when he visited Eastport during the British occupation to conduct business. When his friends met him at the beach, they had difficulty keeping straight faces as they escorted him on his business, in no small part because of the smuggler's long gait and lack of grace. Far from being a disguise, Mowry's appearance attracted attention when he did not wish to be recognized. Happily for Mowry, his friends and neighbors successfully shielded him from the British garrison, and he slipped back across to American territory.[60]

The British commander usually ignored smuggling, an approach that made it considerably easier to govern the populace and provided the garrison with smuggled American provisions. By 1817 it became evident that Eastport's population was introducing large quantities of American contraband not only onto the island but into New Brunswick proper as well. Predictably, Saint John merchants complained that this deprived them of business. Whereas people from as far away as Windsor, Nova Scotia, used to come to their city for provisions, they now bought them illicitly at Lubec and Moose Island.[61] New Brunswick's lieutenant governor, a military man himself, complained that "it is notorious that in the present state of that Island, under colour of providing supplies for its Inhabitants, it is made a Depot for the reception of American manufactures and merchandize of every description."[62]

British military officers' attitudes toward smugglers are illustrated by an incident in 1817, when Saint John's new customs collector, Henry Wright, came to Moose Island to search for contraband from Lubec. On arrival he immediately informed the commander of the garrison why he was there and asked his permission to search for the smuggled goods, which was granted. The collector and his men searched the store of Leonard Pierce and seized two chests and two boxes of tea, a bag of cotton wool, a quantity of saddlery, and several casks of cut nails. In another store belonging to a merchant named Child, he seized a cask of French red wine. Both Pierce and Child freely admitted these goods came from Lubec. Wright put the contraband goods in a military warehouse that was always guarded by a sentry and continued his search. But when Wright attempted to enter other stores in Eastport, he found their doors and windows closed and barred. Wright asked the garrison commander for a writ of assistance or search warrant, but the officer refused, thereby stopping the search for smuggled goods. Much to the disgust of the collector, Leonard Pierce later broke into the military warehouse "in defiance of the sentry" and rescued his goods.[63]

Nor did Wright's problems end there. His crackdown raised the ire of many powerful locals, including John Coffin, a member of the governor's council, former commander of the New Brunswick Fencible Regiment during the War of 1812, and brother of a member of the House of Commons. Despite this, Wright's men seized a boat belonging to Coffin at Passamaquoddy Bay because they found American contraband on board.[64] Coffin then stole his boat back from the customs officers one night, setting off a major scandal. The ensuing public power struggle embarrassed many of the colonial elite, including Wright, Coffin, and the influential lawyer Ward Chipman the younger, who had just married Wright's daughter. Coffin even challenged Wright's comptroller to a duel on Moose Island (the comptroller declined).[65] Coffin traveled to England and personally brought his complaints before the customs commissioners. The customs commissioners supported Wright's position but also launched an investigation into his conduct that led to a curtailment of the fees charged by the New Brunswick customhouse.[66]

From 1812 to 1814, Ulmer's regiment failed to suppress smuggling. British military occupation of Moose Island from 1814 to 1818 also failed to stop smuggling. On this borderland, armed force was no match for market forces. In the end, the War of 1812 made little material difference to Passamaquoddy residents. By 1818, arbitration by the king of the Netherlands restored the border to its pre-1814 form. Perhaps the only tangible difference was that a commercial center sprung up in Lubec, Maine, during the British occupation of Eastport. There Jabez Mowry and fellow smugglers resumed their business, especially in the plaster trade. Less tangible was a renewed determination by American, colonial, and imperial officials to assert their control over trade and the border. Whereas during the embargo and War of 1812 American officials faced hostile crowds of smugglers, after the war New Brunswick learned how difficult it was to control the illicit trade at Passamaquoddy.

7

"ACTUAL AND UNQUALIFIED REBELLION"

It was the sort of report every colonial administrator dreaded receiving. In the summer of 1820, a New Brunswick official on the border with the United States reported to Lieutenant Governor George Stracey Smyth "a state of actual and unqualified Rebellion against His Majesty's Government of this Province." Smyth was in a ticklish situation: Overt military action on the border might arouse the ire of the United States, with which Britain had been at peace only a few years. Furthermore, Smyth had only a handful of troops in the colony, and they were needed in the provincial capital at Fredericton where they had suppressed a riot only a month earlier. Beyond that, prudent colonial administrators who wished to continue their careers hesitated before reacting to reports from panicky officials.[1]

Smyth knew that smuggling lay at the heart of this revolt, but like other colonial administrators he knew that there was more to this problem than simply upholding the majesty of the law. Stopping the smugglers at Passamaquoddy was part of a bigger struggle in which the port city of Saint John, New Brunswick, attempted to assert economic dominance over the Bay of Fundy.[2] But the struggle to stop the plaster trade was more than an economic or political contest; it was also closely related to the Loyalist identity of the province. More than one observer noted that the smugglers involved in the plaster trade introduced American ideas of free trade and democracy into the province.[3]

The effort to suppress smuggling at Passamaquoddy resulted in a "plaster war," a struggle between Saint John's would-be capitalists and Nova Scotian "plastermen" and their allies in Charlotte County, New Brunswick, and nearby Washington County, Maine.[4] It was an armed struggle, in which New Brunswick officials, occasionally aided by the British navy, faced the plastermen and fought with a variety of weapons, from hard words to cannon. The region was not immune to violent crowd protest, in either urban or rural settings. Ethnic tensions, social injustice, labor relations, and trade or smuggling created occasional violent clashes or riots.[5] One might think that such a conflict was one-sided; officialdom, after all, had the weapons and infrastructure to impose its will on the mariners, quarrymen, and farmers who opposed them. Yet the plaster war was a struggle the plastermen would win.

Why did Saint John's merchant elite attempt to extinguish Passamaquoddy's plaster trade? Greed is one answer. The city's merchants struggled to adjust to changing economic conditions. They showed little interest in early manufacturing efforts, choosing instead to remain immersed in the timber trade and capturing the Bay of Fundy region as an economic hinterland.[6] But it is incorrect to think that Saint John's merchants were the only actors in this story. Rural regions were not passive participants in the region's changing economy but active players.[7] In this case, rural producers violently resisted Saint John's pretensions to regional economic dominance.

There were three problems with the plaster trade for colonial administrators and those with an interest in economic development. First, the plaster trade produced no revenue for the colonial government. Outgoing products seldom had to pay an export fee in mercantilist political economy; the idea was that exports would be exchanged for specie or, less ideally, that foreign goods would be taxed at the customhouse on arrival. Second, the plaster trade did not produce specie payment, but quite the opposite. When low-value plaster was traded for higher priced goods, such as flour and provisions, tobacco, rum, naval stores, or goods imported to North America in American bottoms, such as tea and molasses, Maritimers had to make up the difference in coin, thereby draining the region of specie.[8] The third problem with the plaster trade was that the profits in terms of eighteenth-century political economy were squandered on small producers. The merchants of Saint John wanted to control the plaster trade to capture its profits and use that concentrated capital to finance more business ventures. This would provide not only the modest profits offered by the gypsum itself but also the more alluring gain from the carrying trade. Saint John's merchants believed that if they controlled the plaster trade, the immense traffic in American goods, especially provisions, would be stripped from the plastermen and placed in their hands. Saint John would become the marketplace for the entire Bay of Fundy, concentrating wealth and mercantile power in the hands of the great merchants at the expense of self-sufficient independent producers.[9]

New Brunswick faced another perplexing question in its pursuit of prosperity: would it become more "American" (egalitarian, tied to American markets), or would it retain a more "British" (hierarchical, tied to British markets) character? No small amount of confusion arose out of the question of New Brunswick's search for its identity. The colony had always possessed some self-contradictory attributes. A British colony, many of its inhabitants were native-born North Americans. While the colony was part of the British mercantile system, from its very founding in 1784 it had trouble divorcing itself from United States markets, especially American foodstuffs such as flour. While it looked to British institutions as social models, New Brunswick was a remote pioneer society with much in common with the newly settled areas of the United States and Upper Canada.

Another problem with the plaster trade was a perception that it induced otherwise loyal provincials to conduct themselves in "the manners of sentiments of modern democrats." Even after the War of 1812, New Brunswick officials intermittently fretted over the "Americanization" of Charlotte County.[10] Smuggling, trading as one wanted without regard for the government, was feared as a harbinger of egalitarian politics by the political and economic leaders of New Brunswick and Nova Scotia—except, apparently, when they engaged in it themselves, which was frequently. Plaster smugglers certainly were not afraid to flaunt the authority of political appointees, as Stephen Humbert found out to his dismay in 1820.

The plaster trade had long been a mixed blessing to both New Brunswick and Nova Scotia. While it provided a valuable export to the United States that supported many farmers, mariners, and small merchants, it also encouraged large-scale smuggling, as these same entrepreneurs returned from the border with holds full of American produce illegally brought into the province without paying the stiff customs duties placed on foreign goods. This problem was not small; economic historians estimate that plaster was British North America's most valuable export to the United States in the first decades of the nineteenth century.[11]

New Brunswick had attempted to control the illicit trade before. As early as 1806, the provincial Assembly passed a law forbidding colonial merchants to land plaster east of Boston. This would have restricted the trade to the larger vessels that only Saint John's merchants could afford to build, equip, man, and insure. But despite the efforts of George Leonard and others, the law proved easily evaded, and the plaster trade continued unabated at Passamaquoddy. These efforts also failed because they had no effect on neighboring Nova

Scotia, where most of the plaster came from, and that province's governor, Sir John Wentworth, had no intention of making himself unpopular by suppressing the plaster trade.[12] After the War of 1812, they tried again, this time operating in conjunction with Nova Scotia's Assembly, with both provinces passing identical legislation that forbade landing gypsum east of Boston and attempted to tax all gypsum leaving the provinces at the rate of five shillings per ton, which equaled more than $1 per ton on a commodity that was worth about $2 per ton at the wharves of plaster-producing communities like Windsor, Nova Scotia.[13]

The laws went into effect in the spring of 1817. The taxation produced predictable evasion and howls of outrage from the plastermen of Nova Scotia and plaster merchants at Passamaquoddy.[14] It directly threatened the prosperity of Saint Andrews plastermen, who overwhelmed an official attempting to interfere with their smuggling. They took his boat and pointedly used it to smuggle plaster.[15] Even the presence of Royal Navy vessels had little effect. While HM's sloop of war *Wye* made several seizures in July, locals continued to defy the law and even rescued their captured vessels.[16] Predictably, vessel owners petitioned the provincial government for the release of their vessels, citing their poverty.[17] Furthermore, Congress passed legislation that essentially forbade colonial vessels to carry plaster into U.S. ports. This legislation simply encouraged evasion, and plaster smuggling continued at Passamaquoddy as always. The British consulate at Baltimore reported that enough smuggled plaster was reaching the Chesapeake region to significantly drop its price.[18] The provincial Assembly, faced with such overwhelming resistance, withdrew the legislation.

In 1820, New Brunswick attempted once more to curb the illicit plaster trade in the name of good government and greater profits, using worries over provincial identity and loyalty as a further excuse to implement the plaster laws. The individual who stepped forward to enforce these laws was Stephen Humbert. Like many Loyalists, Humbert maintained business connections in the United States despite his loyalist background. In fact, he married his second wife in Boston in the autumn of 1818. He himself had smuggled plaster at Passamaquoddy, as he confessed in his autobiography and as American court records verify.[19] It may well be that this was a case of using a thief to catch a thief, but more certain is that if successful, he would reap the potentially large emoluments of this office and become a hero to the local mercantile community. Whatever the motive, Humbert accepted his appointment as the provincial preventative officer, appointed his son John as his deputy, and converted his forty-ton vessel into a government cutter by hoisting a distinctive red burgee with the word *preventative* stitched on it. Yet even before Humbert set sail for Passamaquoddy, plaster smugglers had seriously embarrassed him by kidnapping his son.

The incident began when a Nova Scotia schooner loaded with plaster (or a "plasterman," a term describing both the vessels and the individuals engaged in the plaster trade) took refuge in the outer reaches of Saint John harbor after having lost its rudder. Humbert and his son John boarded the schooner to ensure its compliance with the new plaster law. The master, however, refused to cooperate by providing his ship's papers, and the preventative officer took the vessel into custody and placed John on board with another guard. That same night plastermen overwhelmed the guards and sailed from Saint John with them as their prisoners. The smugglers inflicted no further violence on the two, but instead chose a practical and effective alternative. They dumped them on the shores of Nova Scotia, some twenty miles below Annapolis. Out of their jurisdiction, lost and without nearby help, the preventative officers had to begin the long and embarrassing process of finding their way home. The elder Humbert posted a £25 reward for the arrest of the kidnappers, but none stepped forward to claim it.[20]

The kidnapping was but the first of a series of embarrassments for the preventative officer. Within minutes of anchoring his vessel with its distinctive flag in Passamaquoddy Bay, a sailor on a nearby plasterman fired a musket at Humbert's sloop. The shot missed, but it alarmed him because his own craft was unarmed. Furthermore, the plasterman lay in American waters, outside of his jurisdiction. An informant soon told Humbert why the shot was fired. James McArthur, captain of the plasterman *Shannon*, challenged his crew to fire at the preventative vessel, promising to give a round of rum to any who would "fire at that D ... D flag." McArthur then boasted of his act in front of several witnesses in the local customs office, including the area's deputy customs officer (who notably was not the informer who told Humbert what transpired).[21]

Faced with violent resistance, Humbert acted with prudence. Instead of creating an international incident by entering American waters, Humbert bided his time, waiting until McArthur reentered New Brunswick waters a few days later before seizing his schooner. McArthur did not give up easily; he refused to show his ship's papers and would not give up the *Shannon*'s tiller. McArthur and Humbert scuffled briefly for control of the helm, but the preventative officer prevailed and the vessel proceeded to Indian Island. As the law only provided that Humbert seize the vessel, McArthur was free to do as he pleased once he was ashore. Bent on mischief, he borrowed the deputy collector's boat and rowed to nearby Eastport in the United States.[22]

McArthur soon returned, leading about fifteen men with the intention of repossessing the *Shannon*. Humbert was also prepared; he had a local constable with him and had hired and armed extra men to support his crew of four. Hard words followed. The constable stepped forward to arrest McArthur, who drew his pistol and fled to the cabin of the *Shannon*. McArthur's confederates engaged in more hard words, but balked at initiating violence, and they eventually returned to Eastport. Meanwhile, the preventative officers cornered McArthur in the *Shannon*'s cabin. Humbert's men beat in the cabin door and arrested him, but the prisoner somehow escaped and fled across the border.

McArthur continued to make trouble for Humbert. He immediately lodged a legal complaint against Humbert with a sympathetic justice of the peace, David Owen of Campobello, who himself had benefited from the plaster trade. He then again recruited armed confederates to rescue his vessel, hoping to ambush the preventative men as they escorted the *Shannon* to Saint John. Humbert managed to avoid the ambush by sailing through the dangerous and little-used Letite Passage, and he arrived at Saint John the next day. On arrival Humbert made a hasty report to the provincial attorney general before taking the next steamboat up the Saint John River to Fredericton to make a report in person to the lieutenant governor.[23]

Humbert's entreaties to Lieutenant Governor Smyth produced few results. He sought British soldiers to support him, but received instead a promise to ask the British naval commander at Halifax for a vessel to patrol Passamaquoddy Bay. The attorney general also agreed to investigate the conduct of the customs officers who actively hindered Humbert.

On returning from Saint John, Humbert recruited additional men for his own cutter and set sail for Passamaquoddy once again at the end of June. The sloop of war *Bellette* arrived to assist him, but the vessel's commander was not inclined to take much interest in his mission and spent only a few days at Campobello. Attorney General Thomas Wetmore's investigation into the conduct of the customhouse officers yielded no results. Henry Wright, the province's senior customs official, stood behind the conduct of Richard Armstrong, the deputy collector at Indian Island, who also happened to be his son-in-law. Humbert was essentially on his own; the inaction of the *Bellette*, the opposition fostered by the customs officer on Indian Island, growing opposition in the provincial press, and his inadequate force only served to encourage the plastermen.[24]

Humbert made a few seizures, but fog hampered both him and the plastermen; there simply was not much traffic on the water due to lack of visibility and light winds. Drier weather in August brought shipping back. Humbert attempted to intercept vessels, but found it impossible in the face of armed resistance. When Humbert approached suspected plaster vessels, the crews appeared on deck brandishing muskets to keep him away. On occasion Humbert found boats full of men pursuing him, and he reported that all the plaster vessels had armed themselves, some with cannon.[25]

With both Humbert and the plastermen arming, confrontation was ensured. The scale of the violence ranged from epithets to bullets and hurled rocks. When Humbert approached the forty-odd plaster vessels off Lubec in mid-August, crewmen from several opened fire with muskets, forcing him to retreat. The following day he pursued two plaster vessels, forcing one aground on the American shore and boarding the other just a few feet offshore. A crowd of about sixty Americans and plastermen gathered on the beach. Brandishing axes, handspikes, and fish shovels (which look a great deal like pitchforks) and throwing stones at Humbert's boat, the crowd forced him to retreat after a rioter stabbed one of his men. The next day Humbert watched helplessly while ten plaster vessels sailed from Lubec, lashed together in one enormous raft. Not possessing force sufficient to take on the combined crews, Humbert had to content himself with picking off a straggler. The day after that, another raft of nine brigs and schooners sailed unopposed. Humbert returned to Saint John despondent, complaining about lack of support and the active interference he endured from the customs officer on Indian Island. He reported to Smyth that the plastermen were in a state of rebellion and again requested a military force to quell the opposition to the plaster laws.[26]

Who were these rebels who so brazenly defied the plaster regulations? Most of the plastermen were from the Fundy shore of Nova Scotia, especially from communities on the shores of Minas Basin, such as Cornwallis, Falmouth, and Horton. Many were "Planters," New Englanders who settled in Nova Scotia in the wake of the Acadian expulsion or, more likely by 1820, their descendents. The mariners who transported the plaster were the neighbors and kinsmen and in some cases the same men who quarried it. This was somewhat unusual in maritime terms; generally cargo producers and ship owners were not the same individuals. But the low unit value of plaster, combined with high freight rates—generally higher than the value of the plaster itself—encouraged ship ownership by the plaster producers.[27] For farmers, quarrying plaster was an activity that gave a high return for their effort, one of several activities that farming families pursued to make ends meet.[28]

Crown officials had some idea with whom they were dealing. The Halifax customs collector had his own opinions about who and what these plastermen were. To him they were an "unprincipled multitude" engaged in a "lawless intercourse" that drew together a "banditti" from both the British provinces and the United States at Passamaquoddy. The collector declared the plaster trade "ruinous to the fair trader, & destructive of the interests & morals of the inhabitants." The collector seemed to accept that the plastermen attempted to terrorize the subcollector at Windsor. What shocked him was that the plastermen attacked the customhouse by petitioning the Assembly and even voted for representatives based on their hostility to the customs establishment. The collector clearly viewed this democratic activity as a threat to political appointees such as himself.[29]

The collector was not alone in condemning Hants County's Planter population. Members of the mercantile and religious elite also criticized the plastermen. Merchants bridled at the thought of countrymen engaged in commerce and consistently argued that the plastermen were ruining themselves by speculating in plaster and neglecting their farms. Some plastermen mortgaged their homes to buy vessels to transport gypsum to Passamaquoddy and ended up in debtors prison when their venture failed. When the plastermen smuggled in West Indian, East Indian, and American goods on their return voyage from Passamaquoddy, they also threatened the profits of the "fair trader" who obeyed the law, because the untaxed smuggled goods were cheaper. An additional threat posed by the plaster trade was that the repeated violation of the laws introduced moral depravity, and trade with Americans infected the plastermen with "Yankee principles." Merchants wanted the plastermen to stay on their farms and leave mercantile pursuits to those who knew them best.[30]

The Anglican religious establishment also viewed the plastermen with suspicion. The Minas Basin region was the core of the radical evangelical movement; Henry Alline himself, Nova Scotia's most famous religious dissenter, came from that area. The religious fervor of Nova Scotia's Yankees challenged the ability of the colony's elite to impose British and Anglican senses of order, creating a new conception of the bonds linking individuals, families, and communities.[31]

Little wonder then that the colonial elites regarded Planters with suspicion or that plastermen had little use for authority figures. Yet plaster smuggling was not primarily a means of social protest but a means of survival for small producers. Acquiring a modest living as a yeoman farmer required diversification, including engaging in wage labor and mining gypsum. Both the practice and productivity of Nova Scotia agriculture before 1820 was dismal, a condition compounded by extremely bad weather patterns after 1815.[32] Falling plaster prices further exacerbated the problem. Given these factors, it is not surprising that plastermen reacted violently against the imposition of regulations and taxes.

The economic concerns of the plastermen were not the same as the traditional upholders of the status quo, who sought gain to reinforce social hierarchy, or that of the rising class of capitalists, who viewed the world in terms of profit. The plastermen defied the political economies of mercantilism—in its death throes by 1820—by trading outside of the closed loop of colonial-metropolitan trade. Farmers viewed the chubby coasting craft they built to carry gypsum as a vital aspect of maintaining their independence and local economy, whereas merchants viewed their ships as capital, a source of profit that had little to do with community values. The plastermen, on the other hand, believed that since they produced the plaster, they should be the direct beneficiaries of the gypsum trade, and they claimed freedom from the unpopular Plaster Act.

Luckily for the plastermen, they had allies in their struggle against the dominance of the Saint John merchants, including the inhabitants of Charlotte County, New Brunswick, Crown customs officers in New Brunswick, and American merchants in Lubec and Eastport. These allies actively supported the plastermen, adding their numbers to the crowds that defied Humbert and interfering with the preventative officer's abilities to enforce the plaster law.

Charlotte County's Loyalist population profited from the plaster trade, too, and had no desire to see the trade fall into the hands of the Saint John merchants. Wealthy Saint Andrews plaster merchants such as Harris Hatch were community boosters who wanted to make their port community a major competitor with Saint John. David Owen of Campobello continued his decades-long support of the plaster trade, and he soundly cursed the Saint John merchants who thwarted his ambitions to turn his island estate into a commercial center. Men of substance were just as likely to smuggle as poor ones, and the plastermen often found allies among the powerful. Men like Hatch and Owen wanted to prosper, but they were motivated by a local paternalist vision that resented and resisted the intrusion of external forces into what they regarded as "their" communities.

A more surprising ally of the plaster smugglers were New Brunswick's imperial customs officers, the very officials dedicated to stopping smuggling. The province's customs officers only concerned themselves with imperial statutes and did not feel bound to enforce provincial laws, such as the Plaster Act. Furthermore, New Brunswick's senior customs officers were fending off a provincial investigation into customhouse fraud and corruption in 1820, and thus were not inclined to assist Humbert's efforts. The customs officer at Passamaquoddy, Richard Armstrong, resented the provincial inquiry into his conduct and profited from the plaster trade by collecting a small fee from plaster vessels that entered his jurisdiction. The plastermen gladly paid this fee because it gave their activities a veil of legitimacy. Armstrong's office on Indian Island was commonly crowded with the masters of plaster vessels, who even boasted to him about their defiance of the plaster law. Armstrong also warned plastermen when Humbert arrived in the bay, on occasion lent his boat to the plaster smugglers, and wrote venomous reports about the preventative officer, accusing him of "timidity and incapacity."[33]

William Wanton, Saint John's creole customs collector, had long supported the plaster trade because it was enormously profitable to himself. While his annual salary was only £50, the collector was also entitled to gather fees for every service rendered to shipping, such as an entry or clearance certificate. While these fees were usually just a few shillings per transaction, they were numerous enough to provide a substantial income for the collector. Between 1807 and 1808, the collector's income averaged £800; by 1816, the collector garnered a stunning £2,900—£900 more than the lieutenant governor's salary—thereby initiating an extensive investigation by the Assembly into the fee structure at the Saint John customhouse. The Assembly committee found extensive abuse in the fee system, and the Treasury censured him and fined him £250; nonetheless, he remained in office until his death later that year.[34]

Henry Wright, an Englishman who succeeded Wanton, shared his views on officeholding as a personal privilege. Wright had no interest in reforming the customs system. He wanted to harness it more effectively for his own gain. Wright proved far more rapacious than his predecessor. In his first year in office, he collected more than £1,000 in fees above what Wanton had by arbitrarily raising them by a third.[35] Furthermore, Wright installed his son-in-law as the deputy collector at Indian Island at Passamaquoddy and installed his son—not yet age twenty-one and therefore ineligible for office—as the deputy collector at Miramichi. He also dismissed the deputy collector at Saint Andrews, an act later found to be illegal.[36] Wright was not a perfect creole in that he was an outsider and possessed an Englishman's disdain for colonials, but he also recognized the power of the older Loyalist clique and was probably delighted to see his daughter marry into the influential Chipman family in 1817, thereby giving him a measure of protection from other powerful Loyalists like General Coffin.

New Brunswick's Council and Nova Scotia's Assembly launched their own investigations into customhouse corruption in 1820. The investigations produced some startling results. For example, Windsor, Nova Scotia, may have produced only eighteen shillings in revenue for the Crown between 1816 and 1819, but it produced an estimated £3,000 in fees that went directly into customs officials' pockets in the same interval.[37] These reform efforts were part of an effort to rationalize government and reduce the old sinecures. Crown customs officers, fearful of losing their prestige and profitable offices, opposed regulating the plaster trade at every turn, a fact that was to embarrass the provincial officials enforcing those laws time and again during the Plaster War.[38]

The American merchants and others engaged in the plaster trade at Passamaquoddy also aided and abetted the plastermen. Plastermen sought out and received shelter on the American side of the border, within sight of Humbert but outside of his jurisdiction. Americans also effectively prevented U.S. customs officers from assisting the preventative officer.

Stephen Thacher, Eastport's collector of customs after 1818, was very different from Delesdernier or Trescott. Thacher was neither a Revolutionary War veteran nor a local. Instead, he was a Yale-educated lawyer from southern Maine, appointed to the collectorship of Passamaquoddy as a political favor.[39] True to his training as an attorney, Thacher was inflexible and legalistic, quickly becoming unpopular with a borderlands populace used to his predecessors' lax enforcement. Letters to the local newspaper castigated Thacher as an avaricious political appointee, a poor replacement for the affable Trescott. One local merchant and noted smuggler complained that Thacher was "the most vexatious man I ever saw, or heard of."[40] One newspaper picked up on Thacher's former position as a Massachusetts judge and nicknamed him "Judge Snatcher," a reference to the rapacity with which he seized even boats carrying cordwood.[41] Probably the least popular of his actions was to strictly enforce federal law that banned foreign vessels under thirty tons from entering American ports.

Thacher compounded his unpopularity when he promised Humbert that he would not allow plaster vessels to enter American waters and deployed the local revenue cutter to keep provincial shipping in British waters. The American populace immediately turned on the collector and the crew of his revenue cutter. The local newspaper published angry letters about the collector and even printed an advertisement posting a reward for the capture of the revenue cutter's crew, who were described as pirates and desperadoes. Given this opposition, it is little surprise that American customhouse officials and revenue cutter personnel ignored the plaster trade during Thacher's frequent absences.[42]

Yankees may have allied themselves with the plastermen, but did that mean that they infected the population surrounding the Minas Basin with a leveling American ideology that threatened the colonial social hierarchy? Given their resounding rejection of the American Revolution and alliance with Charlotte County Loyalists and New Brunswick's customhouse officers, there can be no grounds for supposing that the plastermen were somehow becoming political radicals, let alone republicans. When plastermen took up arms to defend their illicit trade, they did not adopt a political ideology but rather utilized pragmatic tactics that answered their immediate needs.[43] This rejection of state authority, reflected in their evangelical religion, was the result of the localized worldview of a people fully engaged in the struggle to acquire a subsistence for their families. They were not rebelling; they were fighting for their survival.

Humbert returned to Passamaquoddy one last time to try to stop the plastermen. In late September 1820, he returned to Indian Island and awaited the return of HM's sloop of war *Bellette*, whose commander now had strict orders to support Humbert. Most of the plaster vessels lay within admittedly American waters close to Lubec, Maine, but in one of his few victories, Humbert secured Thacher's promise not to interfere when he boarded provincial vessels, even if they were in United States waters. Humbert boarded a number of vessels off Lubec in company with Royal Navy officers and crewmen. When angry plastermen refused to pay the New Brunswick plaster duty, the naval boarding party immediately stripped the vessel's sails. Most plastermen quickly submitted to the law in such cases, but it caused a great deal of anger among them.[44]

Things came to a head on September 29, when Humbert seized one of the smuggling craft and anchored it under the stern of *Bellette* to prevent any rescue attempts by the plastermen. The next day the plastermen anchored as close as possible to the American shore at Lubec. There the smugglers landed a cannon, stacking bars of pig iron next to it for ammunition to defend their fleet of twenty-odd craft. Undeterred and supported by two boats from *Bellette*, Humbert boarded a small plaster vessel. The smugglers did not open fire with their cannon, but used an infinitely more subtle, acceptable, and effective means of resistance. Knowing that Humbert acted out of his jurisdiction when he seized the vessel the day before, the smugglers had an American magistrate issue a warrant for his arrest. As Humbert attempted to seize another plasterman in Lubec harbor, a boat with a magistrate and a deputy sheriff put off from shore with the intent of arresting the preventative officer and putting him in the jail in Machias. Humbert retreated to British waters to guard the seized vessel anchored near *Bellette* and took shelter on the warship.

Both Humbert and the captain must have suspected the plastermen would make an attempt to rescue the captured plaster vessel. The captain of *Bellette* mounted a cannon on his poop deck aimed at it and placed an armed guard to watch the craft. But somehow by 4 a.m., the plaster smugglers had spirited away the guarded vessel. Compounding Humbert's consternation, *Bellette*'s commander informed him that the warship was immediately getting under way for Halifax and would not return that year. *Bellette* sailed at 10 a.m.; the vessel was hardly out of sight at noon when three boatloads of plastermen came to Indian Island and took by force a suit of sails Humbert had seized from another plaster vessel. The preventative officer lacked the force to stop them, both in terms of numbers and armament. Fearing that a mob would destroy his boat and cutter, Humbert sent them back to Saint John, but remained on Indian Island a few days more before returning to report his complete defeat at the hands of the plaster smugglers. As a final humiliation, plastermen entered fabricated complaints at the Indian Island customhouse against Humbert for smuggling American foodstuffs into the province.[45]

Humbert's defeat was also a defeat for Saint John merchants, as the plaster trade continued to elude their grasp. The means of production in this case remained in the hands of independent small producers, who followed up their victory with an aggressive political agenda by electing fellow plaster traders such as Richard Cunningham to the Nova Scotia Assembly, where he busied himself defending the plaster trade, aided by numerous petitions from his constituents.[46] In effect, the Plaster Act forced plastermen to engage in provincial politics. This mobilization led to accusations that the plastermen had "Yankee tendencies," which can be dismissed as the hyperbole of a colonial leadership still traumatized by the American Revolution. Far from indicating Planter disloyalty, the plaster trade engaged them with the provincial government on a cooperative rather than an antagonistic level. It was the plastermen's grievances that led to Nova Scotia's lieutenant governor taking the unusual step of encouraging New Brunswick's lieutenant governor to repeal the plaster laws in early 1821.[47] He wrote to his New Brunswick counterpart concerning the plaster laws that he was "fully convinced of the evils which have resulted from their operation" and that they had financially ruined many Nova Scotians. Smyth, who was not in good health and was never very popular, probably agreed.

The New Brunswick Assembly reacted to Humbert's defeat by quietly repealing the Plaster Act early in 1821, much to the relief of all concerned. After 1820, the Assembly concentrated its energies on preserving the privileged status of New Brunswick timber within British markets and continued its assault on customhouse fees and privileges. Few of the Saint John merchants seem to have suffered by their defeat in the Plaster War. They quickly moved on to concentrate their abilities on the already profitable timber and shipbuilding trades, and Saint John eventually succeeded in becoming the marketplace for all the Bay of Fundy.[48]

Small producers on the resource frontier actively sometimes resisted the attempts of large merchants to make them economically subordinate, and sometimes the small producers won their battles. The plastermen did not challenge the entire system of provincial property and power. Instead, they attacked only those specific aspects that aggravated them, suggesting that their crowd protest was really a function of social economy, rather than a revolutionary movement. These contests were also violent physical confrontations in which the small producers displayed unity, bravery, and intelligence to overwhelm a seemingly formidable state apparatus.

On a regional level, the Plaster War is an example of how locals accommodated and supported others who were combating regulation. Passamaquoddy was truly a smugglers' haven. Not only did locals tolerate illicit trade but they turned out in crowd actions to defend it, grabbing whatever weapons were on hand. Shouts, fists, tools, and even cannon made clear where the sympathies of borderlands residents lay. When pushed, borderland residents proved very capable of joining together against state intervention into their livelihoods.

⚐ Conclusion ⚑

THE MEMORY OF SMUGGLING

In 1834, Jonathan Delesdernier Weston, one of Eastport's civic leaders, published a sweeping history that included native Americans, French explorers, Acadian settlers, the Revolutionary War, the War of 1812, and, of course, information on Eastport's founders. Weston was undoubtedly an excellent choice to write Eastport's history. He had been deeply involved with the community's early years, as one of its first attorneys, magistrate, sometimes legislative representative, and assistant in gathering depositions for the border commission that convened to adjust the border between New Brunswick and the United States after the War of 1812. Unfortunately, owing to failing health, Weston was unable to present his completed history personally. Instead, his son delivered his history in two lectures at the Eastport Lyceum in April 1834, and it was published shortly before Weston died on October 3, 1834.[1]

The Lyceum itself was located in Trescott Hall, a public venue named in honor of one of Weston's deceased friends and a fellow local worthy, Lemuel Trescott. As a decorated veteran of the War of Independence and a friend of George Washington, Trescott acquired considerable status within the community. A small town was named after him, as well as a number of babies. Contrast this with Weston's treatment of George Ulmer, another Revolutionary War veteran. Weston, who knew Ulmer, made no mention of him; another local historian who wrote a few years later admitted that "Colonel Ulmer was much disliked" because of his antismuggling activities.[2] Trescott, the crooked customs officer, retained a high position in local memory, meriting an entire chapter to himself in the town's 1888 history.[3] Clearly some Revolutionary veterans merited more praise than others. Trescott retired in 1818, a wealthy man from the emoluments of his eight-year tenure in office as Eastport's customs collector. Five years after his death in 1826, the people of Eastport commemorated his memory by erecting the Lyceum and schoolhouse in his name.

The Lyceum's mission was to educate the people of Eastport, especially those young men who were to be the next generation of leaders. Weston praised this institution as an asset that diffused information and created a taste for reading in the community. The pamphlets and books they read at the Lyceum connected the Passamaquoddy region to the world and, above all, to the American urban centers that published them, allowing the readers to absorb current ideas.

Not surprisingly, when addressing the period before the War of 1812, when Eastport was a leading smuggling haven in North America, Weston strayed from a strictly truthful interpretation of events. Indeed, he conceded, there had been smuggling on a large scale, but it was conducted mostly by adventurers from outside the community who introduced vicious habits and immorality to the community and gave the place "a character somewhat suspicious."[4] While he admitted that there were smuggling problems during the embargo and the War of 1812, he made no mention of the "Plaster War," nor the rampant smuggling of the 1820s and 1830s. Weston seems on the surface to have been a man of upstanding morals himself: a community leader, owner of pews in both the Baptist and the Congregationalist churches in town, and a man trusted and esteemed by nearly all in the community. Given Weston's credentials and the Lyceum's mission, it is little wonder that he blamed smuggling on strangers and discouraged the local youth from taking part in illicit trade.

Judge Weston's moral façade, just like his defense of Eastport's populace, is decidedly thin in spots. He may never have been an active smuggler, but he clearly expedited smuggling in Eastport. Evidence includes Weston's 1814 commission as the vice-consular agent to Sweden at Eastport, which placed him at the center of the questionable "neutral trade" that masked smuggling during the war. During the war, Weston defended himself from accusations that he actively collaborated with the British occupation forces.[5] Furthermore, he was involved in a strange incident in November 1830, when New Brunswick customs authorities seized a boat belonging to one Thomas Bibber. The colonial authorities in turn auctioned the boat to a British military officer. The new owners of the boat took it to Eastport one day, where Bibber saw it and wrested it from the new owner, one Captain Hook of the British Thirty-fourth Regiment. Bibber then dragged the boat up the streets of Eastport, assisted by a yoke of oxen and numerous locals, while a crowd assembled to enjoy Hook's discomfort. Hook looked to Eastport's assistant customs collector for assistance in getting back his boat. However, that official was Jonathan D. Weston, who also served as Bibber's attorney and had advised him to seize the boat. Weston offered no support to the hapless British officer. Eastport's magistrates also proved no help; they insisted that Bibber's actions were justifiable. Hook had to find his own way back to Saint Andrews.[6]

More ironic yet is that Trescott Hall was named after a crooked customs official. Lemuel Trescott died in possession of fantastic wealth for that time and place: probate records gauged his estate at $31,279.30, no small proportion of it in cash.[7] Thus we have Weston twisting the facts about Eastport's smuggling past, in a building constructed in the memory of a corrupt customs officer, to an audience that undoubtedly knew a thing or two about smuggling.

Weston would also have known that smuggling became more brazen and violent in the 1820s and 1830s, especially in New Brunswick. In 1822, two smugglers badly beat a customhouse officer at Saint John. Later that year there was a gun battle between smugglers and the provincial revenue cutter in the Bay of Fundy that reportedly resulted in several deaths.[8] The following year there was more violent resistance, and troops from the Seventy-fourth Regiment had to defend customhouse authorities from a crowd armed with boathooks and bludgeons.[9] In August 1824, an American captain forced the crew of the provincial revenue cutter to leap back into their boat from his vessel, which they had attempted to seize.[10] Timber smuggling continued at Saint Andrews; one English timber ship escaped a vigilant customs officer in October 1824, only after pointing a loaded gun at him. The captain apologized for the use of force, but explained that he had to because he feared the power of the Saint Andrews merchants engaged in the trade.[11] In 1827, an American captain struck a customhouse officer on a wharf in Saint John after "damning the Customs and the laws."[12] In addition to these smuggling tumults, there were other border-related frays, such as a cross-border "raid" by Eastport fisherman in 1824. A Royal Navy vessel seized several Eastport fishing boats for violating British sovereignty as they worked the grounds near Grand Manan. Outraged Eastport residents quickly armed themselves and took the boats back by force.[13]

Particularly striking are the number of crowd actions involving smugglers disguised as Indians in the 1830s, especially in the Calais–Saint Stephen area. In January 1830, New Brunswick customs authorities seized some American contraband in a barn in Saint Stephen. While they were transporting the goods to a secure warehouse, about twenty-five armed men, disguised as Indians with blackened faces, red shirts over their clothes, and black hats with feathers in them, attacked the officials and carried the goods across the Milltown bridge to American territory. In mid-December 1830, about twenty armed men disguised as Indians broke into a Saint Stephen store that contained contraband seized by New Brunswick customs officials and carried it across the river to Calais. In 1832, another crowd disguised as Indians rescued contraband goods from colonial customhouse officers and brought them to the American side of the border. However, these "Indians" did not just attack colonial customs officers. In July 1837, about forty men dressed as Indians seized two American customs officials at Calais and took them across the border into New Brunswick in a wagon. As the wagon wheels rolled, one of the "Indians" sharpened his bayonet on the iron rim to intimidate the officers. When they reached the woods, they terrorized the officials, demanding to know the identity of an informant. They also threatened to burn down the house of one of the officers. As late as 1846, armed smugglers at Saint George's chased away an overly curious customs officer at gunpoint.[14]

The disguises are themselves significant in that they not only assured anonymity but also provided a sort of theater that terrified the intended victims. By 1830, this sort of theatrical protest had largely been abandoned by Maine's pioneering squatters, but borderland smugglers picked it up in the Calais–Saint Stephen area. They may well have been influenced by the mid-Maine squatter protests; many American settlers in Charlotte County were from the very region where these struggles had been fiercest.[15] Notably, these smuggling Indians practiced the same restraint as the squatter Indians, frequently threatening violence but seldom acting on those threats.[16] Disguises and a reluctance to engage in killing mark these smugglers as "social bandits": self-help activists acting with the approval of the community in breaking the law in accordance with traditional values that were at odds with the state.[17] At Passamaquoddy, the smugglers effectively defended their "right" to trade across the border and consistently intimidated those who opposed them. Smugglers meted out harsh treatment to informers; one man went so far as to publish a statement sworn to by revenue cutter and customhouse officers that he was not the informer in one seizure.[18]

The plastermen, too, continued their smuggling and their violent defense of that trade. On August 8, 1833, New Brunswick customs officers seized the Nova Scotia plasterman schooner *Shannon* in the waters between Campobello and Eastport. The stated reason for the seizure was that the vessel had cleared for a return voyage to Nova Scotia in ballast without a cargo, but revenue officers discovered a cargo of contraband American goods consisting of tea and gunpowder, and they impounded the vessel. The following day, as the four customhouse officers sailed the *Shannon* to Saint Andrews for adjudication, one or more boats put off from Eastport, seized the vessel, and brought it to Union Wharf, safely in American territory.

The community managed to display a remarkable case of collective amnesia regarding this event. The British vice-consul for the region arranged for a local lawyer to collect depositions. The results of his inquiries varied dramatically. While New Brunswick customs officers swore that some fifty to sixty men in three boats seized the *Shannon*, American witnesses claimed only five or six men in one boat did. The colonials also claimed the vessel entered the harbor after 4:00 p.m., that the men who seized the vessel cheered and fired guns until it anchored, and that the crowds on Eastport's wharves shouted verbal abuse at them. They thought at least three or four of the men who rescued the *Shannon* were Americans. The other party claimed that the schooner entered the harbor about 1:00 p.m., that there were no weapons of any sort, and that nobody on Eastport's waterfront said anything to the customs officials. Furthermore, no U.S. citizens were involved in the matter.[19]

Notably, this investigation was conducted by Jonathan Weston's son, also an attorney and the man who read his father's history to the audience assembled in Trescott Hall in April 1834. Yet none of these events found their way into Weston's history, and undoubtedly he would have become quite unpopular had he actually expounded upon the scale of smuggling at Passamaquoddy.

Weston's history, including its errors of omission, exemplified a borderland perspective through its interplay of local and global interests.[20] For Weston, born immediately after the Revolution to a father who had fought in it, but living in a Jacksonian milieu where nationalism and manifest destiny were becoming increasingly the order of the day, explaining his community's relationship with the old Loyalist foes offered some difficult challenges. Weston overcame these problems by downplaying conflict and concentrating on a theme sure to please most: the future prosperity of the community and its recent advances toward that goal. This satisfied locals, who were eager to have their community's praises sung. It also met national expectations because financial success was rapidly becoming a quality Americans attributed to themselves, especially in the commercial North.[21]

Weston's history also fit neatly into a wider pattern of community histories written by local worthies in the early nineteenth century. These works celebrated the success of communities as building blocks in creating national prosperity. In some measure, Weston was also healing the wounds of the War of 1812 and the British occupation of Eastport from 1814 to 1815, when the community as a whole had been demonized in the national press, especially *Niles' Weekly Register*. As early as 1818, immediately after British troops evacuated Moose Island, its American residents tried to redeem the character of the area by addressing the idea that Eastport and Lubec thrived only because of smuggling. A letter submitted to the *New Brunswick Courier* attempted to correct this idea with a rather weak conclusion: "But this notion is not altogether correct." This, no doubt, left the readers to conclude that it was not altogether incorrect, either. More usefully, the article stated, "Near to every boundary line, that is where the fag ends of two governments meet, there is, and always has been and ever will be that sort of unshackled traffic; which in Boston, and N. York and Philadelphia would be called smuggling." The article's author, who may well have been Weston himself, blamed the region's problems on outsiders, for "whenever there has been a prospect of making money by an illicit trade, thither speculators and smugglers have straightway resorted, to the injury of the character of both frontiers."[22] Weston's history was a form of boosterism, designed to heal the wounds of the past and pave the way for a prosperous future. Weston selectively created a local identity and exercised the discretion required of attorneys such as himself.[23]

The same principle operated on the New Brunswick side of the border. An anonymous article published in a Saint John newspaper claimed that Charlotte County's "proximity to the American lines, and the uninhabited state of our coast and of the County generally, render the temptation to smuggle too strong to be easily resisted." The borderland spirit expedited smuggling. The anonymous author complained that British subjects and American citizens assisted one another in smuggling," and described how people on both sides of the border combined in a smuggling trade that brought most of the colony's West India goods through Passamaquoddy.[24] In fact, the plastermen continued their old ways long enough to enter Canadian lore through Thomas McCulloch's *Letters of Mephibosheth Stepsure* and Haliburton's *Sam Slick* tales. Into the 1840s, New Brunswick officials found that the plastermen continued to import large amounts of contraband and that not one barrel of flour in a thousand brought into the province actually paid customs duties.[25]

Lorenzo Sabine, a fellow Eastport resident of Weston's, also wrote history in the mid-nineteenth century. Sabine was a better scholar than Weston and more interested in examining the conflicts raised by living on the border. Sabine admitted that locals engaged in smuggling, although he cautioned, "As the world knows, the tales of smugglers and fishermen are always long and frequently adorned."[26] Sabine was also aware of the many contradictions brought out on the border. As a young clerk to an Eastport merchant, Sabine had noticed the enthusiasm with which Loyalists smuggled and their practice of throwing contraband tea overboard to avoid confiscation of both cargo and vessel. He thought this practice humorously akin to the Boston Tea Party of 1773.[27]

New Brunswick writers also commemorated and mythologized their past in this period. In contrast to American ideals of liberty and independence, New Brunswick's ideology typically extolled the prosperity and order inherent to British colonial society. On May 18, 1833, New Brunswickers celebrated the fiftieth anniversary of the first landing of Loyalists at Saint John. Among the speakers was Supreme Court Justice Ward Chipman. Chipman's father had suffered cruelly during the Revolution and had found refuge in New Brunswick after the war. Yet the elder Chipman sent his own son to Harvard, participated in several border commissions, and was accused of engaging in smuggling himself. Little wonder then that his American educated son had a conciliatory message for his audience that was devoid of anti-Americanism.[28]

In Charlotte County, formal historical consciousness developed much later; community histories did not appear until after Confederation in 1867. But more casual inquiries sometimes touched on the smuggling issue. One of the earliest statements made by a local was in 1835, when an old Loyalist named Patrick Clinch wrote that smuggling was one of the region's major trades, "which some are in the habit of styling Contraband—but which we call *free trade*. Our geographical position exposes us to great temptations in this respect."[29]

None of these histories emphasized the differences between American citizens and colonial subjects. Because Maine and New Brunswick were culturally very similar, even in terms of religion, awareness of their distinctiveness could easily be lost. In this sort of milieu, national declarations become changeable, shaped according to the current state of affairs.[30] In some ways a much better place to look for declarations of ideology is not in the allegedly factual community histories but in the realm of fiction. In novels and short stories, authors could safely rise above the immediate community's consciousness and make sweeping declarations with little fear of unpleasant repercussions. For Passamaquoddy, the fictional adventures of "Sam Slick," a Yankee clockmaker who frequently traveled to Nova Scotia from his Connecticut home, offers an intriguing glimpse into how Maritimers felt about the region. Written in 1835, these stories invariably connected Passamaquoddy with smuggling and the ruinous temptation for Nova Scotians to engage in the plaster trade.

The suppression or absence of nationalistic prejudice is perhaps more understandable in the Maritimes. These colonies had no or little affiliation to one another, usually had limited contacts with distant Britain, and were often dominated by elitist cliques that did their best to control the political, economic, and social agendas. In the United States one might expect a more bombastic attitude, especially during the heady Jacksonian era, but this does not seem to be the case for Passamaquoddy. In part this was a result of the War of 1812, during which the British military occupied all of eastern Maine, thereby muting Yankee pretensions to manifest destiny long after the war ended. Direct conflict did not arise between Maine and New Brunswick until the late 1830s with the events leading up to the so-called Aroostook War.

Selective memory at Passamaquoddy did not lie in the public sphere alone. Individuals and families twisted events as well. This is best illustrated in the death of William Newcomb in 1796. Newcomb attempted to rescue a schooner seized for smuggling by New Brunswick customs officers. On the night of October 2, 1795, Newcomb and eight to eleven others attempted to take the schooner back from the authorities and fired at the men guarding the vessel. The guards, "being hard pushed and fired at with three musquets, were unavoidably obliged to defend themselves." They returned fire and shot Newcomb dead on the vessel's forecastle. A New Brunswick court subsequently acquitted the guards of murder charges. Yet the published Newcomb family genealogy makes no mention of his death, while faithfully recording its date. Clearly someone in the Newcomb family decided that William's violent death was unseemly and actively changed the record.[31]

While local historians celebrated Passamaquoddy's transition from a frontier to a settled region with modern railroads, steamboats, banks, insurance companies, and other hallmarks of capitalist enterprise, smuggling continued. How are we to understand the rituals of smugglers dressed as Indians with the community's increasing economic development?

The answer seems to be that community goals of self-help easily fused with capitalistic individualism at Passamaquoddy, in part because the loser in smuggling was not an individual but the state. This was particularly noticeable in the 1833 *Shannon* incident, in which the entire community either maintained silence or altered events to stymie customs authorities who interfered with smuggling. Furthermore, the smugglers who styled themselves "free traders" could also claim to be at the forefront of early nineteenth-century economic thought, which increasingly insisted on reducing trade barriers, such as British preferences for New Brunswick timber. However, these same "free traders" were pragmatic and self-serving in their approach. Saint Andrews timber merchants had long benefited from illegally shipping American timber to Britain while claiming it was from New Brunswick. When these colonial preferences were endangered, Saint Andrews merchants engaged in boisterous protests that peaked with the burning of a member of Parliament in effigy and the fiery destruction of a boat in the harbor.[32]

Furthermore, when the United States and Britain finally agreed to open colonial ports to American vessels in 1830, creating the long sought-after "free trade" and reciprocity some merchants wanted, it yielded new opportunities to smuggle because tariffs remained high, especially on manufactured goods. Other merchants, especially New Brunswick's timber barons, opposed free trade and industrial development not based on timber.[33] Merchants wanted both protection from foreigners at home and unrestricted access to foreign markets. When they could not trade honestly, they easily made the transition to illicit trade, and laborers, fishermen, and others seemed glad to assist for a cut of the profits. In part, this may have been a result of the occupational pluralism practiced by borderland residents; they had to weave together a number of occupations to provide themselves with a living. Eventually the call for free trade overwhelmed the protectionist ideals, culminating in the Reciprocity Treaty of 1854, which permitted natural products to cross the border duty-free.

Passamaquoddy provides ample evidence that governments continued to have difficulty controlling their borders after 1820. There was often an American garrison at Fort Sullivan in Eastport and a British garrison at Fort Tipperary in Saint Andrews. The British and American navies and revenue cutters increasingly patrolled the border to suppress smuggling and regulate fisheries, but with little result, for they could not distinguish colonial fishermen from their American counterparts.[34] The number of customs officers on both sides grew, and in 1821 Saint Andrews finally became a customs district in its own right, distinct from Saint John. Yet despite the growth of state intervention, resistance continued. The British, colonial, and United States governments failed to adequately cope with or control the growing numbers of impoverished Irish immigrants flooding through the region on their way to American urban centers, and on occasion unscrupulous shipmasters unceremoniously dumped entire shiploads of foreigners at Passamaquoddy and left them to fend for themselves.[35] Criminals, deserters, and debtors continued to slip across the boundary, as they did all along the United States–British North American border. Moreover, contraband unrelentingly moved across the border.

In a bigger context, smuggling at Passamaquoddy indicates the futility of attempting to understand United States and Canadian history separately. Britain continued to have an enormous influence on both; British capital spurred American development, and British North America never broke entirely free from the economic influence of the United States. American and colonial economies remained intertwined after the Revolution, for capitalism tends to ignore borders. From an early date this meant that American corporations penetrated New Brunswick. One example was the Aetna Insurance Company, based in Hartford, Connecticut, which advertised in Saint John newspapers in the 1830s.[36] The strength of these cross-border flows of commerce, goods, and people meant that informal, and often illicit, exchanges continued at the border.

The settlers who came to Passamaquoddy after the American Revolution soon found they had more in common with one another than they had with their respective metropoles. Rituals of allegiance continued on both sides of the border, but with some startling deviations. Calais saluted the Fourth of July with gunpowder borrowed from Saint Stephen's armory, and Calais children insisted on taking a half-day off from school on Queen Victoria's birthday.[37] These popular demonstrations indicate the subtle and benign power of the borderland accommodation.

More alarming were the street rituals of smugglers as they intimidated and assaulted both colonial and federal customs authorities. The white "Indians" who struck terror in the hearts of customs officers indicated the disdain, and even contempt, that borderland residents felt for the state. This sentiment was common throughout North America, but on the border, where governing agencies were weak, it further undermined the already feeble authorities. Furthermore, representatives of state power often sympathized with the local populace. They subverted the laws themselves, thus benefiting the periphery at the expense of the center. The increased politicization of officeholding in New Brunswick under the guise of "responsible government" and in the United States as part of "Jacksonian democracy" may have worsened the problem. It was not until after Canadian Confederation in 1867 and the American Civil War that bureaucrats became more professional and detached from local interests.

The borderland population continued to build transborder ties, based on family, trade, and a shared culture. At times this sentiment was strained, as during the Aroostook War, but friendly relations were the norm. Governments at times unwittingly encouraged cross-border ties, as with the reciprocity agreements of 1830 and 1854, which substantially freed trade from bothersome tariffs. But at other times governments suddenly attempted to close the border. Meanwhile, the borderland populace insisted on de-emphasizing the importance of the border; it was the various governments that frequently changed their policies. This complex set of borderland attitudes encouraged outsiders, including criminals and economic adventurers, to come to Passamaquoddy. Conversely, it also attracted state agencies, such as military units, revenue cutters, and customs officers. The borderland populace developed ways of dealing with both, essentially rejecting troublemakers and co-opting outsiders' values to their own advantage. Frequently this meant paying lip service to the state even as locals undermined its local representatives. The smuggling trade reveals the effectiveness of locals in so doing.

Jefferson's embargo, remembered locally as the "Flour War," was one manifestation of the local ability to overwhelm and subvert government agencies that interfered with smuggling. Notably, competing governments undermined their counterpart's efforts to control the border, as when British imperial and colonial governments actively worked against Jefferson's embargo. The War of 1812 saw a repeat of the embargo, but with an even larger military intervention. As occurred during the embargo, a considerable number of adventurers appeared at Passamaquoddy. Their often troublesome presence is one indicator that the local views concerning illicit trade were held by many others in North American society, some of them destined to become the leading lights of nineteenth-century commerce in both British North America and the United States. The third conflict, known as the "Plaster War," revisited many of these themes, but on this occasion colonial smugglers defied British and colonial authorities and defeated elite Saint John merchants who aspired to dominate the region economically. Accustomed to operating under the privileges of the mercantilist system, they found themselves ill-equipped to fight the economic principles of free trade that the American government advocated. Nor did New Brunswick's merchant community forget this bitter lesson about American economic power. The result was a deep insecurity about their reliance on British trade preferences.[38] Despite frequent lip service to British mercantilism, the size of the American economy and its cheaper foodstuffs forced colonial businessmen to compromise their principles, even if they had to engage in smuggling.

Smuggling was thus an ongoing problem at Passamaquoddy, one that is still not resolved and may never be, so long as a border runs through the region. Nor have borderland attitudes diminished in the region. Native Americans, Mainers, and New Brunswickers continue to reassess their relationship with the invisible line through Passamaquoddy Bay that separates Canada from the United States. Both Canadian and American governments maintain numerous officials and agencies to control the border that remains contested around Machias Seal Island. The benefits of capitalism have proved elusive to the region, which is now an impoverished corner of Maine and New Brunswick, which are respectively a poor state and province in national contexts. Poverty and the region's geography have combined to make drug smuggling a common practice into the twenty-first century. Passamaquoddy residents retain a strong regional identity that spans the border, assisted by transborder cultural groups such as the Border Historical Society, the Quoddy Regional History Board, and the Tides Institute. One is left to wonder what the smugglers themselves, the rogues of 'Quoddy, would have made of these formal efforts to institutionalize cross-border bonds.

APPENDIX A

State of Settlement on Moose, Dudley, and Frederick Islands, c. 1800

Inhabitant	Occupation	Oxen	Cows	Acres Cleared	Acres Wild	Women	Children
Moose Island							
1 William Tater	fisherman		2	1	19	1	3
2 John Kendle	fisherman			3	32		
3 Moses Norwood	fisherman		4	13	59	1	5
4 David Parson	fisherman		1		17	1	3
5 James Carter	fisherman		3	2	23	1	4
6 Nathaniel Clark	fisherman		3			1	3
7 Paul Johnson	fisherman	2	7	9	91	1	5
8 John Lane	fisherman		3	1	16	1	3
9 Daniel Holmes	fisherman		4	4	137	1	5
10 John Newcomb	fisherman	2	2	5	95		
11 Charles Vandiford	shoemaker					1	3
12 Eben'r Mabee	fisherman		4	3	11	1	5
13 William Ricker	fisherman	2	3	16	54	1	
14 Samuel Tuttle	farmer	2	4	37	100	1	7
15 Solomon Mabee	fisherman		2		15	1	3
16 Andrew Herrington	fisherman		4	7	93	1	4
17 Andrew Herrington	fisherman		1		20		
18 Stephen Fountain	fisherman						
19 William Soudy	fisherman			3	75		
20 John Tucker	fisherman						
21 Nathaniel Clark	fisherman		2	4	21	1	5
22 Henry Bowen	fisherman						
23 Andrew Boman	fisherman					1	6
24 Samuel Coombs	fisherman		1	1	5	1	4
25 Wentworth Kennison	fisherman					1	3
26 Jacob Clark Sr.	fisherman					1	1
27 Joseph Clark	fisherman	2	2	15	85	1	5

(continued)

Appendix A (continued)

Inhabitant	Occupation	Oxen	Cows	Acres Cleared	Acres Wild	Women	Children
28 Hume Nostrom	fisherman						
29 John Brown	fisherman					1	5
30 Jacob Lincoln	fisherman	2	2	6	84		
31 William Hammond	fisherman	2	2	5	75		
32 John Stewart	trader						
33 Edward Coombs	fisherman						
34 John Tumbleson	fisherman					1	7
35 James Bradbury	trader		2	6	267	1	4
36 William Hammond	fisherman					1	3
37 John Wortman	fisherman					1	2
38 Wm. & Patrick Egan	traders		2	3	23		
39 Wm. Clark	fisherman	2	4	9	91	1	5
40 Hayden & Shed	traders						
41 Samuel Lughton	fisherman					1	6
42 Caleb Boynton	fisherman	2	5	30	70		
43 John Curry	fisherman						
44 Richard Hall	fisherman						
45 David & Robt. Gilmore	traders						
46 John Burgin	trader					1	1
47 Thomas Burnham	fisherman					1	6
48 John Shackford	fisherman		6	10	196		
49 Alex'r Hacket	fisherman					1	5
50 James Cockin	fisherman	2	8	13	87		
51 Ebenezer Gouge	parson					1	3
52 Elbinah Morton	fisherman						
53 James Young	fisherman					1	4
54 Laben Stoddard	fisherman	2	2	3			
55 Richard Sanborn	fisherman						
56 Jacob French	fisherman						
57 Henry Ward	shoemaker		1				
58 Jonathan Levitt	trader		1		100	1	3
59 John Prince	trader					1	4
60 Levi Covel	fisherman						
61 John Brown	fisherman						
62 William Bowen	fisherman						
Subtotal		22	87	209	1,961	33	129
Dudley Island							
66 William Allan		2	4	20	154	1	6
Total		24	91	229	2,115	34	135

Source: Public Records Office C.O.188/10: "Original Correspondence, Secretary of State: New Brunswick."

APPENDIX B

Deputy Marshal's Records of Enemy Aliens, Eastport, c. 1812–1813

Name	Age	Years in U.S.	Family size	Trade	Took loyalty oath to U.S.	1810 Census	Served in Mass. Militia
Aymor, Daniel	26	5	4	blockmaker	yes	yes	
Boice, Joseph	68	1	4	housewright	no	no	
Bostwith, John S.	42	3	8	mariner	yes	no	
Brown, Samuel	58	8	3	laborer	yes	yes	
Burns, Patrick	30	3	0	laborer	no	no	yes
Cope, Richard S.	30	8	0	cordwainer	yes	no	
Copp, David	60	8	4	trader	no	yes	
Cormie, Joseph	28	8	0	merchant	no	no	
Crawford, Levi	43	4	6	laborer	yes	yes	
Crawley, Philip	25	7	0	fisherman	no	no	
Curry, Andrew	48	2	6	victualer	yes	yes	
Deckle, George	23	.25	4	mason	no	no	
Finch, Simon	55	4	8	laborer	yes	yes	
Greason, Thomas	24	3	2	laborer	yes	no	
Harris, Eli	26	1	4	cordwainer	yes	no	
Harris, Gilbert	47	.10	7	preacher	yes	no	
Haycock, Thomas	27	3	4	baker	yes	yes	
Hunt, Henry	30	2	0	tallow chandler	no	no	
Lawrence, John	23	1	0	painter	no	no	
Lunt, Joseph	23	12	0	seaman	no	yes	yes
McKinley, John	20	8	0	cordwainer	no	no	
Morgan, James R.	24	16	4	fisherman	no	yes	yes
Morris, Robert	45	2	9	laborer	no	yes	
Murray, John	25	3	0	laborer	no	no	
Nowlin, Robert	31	9	3	laborer	yes	no	
O'Donald, Michael	35	.75	3	cooper	no	no	
Parker, Timothy	53	2	5	victualer	yes	no	

(continued)

Appendix B (continued)

Name	Age	Years in U.S.	Family size	Trade	Took loyalty oath to U.S.	1810 Census	Served in Mass. Militia
Pendlebury, Thomas	24	1	3	laborer	no	no	yes
Strut, George	23	16	0	cordwainer	no	no	
Taylor, William	40	23	11	fisherman	yes	yes	
Van Buskirk, Abraham	50	6	10	cooper	yes	yes	
Walker, James	50	2	9	laborer	yes	no	
Whilpley, Joseph	34	2	5	blacksmith	yes	yes	
Woodwith, James	34	6	6	seaman	no	yes	
Woodworth, Samuel	64	6	5	victualer	yes	yes	

35 Heads of households
208 Enemy aliens total

Source: Returns of enemy aliens from Eastport in the District of Maine extracted from the returns of enemy aliens by Maine's U.S. marshal, Thomas G. Thornton, in the autumn of 1812, found in National Archives RG 59, M558, "U.S. Department of State: War of 1812 Papers." Statement of aliens taking oaths of loyalty to the United States in January 1813 found in William King Papers, Maine Historical Society. Militia rolls in Eldridge Collection, *Eastport Sentinel*, February 20, 1907.

NOTES

Abbreviations

EWP	Edward Winslow Papers, Special Collections, Harriet Irving Library, University of New Brunswick, Fredericton
MeSA	Maine State Archives, Augusta, ME
NAC	National Archives of Canada, Ottawa, Ontario
NSARM	Nova Scotia Archives and Records Management, Halifax
PAG	Papers of Albert Gallatin. Microfilm. 46 reels.
PANB	Provincial Archives of New Brunswick, Fredericton
MaDC	Massachusetts Federal District Court Records, National Archives and Records Administration, Waltham, Massachusetts
MeDC	Maine Federal District Court Records, National Archives and Records Administration, Waltham, Massachusetts
MeHS	Maine Historical Society, Portland
MHS	Massachusetts Historical Society, Boston
MCC	Massachusetts Federal Circuit Court Records, National Archives and Records Administration, Waltham, Massachusetts
MSA	Massachusetts State Archives, Boston
NYDC	New York Federal District Court Records, National Archives and Records Administration, New York City
NYPL	New York Public Library, Manuscripts and Archives Division, Astor, Lennox, and Tiller Foundations
SJC	Supreme Judicial Court
TGTP	Thomas G. Thornton Papers, Maine Historical Society, Portland
T92/261	"Report of the Commissioners of a Special Revenue Inquiry during the Years 1812, 1813, and 1814," National Archives, Kew, England
WKP	William King Papers, Maine Historical Society, Portland

Chapter 1. "The Habit of Smuggling"

1. Marsden, *Mission to Nova Scotia*, 56–57.
2. See Marsden, *Grace Displayed*.

3. Humbert, *Rise and Progress of Methodism*, 35–36.
4. Allen, *Works of Fisher Ames*, 617.
5. Cuthbertson, *Old Attorney General*, 76–77.
6. Taylor, "The Smuggling Career of William King."
7. Smith, *Wealth of Nations*, 397.
8. Matson, *Merchants & Empire*, 204.
9. Bailyn, *Atlantic History*, 88.
10. See Lunn, "Illegal Fur Trade"; Griffiths, "Golden Age"; Johnson, "Fair Traders and Smugglers"; Grahn, *Political Economy of Smuggling*; Cooney, "'Doing Business in the Smuggling Way'"; Cooper, *Ned Myers*; Graham, "Gypsum Trade"; Stafford, "Illegal Importations."
11. Bolingbroke, *Voyage to Demerary*, 166; Eves, "Poor People"; Graham, "Gypsum Trade."
12. T92/261, 82–83.
13. Thompson, "Moral Economy of the English Crowd in the Eighteenth Century," 50, and Linebaugh and Rediker, *Many-Headed Hydra*.
14. Nicolas, *Dispatches and Letters*, 171–89.
15. Philp, *Coast Blockade*, 3.
16. Parliament, *First Report*, 6–7.
17. Williams, *Contraband Cargoes*, 151.
18. Ibid., 180–87, 204.
19. Winslow, "Sussex Smugglers," 149.
20. Nicholls, *Honest Thieves*, 217; Morley, *Smuggling War*, 125–62.
21. Bailyn, *Atlantic History*, 88.
22. Leamon, *Revolution Downeast*, 43.
23. Hersey, "Tar and Feathers."
24. Leamon, *Revolution Downeast*, 65.
25. Raymond, *Winslow Papers*, 502–3.
26. Butler, "Rising Like a Phoenix," 21.
27. "Ten Dollars Reward," *New Brunswick Courier* (Saint John), July 22, 1814.
28. Sabine, *Biographical Sketches*, 13.
29. Wright, *Loyalists of New Brunswick*, viii, 217.
30. Bourque and Whitehead, "Trade and Alliances," 131–47.
31. Faulkner and Faulkner, *French at Pentagoet*, 28, 168.
32. Reid, "International Region," 17.
33. Bell, "Melancholy Affair," 23, 35–37.
34. Leamon, *Revolution Downeast*, 178.
35. Davis, *International Community*, 42.
36. Lodge and Armstrong to the Board of Trade, September 9, 1787, B.T.6/59, quoted in Graham, *Sea Power*, 154–55.
37. Deposition of John Black, "Goods seized by the Collector of Halifax as Enemies Property," RG 8–IV/166.6, NAC.
38. HAS Dearborn to Secretary of the Treasury Alexander J. Dallas, Dec. 15, 1814, M178.
39. In two incidents the cannon of Fort Sullivan fired on smugglers. The first was on No-

vember 7, 1813 (see *United States v. the Sloop Venture*, June Term, 1814, RG 21/MeDC), the second in April 1814 (see Zimmerman, *Coastal Fort*, 38).

40. Graham, *Sea Power*, 153–76.
41. Graham, "Gypsum Trade," 209–23.
42. Humbert to Smyth, August 18, 1820, RS24, PANB.
43. Smith, *Wealth of Nations*, 362.
44. The *Agnes*, RG 8–IV/154.2, NAC.
45. Matson, *Merchants & Empire*, 203–14.
46. *United States v. John Clap of New York*, December Term, 1808, RG 21/MeDC.
47. Gregory, *Nathan Appleton*, 87–106, passim.
48. "Reminiscences of a Former Resident of New Meadows," 52.
49. *New England Palladium* (Boston), February 28, 1809.
50. See deposition of John W. Bradley, *U.S. v. A Quantity English Goods*, December Term, 1812, RG 21/MeDC.
51. John Young to William Young, February 6, 1815 in Harvey, "Pre-Agricola John Young," 135.
52. Macmillan, "Christopher Scott," 23–26.
53. "Sir Samuel Cunard," *Dictionary of Canadian Biography Online*.
54. Patrick Clinch to John Saunders, September 4, 1835, EWP.
55. McGregor, *History of Washington Lodge*, 11, 16.
56. *U.S. v. 16 Bales Merchandise*, February Term, 1815, RG 21/MeDC; "Goods seized by the Collector of Halifax as Enemies Property," RG 8, IV/166.6, NAC.
57. Affidavit of John Crumby, January 2, 1815, C.O.217/96.
58. *House Journal*, January 12, 1813. Lewis Tappan's company survives today as Dun & Bradstreet, recently renamed "D&B."
59. See Charles Tappan's letter to Capt. George H. Preble, reproduced in Porter, "Smuggling in Maine during the War of 1812"; *U.S. v. the Sloop "Traveler,"* October Term, 1813, RG 21/MeDC.
60. Thomas, *Liberator*, 10–21. William Lloyd Garrison's father, Abijah, was from a New Brunswick Pre-Loyalist family and worked on coasting vessels that traded with New England.
61. Smith, *Wealth of Nations*, 180.

Chapter 2. "A Sort of Neutrality"

1. Eckstorm, *Indian Place Names*, 227; Hamilton, *Place Names of Atlantic Canada*, 116.
2. *Cumberland Gazette* (Falmouth, Maine), March 20, 1789.
3. Lewis Frederick Delesdernier, "Description and Representation of the present situation of the District of Passamaquoddy," October 1, 1789, Oliver Wolcott Jr. Papers, Connecticut Historical Society, Hartford.
4. George Leonard to Anthony Merry, August 20, 1806, EWP.
5. Bent, "Charles Turner's Journal of His 1802 Trip to New Brunswick," 129.
6. Campbell, *Travels in the Interior*, 285.
7. Kilby, *Eastport and Passamaquoddy*, 151.
8. Even the aid of a pilot might not help. For example, a New Brunswick court stripped a

pilot of his license after he wrecked the mast ship *Britannia* near Campobello in 1798. See *St. John Gazette*, June 22, September 11, and November 16, 1798.

9. "Statement of the Population of the Several Parishes in the County of Charlotte, with the Principal Exports of Each, &c.," c. 1803, EWP.

10. Deposition of Thomas Lesuer Jr., *U.S. v. Sloop Sally of Portland and Cargo*, March Term, 1813, RG 21/MeDC.

11. *Columbian Centinel* (Boston), March 16, 1791; "Petition of Moose Island Inhabitants," *Massachusetts Resolves*, 1791, chap. 90, MSA.

12. Kilby, *Eastport and Passamaquoddy*, 95–96.

13. Davis, *International Community*, 79.

14. February 27, 1810 entry, New Brunswick Executive Council. Draft of minutes with supporting documents, MG9-A1, NAC.

15. Demeritt, "Representing the 'True' St. Croix," 519–22.

16. Joseph Leavitt, diary, August 1814 entry.

17. *Other Merchants and Sea Captains of Old Boston*, 29–30.

18. *Massachusetts Resolves* 1802, chap. 92; *Quoddy Indians v. John Berry* and *Quoddy Indians v. David Nutting & others*, August Term, 1808, Washington County Circuit Court of Common Pleas, and notice concerning compensating the Passamaquoddies for stolen timber dated July 18, 1812, in the Benjamin Lincoln Papers, MHS.

19. Moses Gerrish to Gabriel Ludlow, August 10, 1807, RS637, PANB.

20. *Other Merchants and Sea Captains of Old Boston*, 29–30.

21. Kilby, "Benedict Arnold on the Eastern Frontier"; David Owen to his brother, September 15, 1791, Glansevern Collection, National Library of Wales.

22. Royle, *Pioneer, Patriot, and Rebel*.

23. Aaron Rogers to William King, September 13, 1812, WKP; John Brewer to James Sullivan, November 25, 1796, Northeast Boundary Papers. Sullivan, the future governor of Massachusetts, served on the 1796 boundary commission. While passing Brewer's house, he allegedly observed to Ward Chipman that Brewer was providing information to the British and was therefore "an Enemy to the Commonwealth of Massachusetts where he resided and acted as a publick magistrate."

24. Davis, *International Community*, 70–71.

25. Morse, "Early Records of Eastport, Maine."

26. Lamb, *History of St. Croix Lodge*.

27. Wynn, "New England's Outpost," 65.

28. MacNutt, *New Brunswick*, 165; Davis, *International Community*, 70, 72.

29. "Petition of Moose Island Inhabitants," *Massachusetts Resolves*, 1791, chap. 90.

30. Wright, *Loyalists of New Brunswick*, 160–63, 217–23.

31. George Leonard to Anthony Merry, August 20, 1806, EWP; Temperley, *Lieutenant Colonel Joseph Gubbins*, 55; petition of Jesse Scott and Aaron Hanscom, March Term, 1813, Washington County Circuit Court of Common Pleas, MeSA.

32. Vose, "Col. George Peck," 171–72.

33. David Owen to his brother, July 8, 1788, and December 15, 1788, Glansevern Collection, National Library of Wales.

34. Taylor, *Liberty Men*, 109–12.
35. Condon, *Loyalist Dream*, 43–71.
36. Burrows, *Captain Owen of the African Survey*, 216–17.
37. George Pechelle to unknown, May 28, 1822, Customs 34/6448; see William Owen's "Register-book: Deeds, Leases, etc. for the Estate of Campo-bello."
38. MacKinnon, *This Unfriendly Soil*, 172–76; Condon, *Loyalist Dream*, 153.
39. Wynn, "New England's Outpost," 83; Temperley, *Lieutenant Colonel Joseph Gubbins*, 26, 28, and 45.
40. George Leonard to president of the council, September 27, 1806, EWP.
41. See appendix A.
42. W. Paine to John Wentworth, March 1, 1788, Wentworth Papers, vol. 2, NSARM, quoted in MacKinnon, *This Unfriendly Soil*, 147.
43. Davis, *International Community*, 170–74.
44. Graham, *Sea Power*, 155, 160–62.
45. Campbell, *Travels in the Interior*, 286.
46. Davis, *International Community*, 98–100.
47. Wynn, "Deplorably Dark and Demoralized Lumberers," 68–187.
48. MacNutt, *New Brunswick*, 149–54, 164.
49. Deposition of John W. Bradley in *U.S. v. A Quantity English Goods*, December Term, 1812, RG 21/MeDC.
50. An example of this is Gillam Butler, a Loyalist merchant and smuggler on Campobello who resented Charlotte County's predominantly Scottish officials and blamed his political problems on them. See MacNutt, *New Brunswick*, 62.
51. Macmillan, "New Men," 44–46, 79.
52. Affidavit of Samuel Kelly, December 16, 1802, in David Owen to Lord Hobart, December 29, 1803, C.O.188/12.
53. For timber see MacNutt, *New Brunswick*, 75–76 and 98; for embargo violations see Robert Pagan & Co. to John Millar & Co., May 20, 1808, C.O.217/83.
54. Macmillan, "New Men," 90, and Robert Armstrong to customs commissioners, July 17, 1824, Customs 34/6504, and J. Harper to customs commissioners, April 25, 1817, Customs 34/6571. This report revealed that virtually all ships built in New Brunswick had illegal American components, such as anchors, sails, and rigging.
55. Sabine, *Biographical Sketches*, 543.
56. Sellers, *Market Revolution*, 44.
57. Affidavit of Colin Campbell, *King v. Thomas Ross et al.*, RS 42, PANB.
58. Taylor, *Liberty Men*, 79–82.
59. "Sea Serpent and Whale," *American Advocate* (Hallowell, Maine), August 15, 1818; Dexter, "Cape Ann Visits of the Great Sea-Serpent," 213–20.
60. Sabine, *Report on the Principal Fisheries*, 204.
61. "Gold Mine at Passamaquoddy," *Columbian Centinel* (Boston), July 19, 1809.
62. Wells, *Campobello*, 17–18; Campbell, *Travels in the Interior*, 286; New Brunswick, *Journal of the House of Assembly for 1851*, cxxxix.
63. Kilby, *Eastport and Passamaquoddy*, 145.

64. *Eastport Sentinel*, December 13, 1823.
65. Rawlyk, *Canada Fire*, xvi.
66. Marini, *Radical Sects*, 40–43; Rawlyk, *Canada Fire*, 6.
67. Fingard, *Anglican Design*; Thomas, *Liberator*, 13. Fanny became the mother of famed abolitionist William Lloyd Garrison.
68. Jack, "Biographical Data," 22.
69. Murchie, *Saint Croix*, 265.
70. Journal of Ephraim Abbott, September 19, 1811, quoted in Kilby, *Eastport and Passamaquoddy*, 331.
71. Hebb, *Church of England*, 86.
72. "Extract of a Letter from Eastport to a Gentleman in Newburyport, Dated July 8," *Eagle* (Castine, Maine), July 23, 1811.
73. Bell, *Newlight Journals*, 150; see also "List of Enemy Aliens, Eastport, 1813," WKP.
74. MacKinnon, "Changing Attitudes"; Rawlyk, "Federalist-Loyalist Alliance," 142–60; and Errington, *The Lion, the Eagle, and Upper Canada*, 35–39.

Chapter 3. "A Commerce of Mere Stone"

1. *New Brunswick Royal Gazette* (Saint John), June 8, 1807.
2. Lewis Frederick Delesdernier to James Madison, June 24, 1807, *Annals of Congress*, 1808, 2297–2301.
3. *Eastern Argus* (Portland, Maine), June 25, 1807.
4. *Eastern Argus*, June 25, 1807, and March 31, 1808; Delesdernier to Madison, July 9, 1807, and enclosures, *Annals of Congress*, 1808, 2297–2301.
5. *Eastern Argus*, March 31, 1808.
6. George Leonard to Castlereagh, September 12, 1807, C.O.188/13.
7. David Owen to Francis James Jackson, September 27, 1809, "New Brunswick 'A,'" vol. 21, NAC.
8. David Owen to Mr. Thomas, October 16, 1803, C.O.188/12.
9. "Treasury Department Circular to the Captains of the Revenue Cutters," June 4, 1791, in Syrett, ed., *Papers of Alexander Hamilton*, 8:427–33.
10. Condon, *Loyalist Dream*, 209–10.
11. Graham, *Sea Power*, 175–76.
12. MacNutt, *New Brunswick*, 96.
13. Graham, *Sea Power*, 164.
14. *Acadian Recorder* (Halifax), March 27, 1813.
15. See Sheffield's *Observations on the Commerce of the American States*.
16. George Leonard to John Sullivan, December 14, 1803, C.O.188/12.
17. "American Trade proclamations," November 24, 1784, New Brunswick Executive Council. Draft of minutes with supporting documents, MG9–A1, NAC.
18. MacNutt, *New Brunswick*, 65.
19. Carleton to Sydney, April 6, 1786, C.O.188/3, NAC; "Court Case—Summary of the Charges and Conviction, July 1786," EWP.

20. Lewis F. Delesdernier to James Avery and Stephen Jones, June 26–27, 1786, *Massachusetts Resolves*, July 8, 1786, MSA.

21. Nathaniel Atcheson, *The Question Respecting the Right of the United States to the Islands in Passamaquoddy Bay* [hereafter as *Falmouth* pamphlet], 7.

22. Condon, *Loyalist Dream*, 214–15.

23. Comely sued the official for this act. See *William Comely v. Richard Batchelor and William Comyns*, 1791, RS 42, PANB.

24. Deposition of David Owen, September 13, 1791, C.O.188/18.

25. David Owen to his brother, September 15, 1791, Glansevern Collection, National Library of Wales.

26. "Affidavit of Richard Batchelor," August 8, 1792, RS 23, PANB.

27. Customs commissioners to Gov. Carleton, August 6, 1793, RS 23, PANB.

28. Colin Campbell to Wanton and Parker, December 13, 1795, RS 23, PANB.

29. *Nathaniel Goddard v. Colin Campbell*, 1799, RS 42; Colin Campbell to Saint John Collector and Comptroller, December 13, 1795, RS 23, PANB.

30. Deposition of Colin Campbell, *King v. Wine, Brandy, and Tea*, 1796, and Affidavit of Colin Campbell, *King v. Thomas Ross et al.*, RS 42, PANB.

31. Grand Jury finding, Charlotte County General Sessions, April Term, 1797, RS 148, PANB.

32. Davis, *International Community*, 57, 98.

33. McCusker and Menard, *Economy of British North America*, 77–78; Barrow, *Trade and Empire*.

34. Ibid., 91.

35. Bushman, *King and People*, 151–53.

36. Barrow, *Trade and Empire*, 170.

37. "Report of a Committee on Customhouse Abuses," August 24, 1818, C.O.188/24.

38. "Gross Amount of Fees, 1816 & 1817," C.O.188/24.

39. Barrow, *Trade and Empire*, 81; see also Bushman, *King and People*, 149–54, for an analysis of Barrow's ideas as they applied to Massachusetts.

40. In 1810, Campbell earned £464, considerably more than his counterparts in Britain. See Atton and Holland, *King's Customs*, 2:37.

41. Sabine, *Biographical Sketches*, 401.

42. Deposition of Israel Andrews, August 2, 1821, Customs 34/6446.

43. Lorimer, *History of the Islands*, 78; Bushman, *King and People*, 152.

44. Affidavit of Colin Campbell, *King v. Thomas Ross et al.*, RS 42, PANB.

45. MacNutt, *New Brunswick*, 65, 177.

46. Barrow, *Trade and Empire*, 81.

47. MacNutt, *New Brunswick*, 138.

48. Condon, *Loyalist Dream*, 215.

49. This was the small 33-ton sloop *Union*. See C.O.217/82.

50. Arnell, "Superintendent of Trade and Fisheries," 395–409; Charles E. Leonard's accounts for the revenue schooner *Hunter*, c. 1810, C.O.217/82.

51. John Parr to Lord Sydney, July 4, 1787, Nova Scotia "A," vol. 109, 88–94, NAC, quoted in Arnell, "Superintendent of Trade and Fisheries," 399.

52. Anonymous to Lord Portland, November 8, 1798, C.O.188/9, NAC, quoted in Arnell, "Superintendent of Trade and Fisheries," 408.

53. Leonard to Edward Winslow, December 14, 1805, EWP.

54. David Owen to Mr. Thomas, October 16, 1803, C.O.188/12.

55. See the Agricultural Society of Canada pamphlet *On the Effects of Gypsum* for an enthusiastic 1791 report on plaster as a fertilizer.

56. George Leonard to John Sullivan, November 25, 1802, C.O.188/11.

57. For a description of this process, see deposition of Retire Drinkwater, *U.S. v. 75 Tons Plaster*, September Term, 1812, RG 21/MeDC.

58. See C.O.188/12 for a record of Humbert's trade with the United States.

59. *S. Humbert, claimant of Sloop Industry, apt. v. the United States*, May Term, 1812, RG 21/MCC.

60. George Leonard to Thomas Carleton, March 9, 1803, C.O.188/12.

61. Atcheson, *American Encroachments*, xv; Ward Chipman to Edward Winslow, December 14, 1805, EWP; T92/261, 82.

62. George Leonard to Thomas Carleton, March 9, 1803, C.O.188/12.

63. *Saint John Gazette*, February 7, 1807.

64. Deposition of Israel Andrews, August 2, 1821, Customs 34/6446.

65. Andrews and Campbell to Frederick DePeyster, July 24, and August 26, 1805, DePeyster Papers, NYHS.

66. Royle, *Pioneer, Patriot, and Rebel*.

67. Sprague, "Colonel John Allan," 250.

68. "Extract of a letter to Messrs. Gallatin—Steele—& Wadsworth 30th Jan'y 1800 deliv'd at the Federal City," in John Allan to Joseph Whipple, February 24, 1803, Whipple Papers, MHS.

69. "Moose Island, September, 1807," C.O.217/82, NAC.

70. Admiral George Berkeley to William Marsden, August 14, 1807, Adm. 1/497.

71. *United States v. Schooner Fame*, June Term, 1820, RG 21/MeDC.

72. George Leonard to John Sullivan, December 14, 1803, C.O.188/12.

73. *Falmouth* pamphlet, 21.

74. Leonard to Edward Winslow, December 14, 1805, EWP.

75. Leonard to Castlereagh, February 2, 1806, C.O.188/13.

76. Anthony Merry to Thomas Carleton, April 29, 1806, Barclay Collection, Maine Historical Society, Portland.

77. Gabriel Ludlow to George Leonard, June 26, 1806, C.O.188/13.

78. Leonard to William Windham, October 13, 1806, C.O.188/13.

79. Ibid.; Leonard to Merry, August 20, 1806, and Leonard to president of the council, September 27, 1806, both in EWP; MacNutt, *New Brunswick*, 141.

80. William Wanton and Robert Parker to customs commissioners, June 3, 1808, C.O.188/14.

81. MacKinnon, *This Unfriendly Soil*, 73.

Chapter 4. "The Rascals of Passamaquoddy"

1. *S. Humbert, claimant of Sloop Industry, apt. v. the United States*, May Term, 1812, RG 21/MCC [hereafter as *Humbert v. U.S.*].
2. Deposition of John Swett, *Humbert v. U.S.*
3. See "Final Record Book," RG 21/MeDC.
4. Depositions of John Kendall and Phineas Nevers, *Humbert v. U.S.*
5. Facey-Crowther, *New Brunswick Militia*, 20–21; *Saint John Gazette*, November 2, 1807.
6. Graham, *Sea Power*, chap. 8, "Wheat," 131–41; Gilpin, "American Grain Trade"; Eves, "Poor People."
7. Spivak, *Jefferson's English Crisis*, x.
8. Kilby, *Eastport and Passamaquoddy*, 144.
9. Albert Gallatin to Lewis F. Delesdernier, February 25, 1808, PAG.
10. Albert Gallatin to Delesdernier, March 5, 7, and 29, 1808, Bound Original Reports from the Secretary of the Treasury, Embargo Violations, RG 233.
11. Benjamin Weld to Albert Gallatin, March 22, 1808, quoted in White, *The Jeffersonians*, 444; Joseph Whipple to Gallatin, April 9, 1808, PAG; *New Hampshire Gazette* (Portsmouth), April 26, 1808.
12. *New Hampshire Gazette*, April 26, 1808; *Alexandria Daily Advertiser*, April 13, 1808.
13. Joseph Whipple to Gallatin, April 9, 1808, PAG.
14. James H. McCulloch to Albert Gallatin, April 23, 1808, PAG.
15. Gallatin to Delesdernier, April 26, 1808, PAG.
16. *New York Evening Post*, May 4, 1808.
17. Deposition of Henry Wade, *U.S. v. Andrew Herrington*, September Term, 1808, RG 21/MeDC.
18. *U.S. v. 8 bbls. Flour & 4 bbls. Pork*; *U.S. v. 6 bbls. Flour & 2 Bales Cotton*, both September Term, 1808, RG 21/MeDC.
19. Smith, *Wealth of Nations*, 47.
20. *U.S. v. John Clap*, December Term, 1808, RG 21/MeDC.
21. Kilby, *Eastport and Passamaquoddy*, 78, 144.
22. Deposition of William Sherman, case file, *U.S. v. Robert Webb*, September Term, 1809, RG 21/MeDC.
23. William Coney to Thomas G. Thornton, November 29, 1810, TGTP.
24. Petition of Solomon Mabee to Albert Gallatin, September 20, 1808, PAG.
25. Washington County Jail Calendar.
26. *U.S. v. Solomon Mabee*, September Term, 1808, RG 21/MeDC; Solomon Mabee pardon April 22, 1809, T967.
27. *U.S. v. Paul Johnson, Jun; U.S. v. Paul Johnson; U.S. v. Thomas Johnson*, all December Term, 1808, RG 21/MeDC.
28. *L. F. Delesdernier Jr. v. Paul Johnson*, June Term, 1810, Final Record Book, Hancock County SJC.
29. *U.S. v. Stephen Bruce*, March Term, 1809, RG 21/MeDC.
30. Stephen Bruce pardoned, June 26, 1810, T967.

31. *U.S. v. the Schooner Hiram*, December Term, 1808, RG 21/NYDC.
32. James H. McCulloch to Albert Gallatin, April 23, 1808, PAG.
33. Joseph Whipple to Albert Gallatin, April 9, 1808, M178.
34. Kilby, *Eastport and Passamaquoddy*, 145.
35. *Eastern Argus* (Portland, Maine), June 16, 1808.
36. John Cooper to Thomas G. Thornton, dated Machias, June 10, 1808, and Lewis Frederick Delesdernier to Thornton, April 2, 1808, both in TGTP.
37. Bond for William Coney of Eastport, Gentleman, Samuel Tuttle of Plantation No. 1, Gentleman, and Jabez Mowry of Eastport, Merchant, posted bond for $14,000 on August 12, 1808, TGTP.
38. Kilby, *Eastport and Passamaquoddy*, 145.
39. William Frissell to Jonathan Shortland, May 17, 1808, Adm. 1/498.
40. Whipple to Gallatin, May 22, 1808, PAG; *New York Evening Post*, May 18, 1808; *Columbian Centinel* (Boston), May 21, 1808.
41. *New York Herald*, July 27, 1808.
42. Davis, *International Community*, 71.
43. Thomas Jefferson to Albert Gallatin, May 20, 1808, PAG.
44. *Grand Jury Indictment v. William Sherman*, and *Grand Jury Indictment v. Rueben Glass et al.*, September Term, 1808, RG 21/MeDC.
45. Zimmerman, *Coastal Fort*, 21.
46. *Suffolk Gazette* (Sag Harbor, N.Y.), June 4, 1808.
47. Smith, "So Far Distant," 123–40.
48. Edward Trenchard to Secretary of the Navy Robert Smith, August 9, 1808, M148.
49. D. M. Erskine to James Madison, September 11, 1808, M50.
50. Thomas Jefferson to Albert Gallatin, May 20, 1808, PAG; *Suffolk Gazette*, June 4, 1808; *Mercantile Advertiser* (New York), June 28 and 29, 1808.
51. *Alexandria Gazette*, July 12, 1808.
52. Kilby, *Eastport and Passamaquoddy*, 151; *New England Palladium* (Boston), February 28, 1809; *Commonwealth v. John Manmel*, June Term, 1809, Hancock County SJC.
53. *United States v. the Brig Isabella aka Henrietta*, December Term, 1808, RG 21/NYDC.
54. Isaac Bell to L. F. Delesdernier, May 23, 1808, Isaac Bell Papers, Rare Books and Manuscripts Library, Columbia University. Bell himself was a Loyalist who had lived at Saint John before returning to New York.
55. Delesdernier to Gallatin, June 8, 1808, and Gallatin to Delesdernier, June 27, 1808, both in PAG; Lt. Edward Trenchard to Secretary of the Navy Robert Smith, July 12, 1808, M148.
56. *Eastern Argus* (Portland, Maine), June 16, 1808.
57. Kilby, *Eastport and Passamaquoddy*, 148–49.
58. *Portland Gazette*, June 20, 1808.
59. *New Brunswick Royal Gazette*, August 15, 1808.
60. Robert Pagan & Co. to John Millar & Co., May 20, 1808, C.O.217/83.

61. Ward Chipman to Mr. G. Gallagher, February 25, 1808, H. T. Hazen Collection, New Brunswick Museum, Saint John.

62. For flour prices in the West Indies in 1808, see Spivak, *Jefferson's English Crisis*, 167–69, and Eves, "Poor People."

63. *New Brunswick Royal Gazette*, May 30, 1808.

64. Edward Winslow to Col. E. G. Lutwyche, July 30, 1808, EWP.

65. William Knox to Winslow, May 4, 1808, EWP.

66. George Prevost to J. Howes, customs collector of the Shelburne District, June 24, 1808, RG 1/111, NSARM; Graham, *Sea Power*, 199–200.

67. Lorimer, *History of the Islands*, 78.

68. *Columbian Centinel*, May 28, 1808; Jonathan Shortland to William Frissell, n.d. (July 1808), Adm. 1/498.

69. Shortland to Sir John B. Warren, July 14, 1808, and Shortland to William Frissell, n.d. (July 1808), Adm. 1/498.

70. Chaplin, *Bucknam-Buckman Genealogy*, 59–60.

71. Zimmerman, *Coastal Fort*, 18–19.

72. Richard Hasluck to Lieutenant Governor Hunter, October 12, 1808, RS 23, PANB.

73. George Prevost to Major General Hunter, May 30, 1808, RG 1/138, NSARM.

74. *United States v. Richard Hasluck*, December Term, 1808, RG 21/MeDC.

75. McKee, *A Gentlemanly and an Honorable Profession*, 454.

76. Edward Trenchard to Secretary of the Navy Robert Smith, August 9, 1808, and enclosures, M148; David Erskine to James Madison, September 11, 1808, in Manning, *Diplomatic Correspondence*, 606–7.

77. Richard Hasluck to Lieutenant Governor Hunter, October 12, 1808, RS 23, PANB.

78. Richard Hasluck to B. Ramsay, October 25, 1808, Adm. 1/498.

79. B. Ramsay to Sir John B. Warren, October 26, 1808, Adm. 1/498.

80. Zimmerman, *Coastal Fort*, 22–23.

81. *Commonwealth v. Stephen Kankey*, June Term, 1809, Criminal Files, Hancock County SJC; Washington County Jail Calendar.

82. White, *The Jeffersonians*, 448.

83. *Grand Jury Indictment v. Aaron Olmstead*, December Term, 1808, RG 21/MeDC.

84. Smith, *Wealth of Nations*, 47.

85. Kilby, *Eastport and Passamaquoddy*, 151.

86. Smith, "Murder on Isle au Haut," 17–40.

87. Ibid., 32.

88. Sewall, *Wiscasset Point*, 11–14.

89. Kilby, *Eastport and Passamaquoddy*, 78.

90. *Gazette of Maine* (Buckstown), November 12, 1808.

91. Lewis F. Delesdernier to Silas Lee, June 25, 1810; William Coney to Lee, June 21, 1810, both in case file, *U.S. v. John Kinsley*, December Term, 1809, RG 21/MeDC.

92. David Owen to Jonathan Odell, April 13, 1809, RS 23, PANB.

93. *New Brunswick Royal Gazette*, June 10, 1809.

Chapter 5. "The Pursuit of Ignominious Gain"

1. For St. Mary's, see Ward, "Commerce of East Florida." For Heligoland, see Williams, *British Commercial Policy*, 357–58.
2. Lemuel Trescott to Henry Dearborn, August 21, 1811, *United States v. 110 Tons Plaster Paris*, May Term, 1813, RG 21/MeDC.
3. Report of the Commissioners of a Special Revenue Inquiry, T92/261, 81.
4. Madison to Congress, *House Journal*, 12th Cong., 1st sess., November 5, 1811.
5. Stagg, *Mr. Madison's War*, 25–29, 31; Appleby, *Inheriting the Revolution*, 255–56.
6. Heaton, "Non-Importation, 1806–1812," 193.
7. Heckscher, *Continental System*, 137–38.
8. Graham, *Sea Power*, 199–201.
9. Ibid., 210.
10. William Knox to Edward Winslow, May 4, 1810, and Winslow to George Herrick, late September 1810, EWP.
11. Report of the Commissioners of a Special Revenue Inquiry, T92/261, 83.
12. Graham, "Gypsum Trade," 214.
13. Hall, "Account Book, Schooner *Amphibious*."
14. *Eastern Argus* (Portland, Maine), December 6, 1810, December 12, 1811.
15. George Leonard to Thomas Carleton, March 9, 1803, C.O.188/12; William Gordon to Nathaniel Atcheson, December 27, 1810, MG9–A2, Lieutenant Governor of New Brunswick fonds, NAC.
16. *Eastern Argus*, August 29, 1811.
17. Ibid.; Treasury Department circular, October 7, 1811, in Stagg, ed., *Papers of James Madison*, 3:476–77.
18. "Evasions of the Non-Importation Act," *American State Papers: Commerce and Navigation*, 1:873–74.
19. Fergusson, ed., *Diary of Simeon Perkins, 1804–1812*, xiv.
20. Entries May 26, 1811, and June 22, 1812, New Brunswick Executive Council. Draft of minutes with supporting documents, MG 9–A1, NAC.
21. "Flour Seized by Customs," RG 8–IV/163.14, NAC.
22. C.O.221/32 and C.O.193/2.
23. David Owen to Lt. Gov. George S. Smyth, July 3, 1821, "New Brunswick 'A,'" vol. 27, NAC.
24. *Friends Adventure*, RG 8–IV/158, NAC.
25. See petitions of Jabez Harrison to Congress, November 23, 1811, and David Smith Jr., December 17, 1811, HR 12A-F23, RG 233.
26. Colles gave an account of his earlier life in a sworn deposition in *U.S. v. Schooner Polly*, May Term, 1814, RG 21/MeDC.
27. Unknown to James Colles, March 11, 1811, Colles Papers, NYPL.
28. Unknown [Hugh K. Toler] to James Colles, June 30, 1812, Colles Papers, NYPL.
29. *Boston Repertory*, June 5, 1812.
30. George Ulmer to Henry Dearborn, March 3, 1813, M221.

31. "Items of Seizures Not Settled at the Treasury Dep't Oct. 1, 1814, Taken from Collector Trescott's Schedule March 2, 1815, at Wiscasset," TGTP.

32. *U.S. v. Sloop Marietta*, March Term, 1812, RG 21/MeDC.

33. Lemuel Trescott to Henry Dearborn, August 21, 1811, *United States v. 110 Tons Plaster Paris*, May Term, 1813, RG 21/MCC.

34. Henry Dearborn to Albert Gallatin, August 31, 1811, PAG.

35. Deposition of Nathaniel Kennard, *United States v. the Sloop Eliza*, March Term, 1812, RG 21/MeDC.

36. Anonymous to James Colles, June 30, 1812, Colles Papers, NYPL.

37. King, *Coast Guard under Sail*, 41–43.

38. Joseph Whipple to Albert Gallatin, July 2, 1812, PAG.

39. Deposition of Nathaniel Kennard, *U.S. v. Sloop Eliza,* March Term, 1812, RG 21/MeDC.

40. "Why Are Such Things?" *Portsmouth Oracle* (Portsmouth, N.H.), November 21, 1812.

41. Wells, "U.S. Revenue Cutters," 226.

42. The author stated: "It would be improper of me to recommend a man to support the laws that I knew he himself had violated, but this will not exactly apply to Capt. Morton; [but] it is true that I think he was concerned in the illegal importation of some wine into this district." Joseph Farley to Lemuel Trescott, September 27, 1811, in Farley, "U.S. Customs House," MeHS.

43. Farley to Secretary of the Treasury Albert Gallatin, November 7, 1811, in Farley, "U.S. Customs House," MeHS.

44. See the crew list in *Commodore Barry*, RG 8-IV/80, NAC.

45. George Leonard to Castlereagh, September 12, 1807, C.O.188/13; Arnell, "Superintendent of Trade and Fisheries," 395–409; Charles E. Leonard's accounts for the revenue schooner *Hunter*, c. 1810, C.O.217/82.

46. The *Encouragement*, RG 8-IV/159, NAC.

47. Arnell, "Samuel Cunard," 337.

48. T92/261, "Report of the Commissioners of a Special Revenue Inquiry," 82.

49. Ibid., 4.

50. Lieutenant Governor Hunter to HM's customs commissioners, December 24, 1816, RS 23, PANB.

51. T92/261, "Report of the Commissioners of a Special Revenue Inquiry," 83.

52. George Leonard to William Windham, October 13, 1806, C.O.188/13; Leonard to Edward Winslow, December 14, 1805, EWP.

53. Atton and Holland, *King's Customs*, 37; "Report of Customs Receipts, Duties v. Seizures at Saint Andrews, NB, 1808–1817," Customs 34/6503.

54. Petty Vaughan to Benjamin Vaughan, September 30, 1812, Vaughan Family Papers, MHS.

55. Sabine, *Biographical Sketches*, 401.

56. Graham, *Sea Power*, 160.

57. See *The Question Respecting the Right of the United States of America to the Islands in Passamaquoddy Bay*, 24; *Gazette of Maine* (Buckstown), July 25, 1805.

58. William Frissell to Jonathan Shortland, May 17, 1808, Adm. 1/498.

59. Martin Hunter to Rear Admiral Sir Herbert Sawyer, July 9, 1811, RS 13, PANB; July 10, 1811, entry, Admiral Sir Herbert Sawyer Order and Letter Books, NYPL.

60. The *Boyne*, RG 8–IV/159.2, and the *Sally*, RG 8–IV/159.13, NAC.

61. Gwyn, *Frigates and Foremasts*, 117.

62. John Burgin to Capt. George Hills, July 5, 1809, Hills to Admiral Sir John B. Warren, August 11, 1809, and Warren to William Pole, August 18, 1809, all in Adm. 1/499; Pullen, "Attempted Mutiny," 309–18.

63. *New Brunswick Royal Gazette*, November 7, 21, and 28, 1808; Lawrence, *Judges of New Brunswick*, 106–9.

64. *The King v. Jonathan Watson*, Charlotte County Circuit, August 22, 1811, H. T. Hazen Collection, New Brunswick Museum, Saint John.

65. Provincial Secretary S. H. George to Elkanah Morton, July 16, 1810, and George to Morton, February 25, 1811, both in RG 1/140, NSARM.

66. *New Brunswick Royal Gazette*, February 10, 1812.

67. *New Brunswick Royal Gazette*, August 10, 1812; *Eastport Sentinel* (Eastport, Maine), May 15, 1819.

68. Henry Sewall diary, December 10, 1809. See also Lewis F. Delesdernier to Silas Lee, June 25, 1810, *U.S. v. John Kinsley*, December Term, 1810, RG 21/MeDC.

69. *Eastern Argus* (Portland, Maine), November 1, 1810.

70. Examination of Dennis O'Neal et al., June Term, 1812, Criminal Case Files, Hancock County SJC.

71. *Commonwealth v. William Priest* and *Commonwealth v. John Hutchins*, both June Term, 1811, Hancock County SJC.

72. *Eagle* (Castine, Maine), January 12, 1811

73. *Gazette of Maine*, March 23, 1811.

74. Lorimer, *History of the Islands*, 17–18

75. *Commonwealth v. Peter Berry and Frederick Gray*, June Term 1811, Hancock County SJC, MeSA; Hearn, *Legal Executions*, 194.

76. *Boston Patriot*, May 2 and May 6, 1812.

77. "Recollections of an Old Resident," *Eastport Sentinel*, February 23, 1859; *New Brunswick Royal Gazette*, June 27, 1812; petitions of John and Simeon Perkins, John Barss, and Robert Cummings, RS 24, PANB.

Chapter 6. "Ulmer Was a Rascal"

1. Deposition of William Coney, *U.S. v. the Schooner Polly*, May Term, 1814, RG 21/MeDC.
2. George Ulmer to William King, February 27, 1813, WKP.
3. Deposition of James Colles, *U.S. v. the Schooner Polly*, May Term, 1814, RG 21/MeDC.
4. William Coney to Thomas G. Thornton, April 10, 1813, and Lemuel Trescott to Thornton, April 5, 1813, TGTP.
5. Hugh K. Toler to Thornton, February 15, 1814, TGTP.
6. Taylor, "Centers and Peripheries," 4.
7. 3/6 [H. K. Toler] to James Colles, July 25, 1812, Colles Papers, NYPL.

8. *U.S. v. the Polly*, May Term, 1814, RG 21/MeDC; 3/6 [H. K. Toler] to James Colles, July 24 and 25, 1812, Colles Papers, NYPL; House, *Claim of C. P. Van Ness*, 18.

9. Mathias, "Risk, Credit, and Kinship," 15–35.

10. George Ulmer to Secretary of War John Armstrong, March 29, 1813, M221.

11. Sherman Leland to William King, Eastport, September 17, 1812, WKP.

12. *Boston Repertory*, August 11, 1812; *Boston Patriot*, January 4, 1815.

13. G. Nicolls to Lieutenant General Mann, n.d. (c. 1813), W.O. 55/860; Temperley, *Lieutenant Colonel Joseph Gubbins*, 58.

14. Aaron Rogers to William King, September 13, 1812, WKP.

15. "Proclamation of Major General George Stracey Smyth," *New Brunswick Royal Gazette*, November 9, 1812; H. H. Cogswell to Halifax collector of customs, May 25, 1812, and S. H. George to all Nova Scotia magistrates, July 2, 1812, both in RG 1/140, NSARM.

16. H. H. Cogswell to the Collector and Comptroller of Shelburn, NS, November 11, 1812, RG 1/140, NSARM; Henry Wright to Lieutenant Governor Sherbrooke, October 23, 1812, Colin Campbell Letterbook, 1805–1823, MG 1/2650, NSARM.

17. Ethel Olmstead to Jonathan and Michael Tobin, April 13, 1813, *Richmond*, RG 8-IV/95.1, NAC.

18. Sherman Leland to William King, August 22, 1812, WKP.

19. The *Arab*, RG 8-IV/77.8, NAC.

20. George Ulmer to John Armstrong, March 29, 1813, M221.

21. Ulmer to William King, February 12, 1813, WKP.

22. Ulmer to King, December 27, 1812, WKP; Taylor, "Centers and Peripheries," 6–7; Zimmerman, *Coastal Fort*, 30–34; Kilby, *Eastport and Passamaquoddy*, 161–62; Ulmer to Secretary of War John Armstrong, March 29, 1813, M221.

23. *Commonwealth v. John Campbell*, June Term, 1813, Hancock County SJC, MeSA.

24. Zimmerman, *Coastal Fort*, 34.

25. George Ulmer to Henry Dearborn, March 3, 1813, M221, and "Smuggling and Bonding," *Boston Patriot*, December 1, 1813.

26. House, *Claim of C. P. Van Ness*, 10–11.

27. For an example, see petition of Charles Bird, May Term, 1813, RG 21/MeDC.

28. David Sewall to Thomas G. Thornton, March 9, 1814, TGTP.

29. George Ulmer to William King, March 3, 1813, WKP.

30. *U.S. v. Robert Nowlin*, May Term, 1813, RG 21/MeDC.

31. Deposition of George Manser, *United States v. William Hume et al.*, December Term, 1814, RG 21/MeDC.

32. J. Maule to George Ulmer, March 1, 1813, M221.

33. Zimmerman, *Coastal Fort*, 34.

34. William Stern to William King, July 31, 1813, WKP; *Columbian Centinel* (Boston), July 24, 1813.

35. Capt. Sherman Leland to Col. J. D. Learned, July 10, 1813, *Ulmer v. Leland*, June Term, 1818, Hancock County SJC; *Columbian Centinel*, July 24, 1813.

36. Taylor, "Centers and Peripheries," 8; deposition of Frederick Crone, *Leland v. Ulmer*, June Term, 1821, Hancock County SJC, MeSA.

37. Sherman Leland to J. D. Learned, July 10, 1813, *Ulmer v. Leland*; Taylor, "Centers and Peripheries," 8.

38. Hickey, *Forgotten Conflict*, 169; Banks, *Maine Becomes a State*, 59; Swedish Vice-Consular Papers, Border Historical Society, Eastport, Maine.

39. "Petition to Capt. Hardy and Lt. Col. Pilkington from Spanish and Swedish Owners of Property on Moose Island," n.d. (1814), RG 8-IV/129.2, NAC.

40. Deposition of Constantino Llufrio, *Brig Betsey and Cargo*, February Term, 1816, RG 21/MaDC.

41. Deposition of Valentine Barnard, *Brig Betsey and Cargo*, February Term, 1816, RG 21/MaDC.

42. "Petition to Capt. Hardy and Lt. Col. Pilkington from Spanish and Swedish Owners of Property on Moose Island," n.d. (1814), RG 8-IV/129.2, NAC.

43. The *Rebecca*, RG 8-IV/94, NAC.

44. License from Lt. Gov. George S. Smyth to James Congdon, 1813, M179.

45. Hickey, "American Trade Restrictions," 529.

46. The *Joanna*, RG 8-IV/88, NAC.

47. Snider, *Under the Red Jack*, 63.

48. Crawford, "The Navy's Campaign," 165–72; Kert, *Prize and Prejudice*, 24–33.

49. The *Lucy*, RG 8-IV/89, NAC.

50. Garittee, *Republic's Private Navy*, 113.

51. *Boston Repertory*, November 24, 1813; deposition of Salathial Nickerson, *U.S. v. Sloop Venture & Cargo*, June Term, 1814; Lemuel Trescott to William Pitt Preble, May 24, 1814, and petition of Sherman Leland, both June Term, 1814, all RG 21/MeDC.

52. Deposition of Charles Beeman, *U.S. v. Sloop Venture & Cargo*, June Term, 1814, RG 21/MeDC.

53. Leland, *An Oration*, 10.

54. "Marcellus" to Armstrong, n.d., received March 1814, M222.

55. Zimmerman, *Coastal Fort*, 44–46.

56. Captain Thomas Masterman Hardy's Memorandum, July 17, 1814, *Samuel Leach v. Chebacco Boat S. of Belfast*, October Term, 1814, RG 21/MeDC.

57. Samuel Tuttle and Jabez Mowry to Thomas G. Thornton, May 30, 1816, TGTP; "'Correct' Account of the Capture of Eastport," *Boston Patriot*, August 3, 1814.

58. *Boston Patriot*, April 15, 1815; Ichabod R. Chadbourne to Cyrus King, November 25, 1815, Cyrus King Papers, Manuscripts and Archival Collections, Columbia University, New York.

59. George Smith to Thomas G. Thornton, August 29, 1815, Cutts-Thornton Papers.

60. McGregor, *History of Washington Lodge*, 31.

61. "Petition of Merchants and Other Inhabitants of St. John," April 14, 1817, New Brunswick Executive Council. Draft of Minutes with Supporting Documents, MG 9-A1, NAC.

62. "Case on the Part of the Prosecution, 49 Sides of Leather," Customs 34/6447; George S. Smyth to Earl Dalhousie, September 24, 1817, RS 558, PANB.

63. Henry Wright to customs commissioners, June 15, 1817, Customs 34/6503.

64. Henry Wright to HM's customs commissioners, June 14, 1817, Customs 34/6447.

65. Sabine, *Biographical Sketches*, 324.
66. MacNutt, *New Brunswick*, 177.

Chapter 7. "Actual and Unqualified Rebellion"

1. Stephen Humbert to Smyth, August 29, 1820, RS 24, PANB; *Boston Gazette*, August 18, 1820.
2. Sager and Panting, *Maritime Capital*, 49–50; Acheson, "Great Merchants," 3–27.
3. Sabattis to Chapman, August 31, 1809, vol. 4, Raymond Collection, NAC, quoted in W. S. MacNutt, *New Brunswick*, 175; *New Brunswick Royal Gazette*, May 16, 1820.
4. The term *plaster war* is my own, but see MacNutt, *New Brunswick*, 175, for use of the word *war* to describe the struggle to control the plaster trade; see also *Eastport Sentinel*, July 29, 1820, for "Declaration of War," describing the conflict.
5. For crowd protest in the Atlantic Provinces, see Stanley, "Caraquet Riots"; See, "Orange Order"; Little, "Collective Action."
6. Acheson, "Great Merchants"; Sager and Panting, *Maritime Capital*, 22. Sager and Panting found that colonial merchants sought to make profits by controlling markets rather than engaging in production processes; they also found that many families attempted to live outside of the increasingly capitalist economy.
7. Bitterman, "Hierarchy of the Soil," 242.
8. Atcheson, *American Encroachments*, xv; Ward Chipman to Edward Winslow, December 14, 1805, EWP; T92/261, "Report of the Commissioners of a Special Revenue Inquiry," 82.
9. Sabattis to Ward Chipman, August 31, 1809, Raymond Collection, NAC, quoted in MacNutt, *New Brunswick*, 173.
10. MacNutt, *New Brunswick*, 173–74.
11. Graham, "Gypsum Trade," 210.
12. John Wentworth to Edward Winslow, June 10, 1803, EWP.
13. Graham, "Gypsum Trade," 220.
14. "Petition of Charlotte County Merchants Concerning the Plaster Trade," April 15, 1816, C.O.188/22; "Petition of Hants County Plastermen, February, 1818," RG 5/119, NSARM.
15. *New Brunswick Courier* (Saint John), June 7, 1817.
16. Vessels seized by HM's sloop of war *Wye*, June 14 to August 3, 1817, Adm. 1/510; Captain J. Harper to Admiral Sir David Milne, June 17, 1818, reproduced in Manning, *Diplomatic Correspondence*, 860–61.
17. John Robinson to William Odell, January 21, 1818, RS7, PANB.
18. William Dawson to Harris William Hailes, May 18, 1817, C.O.188/21.
19. Humbert, *Rise and Progress of Methodism*; S. Humbert, claimant of Sloop Industry, apt. v. the United States, May Term, 1812, RG 21/MCC.
20. Stephen Humbert to Thomas Wetmore, May 13, 1820, John Kerr to Thomas Wetmore, May 19, 1820, and Thomas Wetmore to Stephen Humbert, May 23, 1820, all in RS 24, PANB; *Star* (Saint John, NB), June 20, 1820.
21. Stephen Humbert to Thomas Wetmore, May 26, 1820; Stephen Humbert to unknown, May 26, 1820, RS 24, PANB.
22. See "Peter McArthur's Protest," dated May 23, 1820, C.O.188/26, NAC. This version

of events is drastically different from Humbert's; see Humbert to Wetmore, May 26, 1820, RS 24, PANB.

23. Humbert to Wetmore, May 26, 1820, RS 24, PANB; *New Brunswick Royal Gazette*, May 30, 1820.

24. Henry Wright to Thomas Wetmore, May 19, 1820; Humbert to Wetmore, July 21, 1820; Humbert to Smyth, July 27, 1820, RS 24, PANB; *Nova Scotia Royal Gazette* (Halifax), June 28, 1820, and July 26, 1820; *Eastport Sentinel*, July 29, 1820.

25. Humbert to Smyth, August 15 and August 17, 1820; Humbert to Wetmore, August 18, 1820, RS 24, PANB.

26. Humbert to Wetmore, August 18, 1820; Humbert to Smyth, August 29, 1820, RS 24, PANB.

27. See Sager and Panting, *Maritime Capital*, 80, for an analysis of schooner operator-owners.

28. Acheson, "New Brunswick Agriculture," 8–9; Bushman, "Markets and Composite Farms."

29. Thomas Jeffery to customs commissioners, November 22, 1820, Customs 34/6597.

30. *New Brunswick Royal Gazette*, May 16, 1820.

31. Rawlyk, *Canada Fire*, 5; see also Marini, *Radical Sects*, 25–27, 40–43; Sellers, *Market Revolution*, 15.

32. Gwyn, *Excessive Expectations*, 67–73.

33. Humbert to Wetmore, May 26, 1820, Humbert to Richard Armstrong, n.d. [May 1820], Humbert to Wetmore, August 18, 1820, Wetmore to Henry Wright, May 30, 1820, Armstrong to Wright, June 9, 1820, Wright to Wetmore, May 19, 1820, all in RS 24, PANB.

34. Atton and Holland, *King's Customs*, 93.

35. MacNutt, *New Brunswick*, 177.

36. David Owen to Bathurst, November 24, 1817, and John Coffin to Bathurst, November 24, 1817, both in C.O.188/23; "Report of a Committee on Customhouse Abuses," August 24, 1818, C.O.188/24.

37. "Halifax and Outports Receipts of Duties, 1816–1819," Customs 34/6597.

38. "Report of Committee on the Plaster Trade," March 25, 1820, Customs 34/6597.

39. William Pitt Preble to John Holmes, January 21, 1818, John Holmes Papers, MeHS.

40. Jonathan Bartlett to William King, October 2, 1820, WKP.

41. "To Stephen Thacher, Esq. No. 1" and "To Stephen Thacher, No. 2," April 29 and May 13, 1820, and "Celebration at the 'New and Interesting' Town of Alexandria," July 29, 1820, all in *Eastport Sentinel*.

42. *Eastport Sentinel*, April 29, May 13, July 29, 1820; *Nova Scotia Royal Gazette*, July 26, 1820.

43. Bohstedt, "Moral Economy," 274.

44. Stephen Thacher to Humbert, June 26, 1820, RS 24, PANB; "Selections from the Files of the House of Assembly," RG 5/120, NSARM.

45. Humbert to Smyth, October 16, 1820, and Humbert to Wetmore, October 18, 1820, R24, PANB; *Eastport Sentinel*, September 16, 1820.

46. Shand, *Historic Hants County*, 88–89; MacNutt, *New Brunswick*, 175.

47. Lt. Gov. James Kempt to Lt. Gov. George Stracey Smyth, February 27, 1821, RG 1/113, NSARM.

48. Acheson, "Great Merchants," 176. See also Cuthbertson, *Johnny Bluenose at the Polls*, 113–18.

Conclusion: The Memory of Smuggling

1. Kilby, *Eastport and Passamaquoddy*, 243–44.
2. Ibid., 161.
3. Ibid., 440–43.
4. Ibid., 78.
5. Swedish Vice-Consular Papers; *Portland Gazette*, October 6, 1814.
6. *New Brunswick Courier* (Saint John), November 27, 1830.
7. Lemuel Trescott probate, Washington County Courthouse, Machias, Maine.
8. "Battle Royal," *Eastport Sentinel*, September 14, 1822.
9. Atton and Holland, *King's Customs*, 117.
10. *Eastport Sentinel*, August 7, 1824.
11. Jouett to HM's customs commissioners, October 28, 1824, Customs 34/6504.
12. Atton and Holland, *King's Customs*, 147.
13. Kilby, *Eastport and Passamaquoddy*, 476–82.
14. *New Brunswick Courier*, December 18, 1830; Knowlton, *Annals of Calais*, 115–16; Davis, *International Community*, 143; Atton and Holland, *King's Customs*, 340.
15. See "Return of Persons who have come from the United States of America to Reside and Settle in the Province of New Brunswick," dated January 16, 1917, RS 7, PANB.
16. Taylor, *Liberty Men and Great Proprietors*, 192–97, 278.
17. Hobsbawm, *Bandits*, 19–21, 42–43, 50.
18. *Eastport Sentinel*, February 9, 1831.
19. Manning, *Diplomatic Correspondence*, 254–57.
20. Gitlin, "On the Boundaries of Empire," 72.
21. Appleby, *Inheriting the Revolution*, 242.
22. *New Brunswick Courier*, August 29, 1818.
23. Jafee, *People of the Wachusett*, 240–41.
24. *New Brunswick Courier*, August 11, 1821.
25. "Report of Fisheries, Lighthouses, &c.," *Journal of the New Brunswick House of Assembly*, 1841, cxxxvii.
26. Kilby, *Eastport and Passamaquoddy*, 149.
27. Sabine, *Biographical Sketches*, 13.
28. Barkley, "The Loyalist Tradition," 3–4.
29. Patrick Clinch to John Saunders, September 4, 1835, EWP.
30. Koter, "Frontier Peoples," 30.
31. Grand Jury findings, "General Sessions Proceedings Charlotte County," April Term, 1797, RS 148, PANB; Newcomb, *Genealogical Memoir of the Newcomb Family*, 103.
32. *New Brunswick Courier*, April 30, 1831.
33. Acheson, *Saint John*, 57–60.

34. Sabine, *Report on the Principal Fisheries*, 80–81.
35. Spray, "Reception of the Irish," 9–26; *Eastport Sentinel*, September 2, 1820.
36. *New Brunswick Courier*, January 1, 1831.
37. Davis, *International Community*, 304.
38. See, *Riots in New Brunswick*, 17–18.

BIBLIOGRAPHY

Primary Sources

Barclay, Thomas. Barclay Collection. Maine Historical Society, Portland.
Bell, Isaac. Letterbook. Rare Books and Manuscripts Library, Manuscripts and Archival Collections, Columbia University, New York.
Campbell, Colin. Letterbook, 1805–1823. MG1/2650, Nova Scotia Archives and Records Management, Halifax.
Colles, James. Papers. Manuscripts and Archives Division, New York Public Library, Astor, Lenox and Tilden Foundations.
Cutts-Thornton Family Papers. Maine Historical Society, Portland.
Depeyster, Abraham. Family Papers. New York Historical Society.
Farley, Joseph. U.S. Customs House: Waldoboro, Maine, Letterbook, 1803–1816. Maine Historical Society, Portland.
Hall, Thomas, master. Account Book, Schooner *Amphibious*. Manuscripts Collection, G. W. Blunt Library, Mystic Seaport Museum, Mystic, Conn.
Hazen, H. T. Hazen Collection. New Brunswick Museum, Saint John.
Holmes, John. Papers. Manuscripts at Maine Historical Society, Portland.
King, Cyrus. Papers. Manuscripts and Archival Collections, Columbia University, New York.
King, William. Papers. Maine Historical Society, Portland.
Leavitt, Joseph. Diary. Bangor Public Library.
Lincoln, Benjamin. Papers. Microfilm. Boston: Massachusetts Historical Society, 1967.
Morse, Beulah H. Early Records of Eastport, Maine. Maine Historical Society, Portland.
Owen, William F. W. Register-book: Deeds, Leases, etc. for the Estate of Campo-bello. Maine State Library, Augusta.
Sawyer, Admiral Sir Herbert. Order and Letter Books. Manuscripts and Archives Division, New York Public Library, Astor, Lenox and Tilden Foundations.
Sewall, Henry. Diary. Massachusetts Historical Society, Boston.
Swedish Vice-Consular Papers. Border Historical Society, Eastport, Maine.
Thornton, Thomas G. Papers. Maine Historical Society, Portland.
Vaughan Family Papers. Massachusetts Historical Society, Boston.
Winslow, Edward. Papers. Special Collections, Harriet Irving Library, University of New Brunswick, Fredericton.
Wolcott, Oliver, Jr. Papers. Connecticut Historical Society, Hartford.

Bibliography

Documents

Abstract of Charlotte County Petitions, 1765–1842. New Brunswick Museum, Saint John.
Glansevern Collection, David Owen Correspondence. National Library of Wales, Aberystwyth.
Hancock and Washington County Supreme Judicial Court Records. Maine State Archives, Augusta.
Massachusetts Resolves. Supporting Documents. Massachusetts State Archives, Boston.
National Archives and Records Administration. RG 21, *Records of the District Courts of the United States*.
    Records of the U.S. District Court, Maine.
    Records of the U.S. District Court, Massachusetts.
    Records of the U.S. Circuit Court, Massachusetts.
    Records of the U.S. District Court, Southern District of New York.
———. RG 45, *Naval Records Collection of the Office of Naval Records and Library*. M-148: "Letters Received by the Secretary of the Navy from Officers Below the Rank of Commander, 1802–84."
———. RG 56, *General Records of the Department of the Treasury*. M178: "Correspondence of the Secretary of the Treasury with Collectors of Customs, 1789–1833."
———. RG 59, *General Records of the Department of State*. M50: "Notes From the British Legation in the United States to the Department of State, 1791–1906."
———. RG 59, *General Records of the Department of State*. M179: "Miscellaneous Letters of the Department of State, 1789–1906."
———. RG 59, *General Records of the Department of State*. M558, "U.S. Department of State: War of 1812 Papers."
———. RG 77, *Records of the Office of the Chief of Engineers*. M417: "Buell Collection of Historical Documents Relating to the Corps of Engineers, 1801–1819."
———. RG 94, *Records of the Adjutant General's Office*. T967: "Copies of Presidential Pardons and Remissions, 1794–1893."
———. RG 107, *Records of the Office of the Secretary of War*. M221: "Letters Received by the Secretary of War, Registered Series, 1801–1870."
———. RG 107, *Records of the Office of the Secretary of War*. M222: "Letters Received by the Secretary of War, Unregistered Series, 1789–1861."
———. RG 233: *Records of the United States House of Representatives*. "Records of the Ways and Means Committee."
———. RG 233: *Records of the United States House of Representatives*. "Bound Original Reports from the Secretary of the Treasury, Embargo Violations."
———. RG 360, *Records of the Continental and Confederation Congresses and the Constitutional Convention*. M247: "Papers of Continental Congress, 1774–1789."
National Archives, Kew, United Kingdom
    Adm. 1: Admiralty & Secretariat: Papers.
    C.O.188: New Brunswick, Original Correspondence.
    C.O.193: New Brunswick, Miscellaneous, Shipping Returns.

C.O.217: Nova Scotia, Original Correspondence.
C.O.221: Nova Scotia Shipping Returns.
Customs 34: Customs, Plantations Papers.
T92/261: Report of the Commissioners of a Special Revenue Inquiry during the Years 1812, 1813, and 1814. National Archives, Kew.
W.O.55: Ordnance Office Miscellanea.
National Archives of Canada, Ottawa
  MG9–A2, New Brunswick Executive Council. Draft of Minutes with Supporting Documents.
  MG9–A2: Lieutenant-Governor of New Brunswick fonds.
  RG8–IV: Vice Admiralty Court fonds: Nova Scotia.
New Brunswick. *Journal of the House of Assembly*.
Northeast Boundary Papers, 1796–99. Massachusetts Historical Society, Boston.
Nova Scotia Archives and Records Management, Halifax, Nova Scotia.
  RG 1: Provincial Secretary's letter books, 1803–1870.
  RG 5: "Selections from the Files of the House of Assembly, 1758–1841: Series 'P' Assembly Petitions, 1816–1928."
Provincial Archives of New Brunswick, Fredericton.
  RS 7: Records of the Executive Council.
  RS 13: Provincial Secretary, Correspondence.
  RS 23: Customs House Records.
  RS 24: Legislative Assembly: Sessional Records.
  RS 42: Supreme Court Original Jurisdiction Case Files.
  RS 148: General Sessions Proceedings, Charlotte County.
  RS 558: Records of the Regular Military.
  RS 637: Surveyor General Records.
Washington County Circuit Court of Common Pleas Records. Maine State Archives, Augusta.
Washington County Jail Calendar. Sheriff's Office, Washington County Courthouse, Machias, Maine.
Washington County Probate Records. Probate Office, Washington County Courthouse, Machias, Maine.

Published Materials

Acheson, T. W. "The Great Merchants and Economic Development in Saint John, 1820–1850." *Acadiensis* 8 (1978): 3–27.

———. "New Boston to New Brunswick: Anonymous Loyalists in New Hampshire." *Acadiensis* 27 (1997): 3–26.

———. "New Brunswick Agriculture at the End of the Colonial Era: A Reassessment." *Acadiensis* 22 (1993): 5–26.

———. *Saint John: The Making of a Colonial Urban Community*. Toronto: University of Toronto Press, 1985.

Allen, W. B., ed. *Works of Fisher Ames: As Published by Seth Ames*. Indianapolis: Liberty Classics, 1983.

Appleby, Joyce. *Inheriting the Revolution: The First Generation of Americans*. Cambridge, Mass.: Belknap Press, 2000.

Arnell, J. C. "Samuel Cunard and the Nova Scotia Government Vessels *Earl Bathurst* and *Chebucto*," *Mariner's Mirror* 54 (1968): 337–47.

———. "The Superintendent of Trade and Fisheries for Nova Scotia and the Armed Vessels *Union* and *Hunter*, part 1: The Problem Associated with Trade and Fishing after the American Revolution." *Mariner's Mirror* 56 (1970): 395–409.

Atcheson, Nathaniel. *American Encroachments on British Rights; or, Observations on the Importance of the British North American Colonies and on the Late Treaties with the United States with Remarks on Mr. Baring's Examination; and a Defence of the Shipping Interest from the Charge of Having Attempted to Impose on Parliament, and of Factious Conduct in Their Opposition to the American Intercourse Bill*. London: J. Butterworth, 1808.

———. *The Question Respecting the Right of the United States of America to the Islands in Passamaquoddy Bay*. Saint John, New Brunswick: J. Ryan, 1807.

Atton, Henry, and Henry Hurst Holland. *The King's Customs*, vol. 2: *An Account of Maritime Revenue, Contraband Traffic, the Introduction of Free Trade, and the Abolition of the Navigation and Corn Laws, from 1801 to 1855*. London: John Murray, 1910; reprint, New York: Augustus M. Kelly, 1967.

Bailyn, Bernard. *Atlantic History: Concepts and Contours*. Cambridge: Harvard University Press, 2005.

———. *The Peopling of British North America: An Introduction*. New York: Vintage Books, 1988.

Banks, Ronald E. *Maine Becomes a State: The Movement to Separate Maine from Massachusetts, 1785–1820*. Portland: Maine Historical Society, 1973.

Barkley, Murray. "The Loyalist Tradition in New Brunswick: The Growth and Evolution of an Historical Myth, 1825–1914." *Acadiensis* 4 (1975): 3–45.

Barrow, Thomas C. *Trade and Empire: The British Customs Service in Colonial America, 1660–1775*. Cambridge: Harvard University Press, 1967.

Bell, David G. *Early Loyalist Saint John: The Origins of New Brunswick Politics, 1783–1786*. Fredericton, New Brunswick: New Ireland Press, 1983.

———, ed. *Newlight Baptist Journals of James Manning and James Innis*. Wolfville, Nova Scotia: Lancelot Press, 1984.

Bell, Hugh F. "'A Melancholy Affair': James Otis and the Pirates." *American Neptune* 31 (1971): 19–37.

Bent, G. O. "Charles Turner's Journal of His 1802 Trip to New Brunswick." *Acadiensis* 7 (1907): 128–48.

Bitterman, Rusty. "The Hierarchy of the Soil: Land and Labor in a 19th-Century Cape Breton Community." In P. A. Buckeren and David Frank, eds. *The Acadiensis Reader*. Vol. 1, *Atlantic Canada Before Confederation*. Fredericton, N.B.: Acadiensis Press, 1990.

Bohstedt, John. "The Moral Economy and the Discipline of Historical Context." *Journal of Social History* 26 (Winter 1992): 265–84.

Bolingbroke, Henry. *A Voyage to Demerary*. London: Richard Phillips, 1809.

Bourque, B. J., and R. H. Whitehead. "Trade and Alliances in the Contact Period." In Emerson Baker, ed., *American Beginnings: Exploration, Culture, and Cartography in the Land of Norumbega*. Lincoln: University of Nebraska Press, 1994.

Burrows, Edmund H. *Captain Owen of the African Survey: The Hydrographic Surveys of Admiral W. F. W. Owen on the Coast of Africa and the Great Lakes of Canada, His Fight against the African Slave Trade, His Life in Campobello Island, New Brunswick, 1774–1857*. Rotterdam: A. A. Balkema, 1979.

Bushman, Richard L. *King and People in Colonial Massachusetts*. Chapel Hill: University of North Carolina Press, 1985.

———. "Markets and Composite Farms in Early America." *William and Mary Quarterly* (3rd series) 55 (1998): 351–74.

Butler, Joyce. "Rising Like a Phoenix: Commerce in Southern Maine, 1775–1830." In Laura Fecych Sprague, ed., *Agreeable Situations: Society, Commerce, and Art in Southern Maine, 1780–1850*, 15–35. Kennebunk, Maine: Brick Store Museum, 1987.

Campbell, Patrick. *Travels in the Interior Inhabited Parts of North America in the Years 1791 and 1792*. Toronto: Champlain Society, 1937.

Carroll, Francis M. *A Good and Wise Measure: The Search for the Canadian-American Boundary, 1783–1842*. Toronto: University of Toronto Press, 2001.

Chaplin, Ann Theobold. *A Bucknam-Buckman Genealogy: Some Descendants of William Bucknam of Charlestown and Malden, and John Buckman of Boston*. Baltimore: Gateway Press, 1988.

Condon, Ann Gorman. *The Envy of the American States: The Loyalist Dream for New Brunswick*. Fredericton, New Brunswick: New Ireland Press, 1984.

Cooney, Jerry W. "'Doing Business in the Smuggling Way': Yankee Contraband in the Rio de la Plata." *American Neptune* 47 (1987): 162–68.

Cooper, James Fenimore. *Ned Myers; or, A Life before the Mast*. Philadelphia: Lea and Blanchard, 1843.

Copp, Walter Ronald. "Nova Scotian Trade during the War of 1812." *Canadian Historical Review* 18 (1937): 141–55.

Crawford, Michael J. "The Navy's Campaign against the Licensed Trade in the War of 1812." *American Neptune* 46 (1986): 165–72.

Cuthbertson, Brian. *Johnny Bluenose at the Polls: Epic Nova Scotian Election Battles, 1758–1848*. Halifax: Formac Publishing, 1994.

———. *The Old Attorney General: A Biography of Richard John Uniacke*. Halifax: Nimbus, 1980.

Davis, Harold A. *An International Community on the St. Croix (1604–1930)*. Orono: Maine Studies no. 64, University of Maine at Orono, 1950, 1974.

Demeritt, David. "Representing the 'True' St. Croix: Knowledge and Power in the Partition of the Northeast." *William and Mary Quarterly*, 3rd ser., 54 (July 1997): 515–48.

Dexter, Ralph W. "Cape Ann Visits of the Great Sea-Serpent (1639–1886)." *American Neptune* 46 (1986): 213–20.

Eckstorm, Fannie H. *Indian Place Names of the Penobscot Valley and the Maine Coast*. Orono: University of Maine Studies, 2nd ser, no. 55, 1941.

On the Effects of Gypsum or Plaster of Paris as a Manure; Chiefly Extracted from Papers and Letters on Agriculture, by the Agricultural Society in Canada. London: James Phillips, 1791 [CIHM microfiche 20749].

Errington, Jane. *The Lion, the Eagle, and Upper Canada: A Developing Colonial Ideology*. Montreal: McGill-Queen's University Press, 1987.

Eves, Jamie H. "'The Poor People Had Suddenly Become Rich': A Boom in Maine Wheat, 1793–1815." *Maine Historical Society Quarterly* 27 (1987): 114–41.

Facey-Crowther, David R. *The New Brunswick Militia, 1787–1867*. Fredericton, New Brunswick: New Ireland Press, 1990.

Faulkner, Alaric, and Gretchen Fearon Faulkner. *The French at Pentagoet, 1635–1674: An Archaeological Portrait of the Acadian Frontier*. Augusta, Maine, and Fredericton, New Brunswick: Maine Historic Preservation Commission and the New Brunswick Museum, 1987.

Fergusson, Charles Bruce, ed. *The Diary of Simeon Perkins, 1804–1812*. Toronto: Champlain Society, 1978.

Fingard, Judith. *The Anglican Design in Loyalist Nova Scotia, 1783–1816*. London: Church Historical Society, 1972.

Garitee, Jerome. *The Republic's Private Navy: The American Privateering Business as Practiced by Baltimore during the War of 1812*. Middletown, Conn.: Wesleyan University Press for Mystic Seaport, 1977.

Gilpin, W. Freeman. "The American Grain Trade to the Spanish Peninsula, 1810–1814." *American Historical Review* 28 (1922): 24–44.

Gitlin, Jay. "On the Boundaries of Empire: Connecting the West to Its Imperial Past." In *Under an Open Sky: Rethinking America's Western Past*, ed. William Cronon, 71–89. New York: W. W. Norton, 1992.

Graham, Gerald S. *Sea Power and British North America, 1783–1820: A Study in British Colonial Policy*. Cambridge: Harvard University Press, 1941.

———. "The Gypsum Trade of the Maritime Provinces: Its Relation to American Diplomacy and Agriculture in the Early Nineteenth Century." *Agricultural History* 12 (1938): 209–23.

Great Britain. Parliament, *First Report from the Committee Appointed to Enquire into the Illicit Practices Used in Defrauding the Revenue*. London, 1783.

Griffiths, Naomi. "The Golden Age: Acadian Life, 1713–1748." *Histoire Sociale/Social History* 17 (1984): 21–34.

Grahn, Lance R. *The Political Economy of Smuggling: Regional Informal Economies in Early Bourbon New Granada*. Boulder: Westview Press, 1997.

Gregory, Frances W. *Nathan Appleton: Merchant and Entrepreneur, 1779–1861*. Charlottesville: University Press of Virginia, 1975.

Gwyn, Julian. *Excessive Expectations: Maritime Commerce and the Economic Development of Nova Scotia, 1740–1870*. Montreal: McGill-Queen's University Press, 1998.

———. *Frigates and Foremasts: The North American Squadron in Nova Scotia Waters, 1745–1815*. Vancouver: University of British Columbia Press, 2003.

Hamilton, William B. *Place Names of Atlantic Canada*. Toronto: University of Toronto Press, 1996.

Harvey, D. C. "Pre-Agricola John Young, or a Compact Family in Search of Fortune." *Collections of the Nova Scotia Historical Society* 32 (1959): 125–59.
Hearn, Daniel Allen. *Legal Executions in New England: A Comprehensive Reference, 1623–1960*. Jefferson, N.C.: McFarland, 1999.
Heaton, Herbert. "Non-Importation, 1806–1812." *Journal of Economic History* 1 (1941): 178–98.
Hebb, Ross N. *The Church of England in Loyalist New Brunswick, 1783–1825*. Madison, N.J.: Fairleigh Dickenson University Press, 2004.
Heckscher, Eli Filip. *The Continental System*. Oxford: Clarendon Press, 1922.
Hersey, Frank W. "Tar and Feathers: The Adventures of Captain John Malcom." *Proceedings of the Colonial Society of Massachusetts* 34 (1941): 429–73.
Hickey, Donald. *The War of 1812: A Forgotten Conflict*. Urbana: University of Illinois Press, 1989.
———. "American Trade Restrictions during the War of 1812." *Journal of American History* 68 (December 1981): 517–38.
Hobsbawm, Eric. *Bandits*. London: Delacorte Press, 1969.
Humbert, Stephen. *The Rise and Progress of Methodism in the Province of New Brunswick, from Its Commencement until about the Year 1805*. Saint John, New Brunswick: L. W. Durant, 1836 [CIHM microfiche 57341].
Jack, David R. "Biographical Data Relating to New Brunswick Families, Especially of Loyalist Descent." Typed manuscript copy at the Saint John Free Public Library, Saint John, New Brunswick.
Jafee, David. *People of the Wachusett: Greater New England in History and Memory, 1630–1860*. Ithaca: Cornell University Press, 1999.
Johnson, Victor L. "Fair Traders and Smugglers in Philadelphia, 1754–1763." *Pennsylvania Magazine of History and Biography* 83 (1959): 125–49.
Kert, Faye Margaret. *Prize and Prejudice: Privateering and Naval Prize in Atlantic Canada in the War of 1812*. St. John's, Newfoundland: International Maritime Economic History Association, 1997.
Kilby, William Henry, ed. *Eastport and Passamaquoddy: A Collection of Historical and Biographical Sketches*. Eastport, Maine: Edward E. Shead, 1888.
———. "Benedict Arnold on the Eastern Frontier." *Bangor Historical Magazine* 1 (1886–1887): 188–90.
King, Irving H. *The Coast Guard under Sail: The U.S. Revenue Cutter Service, 1789–1865*. Annapolis: Naval Institute Press, 1989.
Knowlton, I. C. *Annals of Calais, Maine and St. Stephen, New Brunswick*. Calais, Maine: J. A. Sears, Printer, 1875.
Koter, Marek. "Frontier Peoples—Origins and Classification." In *Borderlands or Transborder Regions—Geographical, Social, and Political Problems*, ed. Marek Koter and Krystian Heffner, 28–37. Lódz, Poland: University of Lódz, "Region and Regionalism" no. 3, 1988.
Lamb, Harry Edgar. *The History of St. Croix Lodge, No. 46, Free and Accepted Masons, 1821–1931*. Calais, Maine: Advertiser Press, 1931.

Lawrence, Joseph Wilson. *The Judges of New Brunswick and Their Times*. Fredericton, New Brunswick: Acadiensis Press, 1985.

Leamon, James S. *Revolution Downeast: The War for American Independence in Maine*. Amherst: University of Massachusetts Press, 1993.

Leland, Sherman. *An Oration Pronounced at Dorchester, July 4, 1815*. Boston: Rowe and Hooper, 1815.

Linebaugh, Peter, and Marcus Rediker. *The Many-Headed Hydra: Sailors, Slaves, Commoners, and the Hidden History of the Revolutionary Atlantic*. Boston: Beacon Press, 2000.

Little, Linda. "Collective Action in Outport Newfoundland: A Case Study from the 1830s." *Labour/Le Travail* 26 (1990): 37–59.

Lorimer, J. G. *History of the Islands & Islets in the Bay of Fundy*. St. Stephen, New Brunswick: Saint Croix Courier, 1876.

Lunn, Jean. "The Illegal Fur Trade Out of New France, 1713–1760." *Canadian Historical Association Annual Report 1939*, 61–75.

MacKinnon, Neal. *This Unfriendly Soil: The Loyalist Experience in Nova Scotia, 1783–1789*. Kingston and Toronto: McGill-Queen's University Press, 1986.

———. "The Changing Attitudes of the Nova Scotia Loyalists towards the United States, 1783–1791." In *The Acadiensis Reader Volume One: Atlantic Canada before Confederation*, ed. Phillip Buckner and David Frank, 108–19. Fredericton, New Brunswick: Acadiensis Press, 1990.

McCusker, John J., and Russell R. Menard. *The Economy of British North America, 1607–1789*. Chapel Hill: University of North Carolina Press, 1991.

McGregor, James. *History of Washington Lodge No. 37, Free and Accepted Masons, Lubec, Maine*. Portland, Maine: E. W. Brown and James Neagle, 1892.

McKee, Christopher. *A Gentlemanly and an Honorable Profession: The Creation of the U.S. Naval Officer Corps, 1794–1815*. Annapolis: Naval Institute Press, 1991.

Macmillan, David S. "Christopher Scott: Smuggler, Privateer, and Financier." *Canadian Banker* 78 (1971): 23–26.

———. "The 'New Men' in Action: Scottish Mercantile and Shipping Operations in the North American Colonies, 1760–1825." In *Canadian Business History: Selected Studies, 1497–1971*, ed. David S. Macmillan, 44–103. Toronto: McClelland and Stewart, 1972.

MacNutt, W. S. *New Brunswick: A History, 1784–1867*. Toronto: Macmillan, 1963, 1984.

Manning, William R., ed. *Diplomatic Correspondence of the United States: Canadian Relations, 1784–1860*. Washington: Carnegie Endowment for International Peace, 1940.

Marini, Stephen A. *Radical Sects of Revolutionary New England*. Cambridge: Harvard University Press, 1982.

Marsden, Joshua. *The Narrative of a Mission to Nova Scotia, New Brunswick, and the Somers Islands*. Plymouth Dock, England: J. Johns, 1816 [CIHM microfiche 21227].

———. *Grace Displayed: An Interesting Narrative of the Life, Conversion, Christian Experience, Ministry and Missionary Labors of Joshua Marsden*. New York: Author, 1813 [CIHM microfiche 48054].

Mathias, Peter. "Risk, Credit, and Kinship in Early Modern Enterprise." In *The Early Mod-

ern Atlantic Community, ed. John J. McCusker and Kenneth Morgan, 15–35. Cambridge: Cambridge University Press, 2000.

Matson, Cathy. *Merchants & Empire: Trading in Colonial New York*. Baltimore: Johns Hopkins University Press, 1998.

Moore, John Bassett, ed. *Arbitration of the Title to Islands in Passamaquoddy Bay and the Bay of Fundy: Mixed Commission Under Article IV of the Treaty between Great Britain and the United States of Dec. 24, 1814*. New York: Oxford University Press, 1933.

Morley, Geoffrey. *The Smuggling War: The Government's Fight Against Smuggling in the 18th and 19th Centuries*. Stroud, Gloucestershire: Alan Sutton, 1994.

Murchie, Guy. *Saint Croix: The Sentinel River*. New York: Duell, Sloan and Pearce, 1947.

Nason, Roger Paul. "Meritorious but Distressed Individuals: The Penobscot Loyalist Association and the Settlement of the Township of St. Andrews, New Brunswick, 1783–1821." M.A. thesis, University of New Brunswick, 1982.

Newcomb, John Bearse. *Genealogical Memoir of the Newcomb Family*. Chicago: Knight & Leonard, 1874.

New Brunswick, Court of Vice-Admiralty. *The Question Respecting the Right of the United States to the Islands in Passamaquoddy Bay, by Virtue of the Treaty of 1783, Considered in the Case of the Sloop Falmouth, In the Court of Vice-Admiralty for the Province of New Brunswick in the Year 1805*. Fredericton, New Brunswick: J. Ryan, 1806 [CIHM microfiche 92469].

Nicolas, Nicholas Harris. *Dispatches and Letters of Vice Admiral Lord Viscount Nelson*. London: Henry Colburn, 1845.

Nicholls, F. F. *Honest Thieves: The Violent Heyday of English Smuggling*. London: Heinemann, 1973.

Other Merchants and Sea Captains of Old Boston. Boston: State Street Trust Company, 1919.

Philp, Roy. *The Coast Blockade: The Royal Navy's War on Smuggling in Kent & Sussex, 1817–1831*. Horsham, UK: Compton Press, 1999.

Porter, Joseph W. "Smuggling in Maine during the War of 1812." *Bangor Historical Magazine*, 3, no. 11 (May 1888): 201–3.

Prince, Carl, ed. *Microfilm Edition of the Papers of Albert Gallatin*. Philadelphia: Rhistoric, 1969.

Pullen, H. F. "The Attempted Mutiny on Board HMS *Columbine*, 1 August 1809." *Nova Scotia Historical Quarterly* 8 (1978): 309–18.

Rawlyk, George A. *The Canada Fire: Radical Evangelicalism in British North America, 1775–1812*. Montreal: McGill-Queen's University Press, 1994.

———. "The Federalist-Loyalist Alliance in New Brunswick, 1784–1815." *Humanities Association Review* 27 (1976): 142–60.

Raymond, W. O. *Winslow Papers, A.D. 1776–1826*. Saint John, New Brunswick: Sun Printing Company, 1901.

Reid, John. "An International Region of the Northeast: Rise and Decline, 1635–1762." In Stephen Hornsby, Victor A. Konrad, and James J. Herlan, eds., *The Northeastern Borderlands: Four Centuries of Interaction*. Fredericton, New Brunswick: Acadiensis Press, 1989.

"Reminiscences of a Former Resident of New Meadows, Written in 1843." In *Collections of the Penebscot Historical Society*, 46–53. Lewiston, Maine: Journal Office, 1889.

Royle, Edward C. *Pioneer, Patriot, and Rebel: Lewis DeLesDernier of Nova Scotia and Maine, 1752–1838*. Hudson Heights, Quebec: Author, 1976.

Sabine, Lorenzo. *Report on the Principal Fisheries of the American Seas*. Washington: Robert Armstrong, Printer, 1853.

———. *Biographical Sketches of Loyalists of the American Revolution*. Boston: Little, Brown, 1864.

Sager, Eric W., and Gerald E. Panting. *Maritime Capital: The Shipping Industry in Atlantic Canada, 1820–1914*. Montreal: McGill-Queen's University Press, 1990.

See, Scott W. *Riots in New Brunswick: Orange Nativists and Social Violence in the 1840s*. Toronto: University of Toronto Press, 1993; reprint, 1999.

———. "The Orange Order and Social Violence in Mid-Nineteenth Century Saint John." *Acadiensis* 13 (1983): 68–92.

Sellers, Charles. *The Market Revolution: Jacksonian America, 1815–1846*. New York: Oxford University Press, 1991.

Sewall, Rufus K. *Wiscasset Point: The Old Meeting House and Interesting Incidents Connected with Its History*. Wiscasset, Maine: Charles E. Emerson, 1883.

Shand, Gwendolyn Vaughan. *Historic Hants County*. Halifax: Pethoric Press, 1979.

Sheffield, John Lord. *Observations on the Commerce of the American States*. London: J. Debrett, 1784.

Sloan, Robert Wesley. "Loyalists in Eastern Maine during the American Revolution." Ph.D. dissertation, Michigan State University, 1971.

Smith, Adam. *An Inquiry into the Nature and Causes of the Wealth of Nations*. London: William Strahan, 1776; reprint, Chicago: Encyclopaedia Britannica, 1952.

Smith, Joshua M. "'So Far Distant from the Eyes of Authority': Jefferson's Embargo and the U.S. Navy, 1807–1809." In *New Interpretations in Naval History: Selected Papers from the Twelfth Naval History Symposium*, ed. Craig Symonds, 123–40. Annapolis: Naval Institute Press, 1998.

———. "Murder on Isle au Haut: Violence and Jefferson's Embargo in Coastal Maine, 1808–1809." *Maine History* 39 (2000): 17–40.

Snider, Charles Henry J. *Under the Red Jack: Privateers of the Maritime Provinces in the War of 1812*. London: Martin Hopkinson & Co., 1928.

Spivak, Burton. *Jefferson's English Crisis: Commerce, Embargo, and the Republican Revolution*. Charlottesville: University Press of Virginia, 1979.

Sprague, John Francis. "Colonel John Allan of American Revolutionary Fame." *Sprague's Journal of Maine History* 2, no. 5 (February 1915): 233–57.

Spray, William A. "Reception of the Irish in New Brunswick." In *New Ireland Remembered: Historical Essays on the Irish in New Brunswick*, ed. P. M. Toner, 9–26. Fredericton, New Brunswick: New Ireland Press, 1988.

Stafford, Frances. "Illegal Importations: Enforcement of the Slave Trade Laws along the Florida Coast, 1810–1828." *Florida Historical Quarterly* 46 (1967): 124–33.

Stagg, J. C. A. *Mr. Madison's War: Politics, Diplomacy, and Warfare in the Early American Republic, 1783–1830*. Princeton: Princeton University Press, 1983.

———, ed. *The Papers of James Madison: Presidential Series*. 4 vols. Charlottesville: University Press of Virginia, 1984–99.

Stanley, George F. "The Caraquet Riots of 1875." *Acadiensis* 2 (1972): 21–38.

Syrett, Harold C., ed. *The Papers of Alexander Hamilton*. New York: Columbia University Press, 1961–1979.

Taylor, Alan. *Liberty Men and Great Proprietors: The Revolutionary Settlement on the Maine Frontier, 1760–1820*. Chapel Hill: University of North Carolina Press, 1990.

———. "The Smuggling Career of William King." *Maine Historical Society Quarterly* 17 (1977): 19–38.

———. "Centers and Peripheries: Locating Maine's History." *Maine History* 39 (2000): 1–16.

Temperley, Howard, ed. *Lieutenant Colonel Joseph Gubbins: New Brunswick Journals of 1811 & 1813*. Fredericton, New Brunswick: Canada Kings Landing Corp., 1980.

Thomas, John L. *The Liberator: William Lloyd Garrison*. Boston: Little, Brown, 1963.

Thompson, E. P. "The Moral Economy of the English Crowd in the Eighteenth Century." *Past and Present* 50 (1971): 76–136.

Tyler, John W. *Smugglers and Patriots: Boston Merchants and the Advent of the American Revolution*. Boston: Northeastern University Press, 1986.

United States Congress. *Annals of Congress*, 1808.

———. "Evasions of the Non-Importation Act," *American State Papers: Commerce and Navigation* 1:873–74.

———. *House Journal*. 1811. 12th Cong., 1st sess.

United States Congress, House of Representatives. *Claim of C. P. Van Ness*. Washington, D.C.: n.p, 1852.

Vickers, Daniel. "Competency and Competition: Economic Culture in Early America." *William and Mary Quarterly*, 3rd ser., 47 (1990): 3–29.

Vose, Peter E. "Col. George Peck of Eastport, and Lubec." *Bangor Historical Magazine* 5 (July 1889–90): 171–72.

Ward, Christopher. "The Commerce of East Florida during the Embargo, 1806–1812: The Role of Amelia Island." *Florida Historical Quarterly* 68 (October 1989): 160–79.

Wells, Kate Gannet. "David Owen." *Acadiensis* 1 (1901): 21–27.

———. *Campobello: An Historical Sketch*. S.l: s.n., 1892.

Wells, William R. "U.S. Revenue Cutters Captured in the War of 1812." *American Neptune* 58 (1998): 225–41.

White, Leonard D. *The Jeffersonians: A Study in Administrative History, 1801–1829*. New York: Free Press, 1965.

Williams, Judith Blow. *British Commercial Policy and Trade Expansion, 1750–1850*. Oxford: Clarendon Press, 1972.

Williams, Neville. *Contraband Cargoes: Seven Centuries of Smuggling*. Hamden, Conn.: Shoe String Press, 1961.

Winslow, Cal. "Sussex Smugglers." In Douglas Hay, Peter Linebaugh, John G. Rule, E. P.

Thompson, and Cal Winslow, eds., *Albion's Fatal Tree: Crime and Society in Eighteenth-Century England*. London: Allen Lane, 1975.

Wright, Esther Clark. *The Loyalists of New Brunswick*. Hantsport, Nova Scotia: Lancelot Press, 1955; 4th ed., 1981.

Wynn, Graeme. "'Deplorably Dark and Demoralized Lumberers'? Rhetoric and Reality in Early Nineteenth-Century New Brunswick." *Journal of Forest History* 24 (1980): 168–87.

———. "New England's Outpost in the Nineteenth Century." In *The Northeastern Borderlands: Four Centuries of Interaction*, ed. Stephen J. Hornsby, Victor A. Konrad, and James J. Herlan, 60–96. Fredericton, New Brunswick: Acadiensis Press, 1989.

Zimmerman, David. *Coastal Fort: A History of Fort Sullivan, Eastport, Maine*. Eastport, Maine: Border Historical Society, 1984.

INDEX

Acadians, 9
Adams, William P., 75
Allan, John, 22, 44
Alline, Henry, 30, 102
Andrews, Israel, 43
Andrews, Samuel, 31
Anglicans, 30–31, 102
Annapolis, Nova Scotia, 99
Appleby, Nathan, 13
Armidson, Andros, 88
Armstrong, Richard, 100–101, 104
Arnold, Benedict, 23

Baltimore, Maryland, 53, 55, 98
Baptists, 31
Barclay, George, 71
Barclay, Thomas, 71
Bartlett, Jonathan, 85
Batchelor, Richard, 36–37
Bethune, Divie, 59
Bibber, Thomas, 110–11
Bird, Charles, 86
Blackford, Edward, 83
Bodfish, William, 71
Boston, 52; customs officers, 6, 7; gypsum trade, 42, 98; Loyalists, 7
Botsford, William, 46–47
Brewer, John, 23, 83
Bruce, Stephen, 55
Bucknam, Benjamin, 91
Bucknam, Samuel, 61
Butler, Gillam, 36, 129n.50

Calais, Maine, 20, 112, 113
Campbell, Colin, Jr., 43, 46
Campbell, Colin, Sr., 28, 37, 39, 46, 77
Campobello, New Brunswick, 29, 42, 45, 62, 71, 93; population, 19; preventative officer, 77; settled, 22; smuggling at, 36, 37, 43, 74, 76, 78; Wilson family, 25
Carleton, Thomas, 36, 37, 38
Castine, Maine, 14, 64, 79, 85
Chipman, Ward, Jr., 94, 105, 115
Chipman, Ward, Sr., 115, 128n.23
Clap, John, 13, 53
Clinch, Patrick, 115
Coffin, John, 94, 105
Colles, James, 72, 81–83, 86
Comely, William, 37
Coney, William, 55, 81, 85, 92
Congdon, James, 89
Cooper, John, 83, 85
counterfeiters, 79–80
Croke, Alexander, 35
Cunard, Samuel, 15
Cunningham, Richard, 107

Dana, Josiah, 43
Dearborn, Henry, 73, 74
Deer Island, New Brunswick, 19, 31, 57
Delesdernier, Lewis, Jr., 63
Delesdernier, Lewis Frederick, Sr.: betrayed, 62–63; and border, 17–18; corrupt, 43–45; cross-border ties, 23; and embargo, 49, 52–58, 62, 65; and *Porgey* incident, 33; removed, 73
DeWolf, Mary, 43
Digby, Nova Scotia, 1, 79
Dunn, John, 39, 45, 77, 78
Dunn family, 31

Index

Eastport, Maine, 31, 42, 44, 51, 65, 67, 76, 79, 87, 88, 89, 100, 109–11, 113–14, 117; captured, 92; declaration of war, 80; embargo of 1808–1809, 53–56, 58–59, 62–63, 65; enemy aliens, 84, 85; lyceum, 109–10; occupation, 92–93; reputation, 18, 114; riots, 19, 87, 110–11, 113; settled, 19, 22, 24; smuggling at, 49, 53–54, 67, 81, 86, 115
Edgecomb, Noah, 91
Elliot, Daniel, 76
Embargo: of 1807–1809, 50–51, 65, 119; of 1812, 68, 80
enemy aliens, 84, 85
England. *See* Great Britain
evangelicals, 30–31, 102

Falmouth, Maine, 6, 7
Faxon, John, 22
fishermen, 26–27; as smugglers 14, 16–17, 30; superstitious, 29
Flintoph, James, 33, 34
Fort Sullivan, 11, 65, 79, 87, 90–92, 117
Fredericton, New Brunswick, 95, 100
Fundy, Bay of, 2, 8–10, 12, 15, 37, 67, 96, 111

Gallatin, Albert, 34, 52, 54, 56, 63, 70
Garrison, William Lloyd, 16, 130n.67
Goddard, Nathaniel, 21, 22
Grand Manan, New Brunswick, 22, 37, 80, 84, 89, 90
Great Britain: commercial policy, 4, 10, 12, 35, 59–60, 68–69; customs commissioners, 40, 94; Parliament, 4; smuggling 2–4
gypsum, 11, 41–44, 66, 69–70, 95–98, 103

Halifax, Nova Scotia, 2, 9, 71, 78, 89; customs officers, 102; vice-admiralty court, 5, 35
Hamilton, Alexander, 17, 34
Harris, Gilbert, 31
Harrison, Jabez, 72
Hasluck, Richard, 61, 64, 71
Hatch, Christopher, 28–29, 43
Hatch, Harris, 103–4
Henderson, Thomas, 39, 43
Hills, George, 78
Holroyd, John Lord Sheffield, 4, 35
Humbert, John, 99

Humbert, Stephen: Methodist deacon, 1; preventative officer, 12, 97, 98–101; smuggler, 42, 50, 101, 104, 106–7
Hutchins, John, 79

Indian disguises, 112
Indian Island, New Brunswick, 59, 60, 80, 100–101, 104, 106
Indians, 8, 17, 21–22. *See also* Passamaquoddy Indians
Irish, ethnic group, 79, 118
Isle au Haut, Maine, 64

Jefferson, Thomas, 51, 56, 57, 61, 65
Johnson family, 54

Kankey, Stephen H., 63
Kendall, John, 49
King, William, 2

Leavitt, Jonathan, 54
Leland, Sherman, 87–88, 91
Leonard, Charles, 40
Leonard, George, 30, 34, 36, 40–41, 43, 45–47, 76, 77, 97
Little, Josiah, 86
Little, Robert, 54
Livermore, Joseph, 55
Lloyd, Fanny, 31
Llufrio, Constantino, 88–89
Lock, Ebenezer, 46
Loyalists: arrival, 9, 22, 48; celebrated, 115; dogmatic, 40; merchants, 28–29, 103; settlers, 8, 25; as smugglers, 7–8
Lubec, Maine, 15, 71, 93, 94, 101, 106, 107, 114

Mabee, Solomon, 54
Machias, Maine, 63, 79, 87
MacKinnon, Neil, 48
Macon's Bill No. 2. *See* Non-Intercourse Act
Madison, James, 51, 67–68, 90
Malcolm, John, 6–7
Marks, Nehemiah, 23
Marsden, Joshua, 1
Massachusetts, 5–6
McArthur, James, 99–100
McColl, Duncan, 31

158

McMaster, James, 58
McMaster, John, 63–64
merchants, as smugglers, 27–28
Merritt, Nehemiah, 83
Merry, Anthony, 47
Methodists, 1, 15, 31
militia, 51, 84, 87
Moose Island. *See* Eastport
Mowry, Jabez, 15, 43, 71, 73, 81–83, 86, 91, 94; disguises self, 93; flees to Lubec, 92–93
Murphy, James, 31

Navigation Acts, 5, 34–35, 38, 39, 40, 46
Nevers, Phineas, 50
New Brunswick: assembly, 35, 47, 97, 104–5, 108; corrupt officials, 11, 38–39, 41, 47, 94; council, 70, 105; founded, 8–9; lieutenant governor, 36, 47, 95, 108; scale of smuggling, 29, 76; trade, 36, 70; vice-admiralty court, 46–47
Newcomb, Alexander, 89–90
Newcomb, William, 116
Non-Intercourse Act (1809), 67–68
Nova Scotia, 103; agriculture, 102; assembly, 98, 102, 105, 107; gypsum production, 11, 41, 101–2; lieutenant governor, 60, 109
Nymann, Johan, 88

Olmstead, Aaron, 63
Olmstead, Ethel, 84
Owen, David, 21, 25, 34, 37, 65, 79; and plaster trade, 100, 103–4

Pagan, Robert, 20, 28, 59, 80, 83
Parker, Robert, 47
Passamaquoddy Bay, 18–19, 20
Passamaquoddy Indians, 17, 21–22
Patterson, William L., 78
Peck, George, 24
Peel, Robert, 4
Perkins, Simeon, 70
Pettigrove, Thomas, Jr., 56
Pierce, Leonard, 93–94
Piracy, 79
plaister. *See* gypsum
planters, 101, 102
Porter, Joseph, 23
Portland, Maine, 80

Priest, William, 79
privateers, 85, 89–90

'Quoddy. *See* Passamaquoddy Bay

religion, 30–31
revenue cutters: American, 34, 52, 53, 55, 66, 74–75, 106, 117; British, 11, 40, 66, 76, 117
Rice, Solomon, 74
Robbinston, Maine, 86
Rogers, Aaron, 84
Romagné, James, 31
Roman Catholics, 31
Royal Navy, 4, 5, 9, 11, 48, 55, 60–61, 62, 77–79, 85, 90–91, 92, 98, 100, 106–7, 111

Sabine, Lorenzo, 8, 115
Saint Andrews, New Brunswick, 7, 20, 31, 51, 57, 59, 71, 79, 86, 91, 111, 113; customs officers, 45, 105, 117–18; founded 10, 20; plaster trade 98, 103; smuggling at, 14, 81, 99, 111; timber trade, 59, 111, 117
Saint Croix River, 20, 21, 37, 54, 56, 61, 69
Saint John, New Brunswick, 100, 115; customs officers, 7, 17, 37, 40, 41, 47, 104, 111; resented, 103–4; smuggling at, 2–3, 36, 71–72, 88, 89, 111; trade, 35, 42, 93, 95–96, 107, 108, 117, 118, 119–20
Saint Stephen, New Brunswick, 20, 23, 31, 111–12, 118
Scots, ethnic group, 27–28, 39
Scott, Christopher, 14, 15, 28
Sevey, Nathaniel, 62
Sheffield, Lord. *See* Holroyd, John Lord Sheffield
Sherman, William, 54, 56
ships, merchant vessels: *Amphibious*, 69; *Boyne*, 78; *Britannia*, 128n.8; *Eliza*, 62, 64; *Encouragement*, 76; *Falmouth*, 45–48; *Fortune*, 86; *Harmony*, 33–34, 45; *Hiram*, 55; *Industry* 49–50; *Isabella*, 58; *Joanna*, 89; *Liberty*, 6; *Lucy*, 90; *Marietta*, 74; *Mark*, 64–65; *Mary*, 37; *Nancy and Sally*, 9; *Peggy*, 64; *Polly*, 81–82, 83; *Rebecca*, 89; *Sally*, 78; *Shannon* (1), 99–100; *Shannon* (2), 112–13, 117; *Venture*, 90–91
ships, privateers: *Dart*, 89–90; *Mary*, 91
ships, revenue cutters: *Hunter*, 76; *New Hampshire*, 52, 53, 55, 75; *Union*, 40, 45

Index

ships, Royal Navy: *Bellette*, 100–101, 106–7; *Canceaux*, 7; *Cleopatra*, 61; *Columbine*, 78–79; *Cuttle*, 78; *Gaspee*, 6; *Leopard*, 48, 50–51; *Martin*, 90; *Plumper*, 57; *Porgey*, 33, 34, 48, 50, 60, 77; *Squirrel*, 57, 60; *Wye*, 98

ships, U.S. Navy: *Chesapeake*, 48, 50–51; gunboat No. *42*, 57; gunboat No. *43*, 57, 61, 62; *Wasp*, 57, 58, 60

Smith, Adam, 2, 4, 12, 16, 34, 63

Smith, David, 72

Smith, Freeman, 29

smuggling methods: "bonding ploy," 73–74, 85–86; collusive capture, 90–91; free ports, 69; licenses, 89–90, 92; neutral trade, 61, 88, 110; neutral zone, 45–46

Smyth, George Stracey, 95, 100, 108

Spain, 35; flour trade, 89; merchants, 88–89

Staples, Abel, 74

Sullivan, James, 128n.23

Sweden: merchants, 88; neutral, 88; vice-consul, 110

Swett, John, 49

Swett, Moses, 56

Tappan, Arthur, 15

Tappan, Charles, 16

Tappan, John, 15

Tappan, Lewis, 15, 86

Thacher, Stephen, 105–6

timbermen, as smugglers, 14, 27

Toler, Hugh Kennedy, 72

treaties: Jay's (1794), 35; of Paris (1783), 9–10, 17, 20, 21, 46; reciprocity (1854), 12, 117; of Utrecht (1713), 9

Trescott, Lemuel, 66, 80, 93; appointed, 73; corruption, 73–75; dies, 111; flees Eastport, 92; remembered, 109–10; and War of 1812, 81–82, 83, 86

Ulmer, Col. George, 81–83; problems of, 85, 86–88; relieved of command, 88; remembered, 109

United Kingdom. *See* Great Britain

United States Army, 53, 56, 87, 91–92, 117; and Congress, 2, 44, 51, 64, 68, 89, 98

United States Navy, 50–51; and U.S. Supreme Court, 89, 90

United States Supreme Court. *See under* United States Navy

Wanton, William, 38, 39–40, 47, 77, 104

Way, David, 49

Wentworth, John, 98

West Indies, 28, 35, 51, 56, 57, 59, 60, 68, 69, 71, 88, 114

Weston, Jonathan Delesdernier, 50, 109–11, 113–14

Wetmore, Thomas, 100–101

Wheeler, Samuel, 58–59

Windsor, Nova Scotia, 93, 98, 102, 105

Winslow, Edward, 45

Woodward, Thomas H., 84–85

Wright, Henry, 93–94, 100, 104–5

Wyer, Thomas, 7

Yeaton, Hopley, 75

Young, John, 14

Joshua M. Smith grew up on Cape Cod and in coastal Maine. He is professor of humanities at the United States Merchant Marine Academy in Kings Point, New York, and director of the American Merchant Marine Museum.

NEW PERSPECTIVES ON MARITIME HISTORY
AND NAUTICAL ARCHAEOLOGY

Edited by James C. Bradford and Gene Allen Smith

The Maritime Heritage of the Cayman Islands, by Roger C. Smith (2000; first paperback edition, 2001)

The Three German Navies: Dissolution, Transition, and New Beginnings, 1945–1960, by Douglas C. Peifer (2002)

The Rescue of the Gale Runner: *Death, Heroism, and the U.S. Coast Guard*, by Dennis L. Noble (2002; first paperback edition, 2008)

Brown Water Warfare: The U.S. Navy in Riverine Warfare and the Emergence of a Tactical Doctrine, 1775–1970, by R. Blake Dunnavent (2003)

Sea Power in the Medieval Mediterranean: The Catalan-Aragonese Fleet in the War of the Sicilian Vespers, by Lawrence V. Mott (2003)

An Admiral for America: Sir Peter Warren, Vice Admiral of the Red, 1703–1752, by Julian Gwyn (2004)

Maritime History as World History, edited by Daniel Finamore (2004)

Counterpoint to Trafalgar: The Anglo-Russian Invasion of Naples, 1805–1806, by William Henry Flayhart III (paperback edition, 2004)

Life and Death on the Greenland Patrol, 1942, by Thaddeus D. Novak, edited by P.J. Capelotti (2005; first paperback edition, 2014)

X Marks the Spot: The Archaeology of Piracy, edited by Russell K. Skowronek and Charles R. Ewen (2006; first paperback edition, 2007)

Industrializing American Shipbuilding: The Transformation of Ship Design and Construction, 1820–1920, by William H. Thiesen (2006)

Admiral Lord Keith and the Naval War Against Napoleon, by Kevin D. McCranie (2006)

Commodore John Rodgers: Paragon of the Early American Navy, by John H. Schroeder (2006)

Borderland Smuggling: Patriots, Loyalists, and Illicit Trade in the Northeast, 1783–1820, by Joshua M. Smith (2006; first paperback edition, 2019)

Brutality on Trial: "Hellfire" Pedersen, "Fighting" Hansen, and the Seamen's Act of 1915, by E. Kay Gibson (2006)

Uriah Levy: Reformer of the Antebellum Navy, by Ira Dye (2006)

Crisis at Sea: The United States Navy in European Waters in World War I, by William N. Still Jr. (2006)

Chinese Junks on the Pacific: Views from a Different Deck, by Hans K. Van Tilburg (2007; first paperback edition, 2013)

Eight Thousand Years of Maltese Maritime History: Trade, Piracy, and Naval Warfare in the Central Mediterranean, by Ayse Devrim Atauz (2008)

Merchant Mariners at War: An Oral History of World War II, by George J. Billy and Christine M. Billy (2008)

The Steamboat Montana *and the Opening of the West: History, Excavation, and Architecture*, by Annalies Corbin and Bradley A. Rodgers (2008)

Attack Transport: USS Charles Carroll *in World War II*, by Kenneth H. Goldman (2008)
Diplomats in Blue: U.S. Naval Officers in China, 1922–1933, by William Reynolds Braisted (2009)
Sir Samuel Hood and the Battle of the Chesapeake, by Colin Pengelly (2009)
Voyages, the Age of Sail: Documents in American Maritime History, Volume I, 1492–1865, edited by Joshua M. Smith and the National Maritime Historical Society (2009)
Voyages, the Age of Engines: Documents in American Maritime History, Volume II, 1865–Present, edited by Joshua M. Smith and the National Maritime Historical Society (2009)
HMS Fowey *Lost and Found: Being the Discovery, Excavation, and Identification of a British Man-of-War Lost off the Cape of Florida in 1748*, by Russell K. Skowronek and George R. Fischer (2009)
American Coastal Rescue Craft: A Design History of Coastal Rescue Craft Used by the United States Life-Saving Service and the United States Coast Guard, by William D. Wilkinson and Commander Timothy R. Dring, USNR (Retired) (2009)
The Spanish Convoy of 1750: Heaven's Hammer and International Diplomacy, by James A. Lewis (2009)
The Development of Mobile Logistic Support in Anglo-American Naval Policy, 1900–1953, by Peter V. Nash (2009)
Captain "Hell Roaring" Mike Healy: From American Slave to Arctic Hero, by Dennis L. Noble and Truman R. Strobridge (2009; first paperback edition, 2017)
Sovereignty at Sea: U.S. Merchant Ships and American Entry into World War I, by Rodney Carlisle (2009; first paperback edition, 2011)
Commodore Abraham Whipple of the Continental Navy: Privateer, Patriot, Pioneer, by Sheldon S. Cohen (2010; first paperback edition, 2011)
Lucky 73: USS Pampanito's *Unlikely Rescue of Allied POWs in WWII*, by Aldona Sendzikas (2010)
Cruise of the Dashing Wave: *Rounding Cape Horn in 1860*, by Philip Hichborn, edited by William H. Thiesen (2010)
Seated by the Sea: The Maritime History of Portland, Maine, and Its Irish Longshoremen, by Michael C. Connolly (2010; first paperback edition, 2011)
The Whaling Expedition of the Ulysses, *1937–1938*, by Lt. (j.g.) Quentin R. Walsh, U.S. Coast Guard, edited and with an introduction by P.J. Capelotti (2010)
Stalking the U-Boat: U.S. Naval Aviation in Europe during World War I, by Geoffrey L. Rossano (2010)
In Katrina's Wake: The U.S. Coast Guard and the Gulf Coast Hurricanes of 2005, by Donald L. Canney (2010)
A Civil War Gunboat in Pacific Waters: Life on Board USS Saginaw, by Hans K. Van Tilburg (2010)
The U.S. Coast Guard's War on Human Smuggling, by Dennis L. Noble (2011)
The Sea Their Graves: An Archaeology of Death and Remembrance in Maritime Culture, by David J. Stewart (2011; first paperback edition, 2019)

www.ingramcontent.com/pod-product-compliance
Lightning Source LLC
Chambersburg PA
CBHW020852160426
43192CB00007B/888